AI-Enhanced ELT

Innovative Strategies to Transform Your Classroom

By Samaneh Eslamdoost

This book has a companion website.
Go to www.tesol.org/AI-enhanced-ELT-book for additional resources.

tesol press

bookstore.tesol.org

TESOL International Association
1925 Ballenger Avenue, Ste. 550
Alexandria, VA 22314 USA
www.tesol.org

Associate Director of Publications: Tomiko Breland
Copy Editor: Suzy Richardt
Reviewers: Margie Baylon, Amirpooya Dardashti, Jill Hakemian, Rabia Hos, Lilia Savova
Cover Design: Elisabeth Heissler Graphic Design
Interior Design and Typesetting: Citrine Sky Design
Head of Education and Events: Sarah Sahr

Recommended citation:
Eslamdoost, S. (2026). *AI-enhanced ELT: Innovative strategies to transform your classroom*. TESOL Press.

ISBN 978-1-953745-54-5
ISBN (ebook) 978-1-953745-55-2
Library of Congress Control Number 2026933020

Table of Contents

Introduction

The integration of generative artificial intelligence (AI) tools and systems in English language teaching (ELT) presents educators with one of the most noteworthy reforms in the history of language education. This technological transformation is changing how we conceptualize, deliver, and evaluate language instruction. As an educator and researcher with more than two decades of experience in ELT spanning multiple institutions and educational contexts, I have witnessed firsthand the evolution of language teaching methodologies. My journey from traditional classroom instruction to AI-driven teaching has provided unique insights into both the advantages and disadvantages this technological revolution has introduced.

This book emerges from the intersection of academic research and classroom experience. Through my work, I have observed how AI is reshaping the landscape of language education. My research on teacher identity reconstruction in English as a foreign language contexts, combined with my hands-on experience integrating AI tools in language classrooms, has shown me the profound effect of these technologies on both myself as an educator and on multilingual learners of English. More than was the case for previous advances in educational technology, bringing AI into the classroom signifies a shift in how we approach language teaching and learning.

The goals of this book are to address key theoretical foundations for integrating AI tools in ELT and to share practical applications of those tools in language classrooms. Each chapter explores multiple dimensions of AI integration, from concepts to applications, in skills development, language assessment, and curriculum design. This book is a humble effort to offer guidance to readers through the complexities of AI implementation and to provide a critical perspective on its drawbacks and ethical considerations. This balanced approach is indispensable for those seeking a comprehensive understanding of AI's potential benefits for language teachers and learners.

The Evolving Role of the Teacher

From my observation, the rapid growth of AI technologies in education has elicited both excitement and apprehension among language educators and is precipitating a profound transformation in the role of educators. Many teachers find themselves at a critical juncture: They see the potential benefits of AI, but struggle with dilemmas about its proper use.

As AI systems increasingly assume responsibility for routine tasks, such as grading assignments and generating practice exercises and drills, educators are liberated to focus on higher value aspects of language education. This shift can empower English language teachers to dedicate their expertise to guiding learners through personalized learning trajectories, cultivating their critical thinking skills, and offering them essential emotional support that only humans can provide. This aligns closely with sociocultural theory (Vygotsky, 1987), which emphasizes the paramount importance of social interaction for cognitive development. In this new paradigm, educators are increasingly engaged in creating dynamic, interactive, and collaborative learning environments that promote higher order thinking skills and facilitate deeper language acquisition (Hockly, 2023; Schmidt & Strassner, 2022).

> **KEY TERM**
>
> **Personalized learning trajectories:** The individualized and evolving paths of language learning that learners follow, shaped by their contexts, needs, and goals. The term emphasizes the dynamic, developmental, and sometimes nonlinear nature of learning.

The rising use of AI tools in ELT necessitates a parallel advancement in digital literacy and AI proficiency among educators, who must develop a comprehensive understanding of AI systems, their capabilities, and their limitations. Teachers must become adept at evaluating and selecting appropriate AI tools, discerning their pedagogical value, and integrating them effectively into their instructional practices. This newfound expertise involves not only technical fluency but also the skill of discernment in utilizing AI to support improved learner engagement and outcomes.

Although the importance of technology in the modern language classroom cannot be overstated, it must not overshadow the core principles of effective language pedagogy that have been refined over decades of research and practice. The contemporary English language educator must artfully blend pedagogical expertise with digital literacy, leveraging AI tools to enrich traditional teaching methods rather than supplanting them entirely. This delicate balance is critical in guaranteeing that AI serves as a complement to, rather than a replacement for, established teaching practices.

As AI systems become increasingly advanced in their ability to both generate and analyze discrete aspects of language use, such as grammatical accuracy and vocabulary range, educators must focus on helping learners acquire the higher order skills that define human communication. These include the ability to use language creatively, engage in complex discourse, and navigate the subtleties of intercultural communication. The role of English language teachers in the age of AI is evolving into that of a multifaceted facilitator, combining technological savvy with deep pedagogical knowledge. This evolution demands continuous professional development, adaptability in the face of rapid change, and a willingness to embrace innovation while maintaining a steadfast commitment to the core principles of effective language teaching. By skillfully navigating this complex landscape, educators can harness the power of AI to enhance their teaching practices, provide more personalized learning experiences, and ultimately prepare learners for the linguistic demands of an interconnected and technologically driven world.

Purpose and Structure of This Book

Embracing AI has generated both opportunities and challenges for English language educators. How can ChatGPT be used effectively for lesson planning while maintaining pedagogical integrity? When is it the most beneficial to use automated writing feedback systems, and how do we make sure they do not stifle learners' creative ideas? What are our responsibilities about data privacy when using AI-driven pronunciation apps? These questions, together with questions about equity, bias, and the changing role of educators, serve as the basis for this book.

This book is designed for ELT professionals at every level—classroom teachers seeking practical implementation strategies, teacher educators preparing the next generation of AI-literate instructors, curriculum designers integrating technology into language programs, and researchers investigating AI's impact on language learning. In each chapter, it offers adaptable frameworks and practical tools that can be adjusted across various educational contexts.

The book is structured to lead readers on a journey from knowing to implementation. We begin in Chapters 1 and 2 with foundational knowledge: how AI technologies work, what research supports their effectiveness, and how to write efficient prompts that generate pedagogically sound content (Chapter 2's SCRIPT model). Chapters 3 and 4 integrate theory and practice, displaying how AI can enhance everything from curriculum design to classroom differentiation.

The central focus of the book lies in Chapters 5–7, which offer detailed and specific guidance for integrating AI when teaching reading, writing, listening, speaking, and more.

Here you'll find recommendations for specific AI tools and how to use them effectively. Practical "Try It Out" activities show how AI-powered learning platforms, such as Newsela, Grammarly, ELSA Speak, and others, can be implemented purposefully into your instruction. Each chapter also includes a critical analysis of these tools' limitations and their ethical challenges.

These "Focus on Skills" chapters also contain tables with an overview of AI platforms relevant for specific skills. Each table presents a list of pertinent functions and indicates whether each tool provides that function (✔ = yes; ◐ = partially). Here's an example from Chapter 7:

Table 2. Tools for Visualizing Pronunciation Practice

AI Tool	Generates spectrograms	Compares learner speech to model	Identifies spectral phoneme features	Visualizes frequency/pitch	Provides feedback on accuracy	Tracks learner progress	Aligned with CEFR/standards
Praat	✔	✔	✔	✔	◐		
WaveSurfer	✔		◐	✔			
Sonic Visualizer	✔		✔	✔			

Chapter 8 dives more deeply into questions of equity and ethics. This chapter offers strategic suggestions for guaranteeing that AI supports all learners fairly. Chapter 9 tackles the topic of professional development and outlines practical methods for building AI literacy among ELT professionals. The final chapter examines what lies ahead, from immersive virtual learning environments to emotionally intelligent AI tutors, and reflects on how these emerging technologies may fundamentally change the experience of language learning.

Appendix A is designed as a quick visual guide to choosing the AI tool(s) that can best support a certain teaching function or develop a certain language skill. In Appendix B, readers will find a practical glossary listing the AI tools mentioned in this book, with a link to each tool's website and a short description. For ease of reading, I have chosen to provide the website links in the glossary rather than include them repeatedly throughout the text.

Throughout this book, readers will notice a continuing theme: AI is most effective when it empowers educators to focus on inspiring learners, enabling meaningful communication, nurturing critical thinking, and building the cultural bridges that elevate language learning in a meaningful way. This theme underlies every recommendation, with the goal of integrating AI to enhance, not replace, traditional language teaching.

 Companion Site

A library of prompt templates from this book is also available on the companion site (www.tesol.org/AI-enhanced-ELT-book). There, you can find clickable copies of both appendixes: Appendix A, a matrix of recommended AI tools with their functions or features, and Appendix B, a glossary of all AI tools mentioned in this book with descriptions and links to each tool's website.

Professional learning providers may choose to download activities, tables, and figures from the companion site for professional learning sessions with teachers. I also encourage readers to use these online resources to enhance their learning.

Author's Use of AI

In writing this book, I utilized AI tools like ChatGPT (OpenAI, 2025) and Claude (Anthropic, 2025) as collaborative partners through various phases of the writing process. From structuring chapters and generating concepts to exploring relevant research and identifying emerging resources, these tools have acted in the role of a thought partner, which helped enhance my efficiency, foster idea development, and broaden my perspective. However, it is critical to clarify that AI was not a substitute for expertise, analytical reasoning, or pedagogical insight. Every AI-generated output was meticulously examined and revised to align with my professional knowledge and the book's objectives. My approach to using AI is an example of what I view as its responsible and strategic use in education: serving as an assistive resource rather than a replacement for originality, critical thinking, and academic rigor. This acknowledgement is in line with an overall theme of this book, which is to advocate for the thoughtful and ethical use of AI in language education and ensure that the educator stays at the center of the learning process.

Note on AI Tools

The tables in this book describe AI-powered tools as of the time of writing. Because such tools evolve rapidly, the information presented should be understood as a comparative snapshot, not a guarantee of current or complete functionality.

CHAPTER 1

AI in English Language Teaching: Theory, Research, and Impact

The Evolving Landscape of English Language Teaching

Since its beginning, the field of English language teaching (ELT) has evolved along with the contemporary understanding of language acquisition processes and best pedagogical practices. This evolution has been characterized by a shift from a prescriptive, teacher-centered paradigm to more holistic, learner-oriented methodologies and frameworks—a transformation based on research from multiple disciplines, including linguistics, psychology, sociology, and cognitive science. Moreover, the evolution of ELT approaches and methodologies reflects a broader epistemological shift in educational philosophy: the transition from behaviorist models toward constructivist and socioconstructivist paradigms. This transition has triggered a reform in the roles of educators and learners, promoting more collaborative and inquiry-based approaches to language pedagogy (Brown, 1989; Jacobs & Farrell, 2003; Richards & Rodgers, 2014). ELT has also seen a shift toward authenticity, resulting in a focus on real-world communication and learner-centered instruction.

In recent decades, ELT has continued to evolve in response to the digital revolution. The introduction of computers, the internet, and mobile devices has presented teachers and learners with new tools and resources, broadening the possibilities for language learning to extend beyond the walls of traditional classrooms. Online language exchange platforms, digital textbooks, and language learning apps, which facilitate autonomous the atic language input, have become integral parts of many accessibility of language learning resources but has also given rise to new pedagogical approaches, such as blended learning and flipped classroom models (Pokrivcakova, 2019; Yang & Kyun, 2022).

A New Frontier in ELT

Now, we stand at the threshold of another paradigm shift in ELT: the integration of generative artificial intelligence (AI) technology. With its capacity to process vast amounts of data, recognize patterns, and adapt to individual learner needs, AI offers remarkable opportunities to enrich language learning and teaching programs. Research has shown how AI-powered tools significantly improve language learning by providing adaptive learning environments and real-time feedback (Kuddus, 2022; Schmidt & Strassner, 2022). Furthermore, the astonishingly fast adoption of AI tools represents a notable shift in ELT since its start. Historically, changes in dominant ELT methodologies and approaches have occurred gradually, affording educators adequate time to adapt their practice incrementally. In contrast, the emergence of AI has been comparatively sudden. Its rapid arrival has transformed the field and substantially enriched the landscape of available tools and activities for language teaching, but the speed and scope of this change has become overwhelming for many ELT educators. As new AI tools continue to emerge, they evoke a complex mix of excitement and apprehension that challenges our ability to adapt and raises questions about the future of language education. Thus, the integration of AI in ELT presents both opportunities and challenges that must be carefully navigated to ensure that technological advancements enrich, rather than diminish, the quality of language education.

Adapting and evolving in response to the integration of AI in English language pedagogy requires strategic approaches and a flexible mindset from all stakeholders in the field. AI has begun to permeate every facet of our educational system, from teaching methods and curriculum design to administrative tasks. As an example, recent studies (Schmidt & Strassner, 2022; Vijayakuma & Chellapandiyan, 2024) highlight the integration of AI as a transformative factor in providing personalized learning experiences and fostering autonomous learning. These changes have gained attention from policymakers and administrators and affected their decisions at institutional and systemic levels. More broadly, ELT may be influenced by national efforts in the United States to emphasize AI use in education and workforce development, as outlined in President Trump's executive order, "Removing Barriers to American Leadership in Artificial Intelligence" (Exec. Order No. 14179; 2025). For English language teachers, keeping up with these rapid advancements in our field is not merely beneficial but crucial for professional relevance and effectiveness.

Recalling the historical evolution of ELT, however, reminds us of our field's remarkable adaptability. As we explore this novel technological frontier, we must balance innovation with pedagogical wisdom. The transformative potential of AI in language education depends not on technological advances alone, but on their thoughtful use—guided by educators' expertise and learners' needs. By both accepting this change and preserving the interpersonal essence of language learning, the ELT community can harness AI's capabilities to create more equitable, effective, and engaging learning experiences, fulfilling our discipline's lasting commitment to meaningful communication across linguistic boundaries.

Today, understanding and efficiently integrating AI-powered technologies is crucial for educators seeking to improve their teaching methods and learner outcomes. However, it is important to note that AI cannot provide a wholesale replacement of traditional teaching methods or the human element in education; rather, it should be approached as a tool to enrich current pedagogical practices. The empathy, cultural sensitivity, and ability to provide feedback that educators bring to the language learning process remain irreplaceable. Our challenge lies in finding the optimal balance between leveraging AI technologies and maintaining the essential human relationships and interactions that have always been at the heart of successful language teaching.

AI Systems: A Brief Overview

AI refers to computer systems capable of performing tasks that typically require human intelligence. These include natural language processing (NLP), automated speech recognition, machine learning, and adaptive learning systems. Traditional AI systems are intended to examine data to drive predictions or classifications, but generative AI generates new content such as text, images, or code based on patterns learned from training data. The following sections define each of these systems in more detail.

Natural Language Processing

NLP is the most important technology driving AI-powered language learning apps. It helps computers understand, interpret, and generate human language meaningfully. When your learners

> **KEY TERM**
>
> **Natural language processing:** A type of computer technology that helps digital tools understand and use human language, allowing them to read, write, and respond in ways that sound natural.

interact with language learning apps that provide instant corrections and feedback or when they engage with conversational chatbots for practice, they are benefiting from NLP's ability to process linguistic patterns and respond properly to their language use.

Apps powered by NLP have shown significant promise in improving reading comprehension and writing skills by providing instant feedback, error correction, and personalized recommendations for improvement. These AI-powered systems can analyze student writing in real time by offering targeted suggestions for grammar, vocabulary, and style, thus accelerating the learning process and promoting learner autonomy (Manire et al., 2023; Schmidt & Strassner, 2022). Beyond simple correction, large language models such as ChatGPT can simulate human-like dialogue that provides learners with the chance to practice both receptive and productive skills in stress-free environments (Liao et al., 2023). Via sustained interaction with the chatbot, learners benefit from its corrective feedback and scaffolded support. This process fosters confidence, fluency, and continuous engagement.

Advanced NLP technology surpasses basic error correction to support deeper, personalized language learning based on learner input. Transformer-based architectures, such as those underlying ChatGPT, integrate attention mechanisms, learn from human feedback, and employ context-awareness to adjust interactions. These systems can simulate multiturn conversations, provide differentiated instruction, and even offer metalinguistic feedback, which can ultimately assist learners to understand the rationale behind corrections (Kirana & Gupta, 2022; Liao et al., 2023). This supports learners' metacognitive skill development and deeper understanding (Schmidt & Strassner, 2022). By tracking learner input across tasks, such as quizzes, essays, and speaking activities, NLP algorithms can identify persistent errors, generate tailored content, and recommend exercises based on areas of weakness. Furthermore, ChatGPT has been shown to align with six key ELT writing standards (grammar, vocabulary, clarity, organization, revision, and style) by generating targeted feedback and offering rich examples customized to individual performance (Liao et al., 2023).

NLP is also changing the broader pedagogical landscape in ELT. Technology-enhanced language learning environments use NLP to support flipped classrooms, mobile-assisted learning, and game-based learning. In these environments, NLP provides the technology to analyze learner input, assess comprehension, and adapt content delivery in real time, leading to a more immersive and responsive learning experiences (Liao et al., 2023). In addition, educational researchers are leveraging NLP to analyze learner discourse and interaction patterns, identify misconceptions, and widely evaluate the efficiency of instructional interventions.

As NLP technology continues to evolve, its role in ELT is poised to expand. Educators will see an evolution from today's apps that serve as personalized learning assistants to systems that provide real-time class analytics and automated curriculum support. NLP's combination of deep linguistic analysis, adaptive feedback, and learner-centered design establishes this technology as a cornerstone of AI-enhanced language education.

Automated Speech Recognition

Automated speech recognition transforms spoken language into written text, basically giving machines the capability to "hear" and transcribe human speech. For language learners, automated speech recognition technology can evaluate pronunciation, recognize specific phonetic challenges, and deliver targeted feedback on speaking skills. This technology enables the pronunciation assessment features in online language learning platforms that allow learners to practice speaking individually and receive constructive guidance and feedback on their oral production without educator intervention.

Machine Learning

Machine learning refers to systems that improve their performance automatically through experience. In contrast to traditional software with fixed rules, language tools driven by machine learning constantly adapt to learner interactions and become more effective over time. In the ELT classroom, we use machine learning when educational software analyzes patterns across a large number of learners to make predictions about which students might face trouble with specific grammar concepts, pinpoint the most effective sequence of instruction based on collective data, or develop increasingly accurate placement tests by learning from past student outcomes.

Adaptive Learning Systems

Adaptive learning systems generate personalized educational experiences by monitoring learner performance and adjusting content accordingly. Rather than following strict curricula where all learners progress at identical rates, adaptive learning systems respond in real time to individual learner actions during a single session. They can immediately recognize when a learner struggles with specific concepts and automatically offer additional practice, alternate explanations, or simpler examples. In the same way, when learners show mastery of a particular content, these systems offer more challenging material. This guarantees efficient learning pathways exclusively suited to individual capabilities and learning styles.

AI Integration in ELT: Benefits and Challenges

The integration of AI in language teaching brings a multitude of benefits that can significantly improve educational practices and outcomes. Used appropriately, AI can improve student outcomes, improve assessments, and facilitate data analysis.

How AI Improves Student Outcomes

- Creates individualized learning paths for each student based on their proficiency level, learning style, and progress (Manire et al., 2023; Schmidt & Strassner, 2022)

- Assists in creating adaptive lesson plans that automatically adjust based on learners' progress and performance data

- Suggests alternative activities or resources if learners are struggling with certain concepts

- Helps design more interactive and engaging lessons by suggesting resources and strategies that align with lesson objectives, student proficiency levels, and student interests

- Serves as a conversation partner for learners, allowing them to practice their language skills at any time in a low-stakes environment

How AI Improves Assessments

- Generates a wide variety of language tasks and materials based on specific learning objectives, including quizzes, texts, and prompts

- Provides instant feedback on learner performance during lessons by analyzing spoken language, written texts, and even nonverbal cues (Lee et al., 2023; Liang et al., 2021)

- Assists in grading objective questions and provides detailed feedback on subjective responses, such as essays or spoken presentations, improving assessment reliability

- Analyzes learners' spoken and written language production to identify common errors, track improvement over time, and provide targeted suggestions for enhancement (Ali, 2020)

How AI Facilitates Data Analysis

- Informs curriculum design by analyzing vast amounts of data on student performance, learning trends, and global language needs to identify gaps in existing curricula and suggest areas for improvement or expansion

- Analyzes patterns in learner performance and engagement to identify students at risk of falling behind or dropping out, allowing for early intervention or modified instruction
- Provides cross-linguistic analysis, identifying potential areas of interference or transfer between a learner's home language and English
- Analyzes teaching patterns and learner outcomes to provide personalized recommendations for teacher professional development, including suggestions for new teaching strategies, resources, or areas where additional training might be beneficial (Huang et al., 2023)

By integrating these AI-powered tools and strategies, English language teachers can make their teaching practice more efficient, personalized, and effective. However, AI should always be seen as a complement to, rather than a replacement for, skilled human teachers.

Though the potential benefits of integrating AI in ELT are significant, several challenges must be addressed. These include technological barriers, ethical considerations, teacher training, and the need to balance AI assistance with human interaction (Edmett et al., 2023; Lee et al., 2023; Sumakul et al., 2022). I discuss these challenges, among others, at length in Chapters 8 and 9.

Theory and Research

Theoretical Foundations of AI in Second Language Acquisition

The integration of AI in English language teaching finds its theoretical grounding in established second language acquisition theories. Core frameworks, such as the input hypothesis (Krashen, 1985), the interaction hypothesis (Long, 1996), and skill acquisition theory (Anderson, 1982), present foundational concepts that educators can implement and extend through applying AI technologies (Chen, Zou, et al., 2021).

Krashen's (1985) input hypothesis is particularly encouraging for the adoption of AI systems because they can deliver personalized, comprehensible input customized for learners' i+1 level, or input slightly beyond the learner's current proficiency level, which is necessary for language acquisition (Qin & Zhong, 2024). Similarly, the principles of Long's (1996) interaction hypothesis are embodied in AI-powered chatbots and virtual tutors that enable meaningful learner interactions necessary for language development (Zou, Guan, et al. 2023).

DeKeyser's (2007) skill acquisition theory, which highlights the progression from declarative to procedural knowledge, also supports the use of AI tools that can adjust in response to learner input and build personalized and adaptive materials for language learning (Kuddus, 2022). Another compatible framework is Tomasello's (2003) usage-based theory of language acquisition, as AI can provide learners with extensive contextualized input and opportunities for extended practice in meaningful contexts.

Finally, cognitive load theory (Sweller, 1988) introduces another relevant framework, with AI systems capable of dynamically adapting content to learners' cognitive states. Responsive technology minimizes extraneous cognitive load and promotes proper processing demands, which can meaningfully enhance knowledge retention and overall learning outcomes.

Research on AI-Enhanced Teaching Practices and Classroom Management

Sophisticated AI systems employing computer vision and NLP have exhibited the capability to automate routine classroom management tasks. In one example, Aljohnai et al. (2022) investigated an AI-based attendance management system, finding that it offered a more secure and efficient alternative to traditional attendance methods.

Another study (Li et al., 2023) investigated an AI-based classroom behavior analysis system in an experimental setting. The system employed wearable mixed reality glasses worn by teachers in physical classrooms, which captured real-time images of students' faces. Then, the system used a computationally efficient AI model to offer real-time emotion recognition. Results showed that this lightweight model ultimately increased teaching quality, protected student privacy, and enhanced learning outcomes.

Beyond classroom management, content and materials creation is one of the most demanding and time-consuming aspects of language teaching. Rudik & Onyshchuk (2024) examined how NLP-driven large language models, such as GPT-3, can generate tailored and interactive learning materials for English for specific purposes curricula across various professional fields. Results of the study indicated both strengths and limitations when using AI tools for educational content creation. The researchers found that AI can streamline the process of materials development, offer personalized learning experiences, and boost content relevance via real-time updates from related industries. However, the generated materials showed errors with respect to accurate use of domain-specific terminology; further, human oversight was required to guarantee cultural sensitivity and pedagogical appropriateness.

Research on AI-Enhanced Assessment and Feedback Systems

The adoption of AI-driven systems for assessment and feedback is one of the most noteworthy developments in ELT. Although automated grading for complex language tasks has been controversial (Hearst, 2000), recent research underscores the promise of using AI tools to generate initial feedback and grade objective assessments. Flodén (2024) found that ChatGPT 3.5's performance in grading university exams compared favorably with that of human teachers. The results revealed that AI could deliver plausible scores; however, there were some ethical considerations, including variances in scoring consistency and the tendency to assign marginally higher grades.

In addition to providing as-yet limited support for grading assessments, AI-powered writing assistants have become progressively advanced in offering feedback—going beyond simple grammar and spelling corrections. A recent study on the efficiency of an AI-powered writing tool for postgraduate students in an academic writing course suggested that learners who used the writing tool made significant improvements in engagement, self-efficacy, and emotional responses to learning (specifically, reduced anxiety and increased enjoyment) compared to control groups (Nazari et al., 2021). Likewise, a similar study investigated the effect of AI-mediated personalized feedback via Duolingo on learners' levels of English achievement and motivation, finding striking progress on both measures compared to traditional instruction (Wei, 2023). However, assessment reliability remains a significant concern. Schmidt and Strassner (2022) noted that current AI systems struggle to evaluate complex language productions consistently, particularly in areas requiring subjective judgment, such as writing style or speaking fluency. Another study found that teacher evaluations offered higher accuracy than ChatGPT in assessing second language writing, with only weak-to-moderate correlations between AI and human scoring (Shabara et al., 2024). These examples suggest that adopting AI-powered tools in language assessment should be undertaken with caution and under close guidance by the human educator to ensure reliability.

Research on Skill-Specific Applications

Reading Instruction

AI's capacity to generate adaptive texts and build intelligent comprehension assessments is well-suited to support reading instruction on both individual and global scales. One groundbreaking study demonstrates how AI can tackle one of the most fundamental challenges in developing countries: improving literacy at scale. When an AI-powered _____ _____ platform called ReadToMe was employed across thousands of schools in India, researchers documented considerable gains in English literacy among more than 1 million K–12 students (Srinivasan & Murthy, 2021). This example highlights AI's potential to democratize reading instruction, regardless of geographic or socioeconomic constraints.

Various AI applications can offer sophisticated tools for teaching reading in an ELT context (McCarthy & Yan, 2023):

- SMART (Student Mental Model Analyzer for Reading and Teaching; https://smart.cehd.gsu.edu/SMART/) is an AI-powered reading tool that helps learners develop summarization skills and deeply understand assigned readings.

- NLP-powered large language models, such as BERT and ChatGPT, can analyze text complexity and provide advanced readability metrics.

- Intelligent textbooks, such as Pearson's MyLab, adapt to individual learner needs.

Research has consistently shown that personalized, adaptive learning experiences can address persistent challenges in reading comprehension by catering to individual learner needs, with studies demonstrating significant improvements in reading comprehension scores among senior high school students compared to control groups (Hidayat, 2024).

Writing Instruction

AI systems for writing instruction have evolved to design and modify personalized writing materials that match individual language proficiency levels, needs, and interests. These systems develop learners' writing skills through curated feedback and automated evaluation. A systematic review of AI-powered writing assistance tools in language classrooms found that automated writing evaluation and corrective feedback tools can increase learners' writing quality when applied properly, though their long-term learning benefits remain unclear (Alharbi, 2023).

Grammarly has emerged as a particularly well-researched tool in this domain. Multiple studies have demonstrated its effectiveness in reducing specific error types, particularly inflectional morpheme errors and issues stemming from home language interference (Alam et al., 2023). However, there are limitations to Grammarly's accuracy. One study shows that though Grammarly successfully detects some grammatical errors, it misses many others—and sometimes provides incorrect suggestions, particularly for complex grammar structures that human raters can easily identify (Park, 2019).

ChatGPT represents another significant development in AI-powered writing instruction. Research indicates that integrating ChatGPT in the writing process has a significant impact on reducing grammar errors (Mohammad Ali, 2023); however, mixed results have been reported regarding ChatGPT's effectiveness with complex English grammar rules when correcting learner writing, with some students questioning its efficiency in certain areas (Monika & Suganthan, 2024).

Speaking and Listening Instruction

AI technologies have made significant strides in their effectiveness at assessing and providing feedback on spoken language—traditionally a challenging area to address in large classes. For example, AI-powered speech evaluation programs, such as Liulishuo, IELTS Liulishuo, EAP Talk, and Shanbay, have proven efficient in supporting improvements in pronunciation and fluency through various types of personalized feedback, including scores, practice suggestions, and detailed textual feedback (Zou, Du, et al., 2023).

Moving from speaking to listening, intelligent personal assistants have demonstrated particular effectiveness in listening development. Research shows that conversation practice with Amazon's Alexa improved learners' listening comprehension scores significantly in understanding main ideas and supporting details, with experimental groups showing statistically significant gains compared to control groups (Dizon, 2020), and interacting with Google Assistant significantly enhanced learners' listening skills, with the multimodal Google Nest Hub producing the most substantial improvements in adolescent learners' comprehension abilities (Tai & Chen, 2023).

AI chatbots have emerged as powerful tools for both speaking and listening skill development. In one study, learners who engaged in spoken language practice activities with chatbots showed noteworthy improvements in listening comprehension, particularly in understanding conversations and short talks (Kim, 2018). A systematic review of AI dialogue systems (i.e., chatbots) concluded that these systems can significantly increase students' listening comprehension capabilities by providing opportunities for authentic dialogue practice followed by immediate feedback (Zhai & Wibowo, 2023).

A final type of AI-driven technology with the potential to support language learning is virtual reality. Its integration with AI has opened new frontiers in immersive language practice. Studies on virtual reality–based English learning demonstrate indirect enhancement of listening skills through immersive conversations with AI-powered virtual characters in authentic scenarios (Park, 2022). Like other AI-powered tools, virtual reality platforms for language education can offer personalized feedback, interactive practice, and real-time speech evaluation, all of which have been shown to increase learner engagement, reduce speaking anxiety, and foster autonomous learning.

Pronunciation Instruction

The theoretical frameworks supporting pronunciation learning include various models that clarify phonological development. Flege's speech learning model (1995, 2003) asserts that learners form new phonetic categories based on perceived similarity between first language (L1) and second language (L2) sounds, with greater L1–L2 dissimilarity facilitating more accurate L2 production. This principle directly supports the use of AI applications that can analyze learner speech patterns, identify specific areas of L1 interference, and provide targeted practice on problematic sound contrasts. Similarly, Best's perceptual assimilation model (1995) explains how learners initially assimilate L2 sounds to existing L1 categories, suggesting that AI-powered pronunciation study tools should emphasize perceptual training to help learners distinguish between similar phonemes before focusing on production accuracy.

Schmidt's noticing hypothesis (1990) asserts that conscious attention to linguistic forms is necessary for acquisition—a process that AI can facilitate through explicit personalized feedback, visual representations of speech patterns, and repeated exposure to target features. Anderson's skill acquisition theory (1982) proposes that learners progress from declarative knowledge through procedural stages to automaticity. AI-driven pronunciation study tools can operationalize this developmental progression by initially providing explicit instruction about articulatory features, then offering guided practice with immediate corrective feedback, and finally enabling fluency-focused activities once accuracy is established. Together, these frameworks suggest that effective AI pronunciation instruction should combine

- perceptual training based on predicted L1 interference patterns,
- explicit noticing opportunities through multimodal feedback, and
- adaptive scaffolding that adjusts instructional support as learners advance through developmental stages.

Recent research has expanded our understanding of AI's role in pronunciation training through comprehensive meta-analyses. One such study explored AI-powered tools for pronunciation practice, such as mobile apps, web applications, chatbots, and intelligent virtual assistants, finding that using these tools improves learners' intelligibility, heightens their motivation, and reduces anxiety (Vančová, 2024). Tools such as Amazon's Alexa, Apple's Siri, Google Home, and various other chatbots are recognized as efficient providers of personalized pronunciation feedback and promoters of autonomous learning.

Adaptive Learning and Personalization

AI-powered adaptive learning systems demonstrate significant potential for personalized language instruction. Research has indicated that AI-powered adaptive systems for English language learning result in high performance across key factors, such as accuracy of speech recognition, adaptation to learning styles, and personalization of learning paths, which together ultimately lead to significant improvements in learner proficiency (Qin & Zhong, 2024). These systems transform language education by creating more engaging, effective, and personalized learning experiences compared to traditional methods.

Challenges and Limitations

Bias and Equity Concerns

Critically, language assessment tools powered by AI often rely on preexisting datasets that may reflect cultural, linguistic, or gender biases, which can result in skewed evaluations of learners' linguistic skills (Kasneci et al., 2023). Current AI systems usually function within standardized language norms, often failing to sufficiently address dialectal variations or rhetorical patterns unique to different cultures. This standardization can sideline certain writing styles and potentially marginalize discourse patterns that differ from the AI's training data. Such biases can also reinforce the notion that certain language forms, accents, or English dialects are superior, eventually affecting learners' confidence and development. Reinforcing this concern, Mohamed (2024) studied English language faculty members' perceptions of AI-based chatbots, concluding that although these tools offer advantages like personalized instruction and real-time feedback, they also present ethical concerns, including perpetuating language biases and stereotypes.

Technical and Pedagogical Limitations

Despite promising progress, AI-powered assessment and feedback systems pose several pedagogical limitations, such as a lack of contextual awareness, insufficient training data for less common languages, diminished human interaction, and challenges in replicating cultural intricacies (Rebolledo Font de la Vall & Araya, 2023; Loyola Innaci & Helan Jona, 2024; Zaghlool & Khasawneh, 2023). The integration of AI in teaching reading and writing presents multiple challenges that must be critically examined.

First, AI systems, though highly capable of processing natural language, often show limitations in understanding contextual coherence and rhetorical structures that are essential to effective writing. These systems excel at sentence-level corrections; however, they frequently struggle with discourse-level concerns, including argument development, logical flow, and genre-specific conventions. One investigation of AI writing tools, such as automated writing evaluation systems and text generators, found that, despite their efficiency in providing personalized feedback and enhancing writing quality, AI tools were deficient in contextual understanding and required teacher mediation to optimize learning outcomes (Alharbi, 2023). These weaknesses create a risk that learners may receive superficial feedback on their writing that addresses grammatical accuracy but fails to address features of effective written communication.

Second, AI tools exhibit limitations in evaluating creative and divergent thinking in writing, potentially limiting how learners express themselves and pushing them to follow patterns the system sees as "correct" instead of supporting creative language use. In reading comprehension, AI tools can create comprehension questions but often fail to model the metacognitive strategies proficient readers use, such as making predictions, drawing inferences, and critically evaluating an author's viewpoint (Xia et al., 2024).

Pedagogical Implications and Future Directions

The integration of AI tools in ELT is transforming teaching practices. A major shift is occurring as educators transition from traditional knowledge dispensers to strategic learning facilitators. Park and Doo (2024) noted, for example, that teachers now focus on guiding learners through successful and critical use of AI tools while emphasizing development of higher order thinking skills. Today's curricula increasingly include lessons on AI literacy: the ability to use AI tools successfully, effectively, and ethically.

Current trends in curriculum design encourage educators to highlight human–AI collaboration and create learning experiences that combine technological capabilities with human intelligence in language learning processes, especially in blended learning environments (Ejjami, 2024). AI-powered personalized learning at scale can present breakthroughs in language teaching by facilitating individualized instruction for large learner populations (Ramalingam et al., 2022). Through adaptive content delivery systems, learners can receive materials and tasks tailored to their learning pace and style preferences, as AI algorithms analyze learner data to generate optimal learning sequences and offer targeted, immediate feedback.

Although AI tools present promising advances for language learning and assessment, educators must stay cognizant of their limitations and strive for a balanced approach that combine AI's advantages with traditional human-centered teaching methods. Throughout this book, I advocate for careful incorporation of AI tools into instruction while maintaining human oversight and considering how these tools interact with learners, teachers, and educational contexts.

CHAPTER 2

Crafting Prompts for Language Teaching Success

Today's English language classroom is undergoing incredible transformation in response to the introduction of generative artificial intelligence (AI) tools. These tools, ranging from automated grammar checkers to advanced language generation models, are becoming integral to instruction because they can provide students with exposure to authentic language as well as personalized feedback and learning experiences. However, one important factor that defines the success of these tools is the quality of prompt engineering by the educators. We have devoted an entire chapter to prompt engineering because the importance of writing good prompts cannot be understated when it comes to using generative AI in education: The AI output is only as good as the human input.

Prompts set the foundations of our learners' interactions with AI. Poor prompt engineering can lead to confusion and mixed results. Given the increasing integration of AI in ELT contexts, understanding how to design effective prompts is becoming an essential professional skill for educators. Prompts not only guide AI interactions; when well-written, they help to steer conversations with chatbots in meaningful directions, create deeper connections to learning objectives, and keep students engaged at levels that match their proficiency.

> **KEY TERM**
>
> **Prompt:** A clear and specific instruction or question given to an AI system to elicit targeted responses or outputs. In language teaching contexts, prompts act as a critical link between instructional goals and AI-generated content, shaping the quality, relevance, and appropriateness of materials, activities, or feedback for learners.

Understanding Prompt Engineering in ELT

Prompts serve as a critical bridge between educators' goals and the desired learning outcomes. Successful prompts are constructed with the following criteria in mind.

- **Alignment With Instructional Goals:** Prompts must be drawn from instructional goals and curriculum objectives, and prompt writers must keep in mind best practices in language pedagogy. This alignment increases coherence, strengthening the connection between what is taught and what is learned.

- **Contextual Relevance:** Prompts must be relevant to your teaching and learning context, particularly your learners' cultural backgrounds and their authentic experiences. Integrating these elements ensures that the resulting activity resonates personally with learners, increasing their motivation and engagement.

- **Scaffolding:** Strategic prompts act as scaffolds. They accommodate diverse proficiency levels and, at the same time, support inclusive learning environments. These prompts promote differentiated instruction and encourage active participation by incorporating elements that capture learners' attention and sustain their interest.

- **Consideration of Bias:** Prompts require consideration of ethical issues, avoiding bias, and confirming accessibility. As AI systems often lack cultural and contextual sensitivity, thoughtful prompt engineering can guide learners' interactions with AI toward more inclusive and meaningful outcomes. (See Sotlikova's 2023 study exploring how integrating design thinking in ELT classrooms can address ethical concerns and empower students through culturally informed, engaging prompt engineering.)

Effective prompt engineering in ELT is a multilayer process. When thoughtfully and strategically engineered, prompts have the capacity to support instructional objectives, boost learner engagement, and increase inclusivity.

A Review and Comparison of Prompt Design Frameworks

Effective prompts serve as the bridge between teachers' aims and AI output, helping teachers ensure that classroom goals are met efficiently and creatively. This section examines specialized frameworks for AI prompt design drawn from educational, corporate, and technical contexts.

An ELT Framework for Prompt Design

The Five "S" Model for English Language Teachers (TESOL International Association, 2025b) is specifically designed for ELT contexts and is based on the AI for Education 5S Framework (AI for Education, 2024), which includes the following key ideas:

- **Simplify language:** Use simplified language and avoid jargon when possible.
- **Set a role:** Tell AI what role it is playing.
- **Specify a task:** Describe what the language task is, being as specific as possible.
- **Structure the output:** Give specific parameters for what you want AI to produce.
- **Share feedback:** Provide feedback on what you'd like changed.

Additional Educational and Domain-Specific AI Frameworks

EDUCATIONAL FRAMEWORKS	
5S Framework (AI for Education, 2024)	**Set the Scene:** Provide context for the task. **Be Specific:** Use precise language. **Simplify Language:** Keep instructions clear. **Structure Output:** Define the response format. **Share Feedback:** Continuously refine prompts.
CLEAR (University of San Francisco Gleeson Library, 2024)	**Be Concise:** Use the essential words. **Be Logical:** Order ideas clearly. **Be Explicit:** Provide precise information. **Be Adaptive:** Refine prompts based on the results. **Be Reflective:** Evaluate results critically.
7 Ingredients of a Successful Prompt (Oliver, 2024) from Cambridge.org	**Describe the Role:** Define AI's assumed persona. **Give Instructions:** Provide actionable tasks. **Provide Context:** Include necessary details. **Input Content:** Supply relevant materials. **Define Output Format:** Specify desired structure. **Establish Style and Tone:** Clarify tone requirements. **Define Constraints:** Limit response parameters.
The Essentials (MIT Sloan Teaching & Learning Technologies,	**Provide Context:** Frame the task. **Be Specific:** Enhance clarity. **Build on Conversation:** Use iterative follow-ups.

CORPORATE AND TECHNICAL AI FRAMEWORKS	
7 Essential Steps (Cook, 2023) from Forbes.com	**Assign a Role:** Tell AI "who" it should be.
	Give a Task: Use precise instructions.
	Provide Context: Add details and background information.
	Provide Examples: Show samples of desired format or structure.
	Create Rules: Specify formatting, word count, and style.
	Set Constraints: Say what not to do.
	Evaluate and Iterate: Refine prompts for improvement.
Tips for Effective Prompts (Grammarly, 2025)	**Be Clear and Specific:** Define what you want.
	Test Variations: Try multiple versions of the prompt.
	Use Delimiters: Separate parts of your prompt with XML tags or symbols.
	Assign a Role: Tell AI to respond from a particular perspective.
	Provide Examples: Include samples of the desired output.

Reviewing these models for effective prompt writing, several recurring themes emerge: a need for clarity, context, and continuous improvement. These themes must be the foundation for any successful AI integration and implementation; they also lead to the following three best practices for writing effective prompts.

AI Prompt Engineering Best Practices in ELT

Preparation (Clarity and Structure): Goals must be clearly defined, instructions clearly articulated, and responses logically structured. This phase requires educators to establish quantifiable standards and generate descriptive examples that best support the learning process.

Development (Role and Context): Relevant background information must be incorporated, assigning AI a clearly defined role so it can appropriately modify interactions to best fit the learners. In this phase, instruction starts with simple prompts, progressively cumulating in difficulty to match learners' developing proficiency.

Refinement (Iteration and Feedback): There must be an ongoing process of feedback for the AI. This means that educators should progressively develop and refine prompts to improve activity designs and optimize learning outcomes. This phase emphasizes analyzing the whole approach, recording observed patterns, and adjusting prompts as required.

When combined, these principles guarantee that AI prompt engineering—and thus AI integration into teaching—is both effective and adaptable.

The SCRIPT Model for Effective Prompt Design in ELT

Drawing from these best practices on prompt engineering, I have developed the SCRIPT model, which provides English language teachers with a structured approach to designing effective prompts that enrich language teaching and learning through AI integration, while guaranteeing both pedagogical soundness and learner engagement. The SCRIPT model encompasses six key elements:

Strategic foundation
Context and objectives
Responsiveness and inclusivity
Interactive engagement
Pedagogical alignment
Technology and continuous development

Each element of the SCRIPT framework aligns with a critical dimension of generating effective AI prompts for language education:

Elements of the SCRIPT Model

Strategic Foundation
- Align with curriculum goals, instructional aims, and learner needs.
- Consider cultural backgrounds and proficiency levels of the learners.
- Align with learning objectives.

Context and Objectives
- Use specific, unambiguous language.
- Define intended outcomes clearly.
- Provide adequate contextual information.

Responsiveness and Inclusivity
- Provide scaffolding.
- Confirm cultural relevance.
- Include universally relatable content for diverse learners.

Interactive Engagement

- Tailor to learner demographics and motivations.
- Design for active learning.
- Establish authentic connections to real-world context.

Pedagogical Alignment

- Design effective and reliable assessments.
- Integrate with core language skills.

Technology and Continuous Development

- Guide AI tools for comprehensive outcomes.
- Refine based on feedback.
- Ensure adaptability for emerging needs.

Prompt Engineering With SCRIPT: A Breakdown

What does each component of the SCRIPT model mean in practice? To design prompts for AI-powered language teaching and learning, ELT educators must consider key elements of each element of the model throughout the design process. This comprehensive approach guarantees that the resulting prompts are optimally structured to support highly engaging, culturally inclusive, and objectives-aligned tasks for language learning.

Strategic Foundation

Context and Curriculum: It is crucial to align prompts with curriculum goals. Each prompt should clearly target instructional aims and support the intended learning outcomes. Moreover, careful care should be given to how the prompt improves the overall coherence and flow of the learning experience, to ultimately foster an impactful educational journey for learners.

Target Audience: When crafting prompts, it is critical to consider the target audience by being mindful of your learners' cultural backgrounds and experiences. Each task needs to support diverse proficiency levels and promote an inclusive learning environment where all learners can engage. To foster engagement and relevance, prompts should be designed to resonate with learners on a personal level. Moreover, to support inclusivity and accessibility, they should address the diverse learning needs and proficiency levels in the classroom,

Alignment with Learning Objectives: Each prompt should be intentionally crafted to fulfill a specific instructional goal. Whether the instructional goal is to practice a particular grammar structure, expand vocabulary, or enhance conversational abilities, the prompt must be carefully designed to focus on achieving that precise learning objective.

Context and Objectives

Clear and Specific Language: Clarity and specificity in language is crucial to prompt design. Unclear or intricate prompts can easily lead to output that deviates from the intended outcome. To avoid this, prioritize the use of straightforward and unambiguous language and steer clear of idioms or complex sentence structures that might be misunderstood by AI systems.

Defined Outcomes: Defining the expected outcomes in clear language is a critical component of any prompt. Whether the goal is designing a lesson plan or crafting brainstorming ideas, the prompt must explicitly state what kind of outcome is expected. This clarity guarantees that the AI tool, when assisting in these tasks, generates output that aligns closely with the educator's goals.

Contextual Support: Providing adequate contextual information in each prompt is another equally crucial factor, particularly when the desired output will discuss abstract concepts or unfamiliar topics. The added context helps guide the AI to generate more accurate and relevant responses. Also, it is important to guide AI outputs toward culturally sensitive and contextually appropriate responses.

Task Components: Specifying instructions on how tasks should be structured is another factor in successful prompt engineering for language teaching. Include any necessary guidance on scaffolding for differentiated instruction. Activities should be designed to boost learner engagement.

Responsiveness and Inclusivity

Scaffolding and Differentiation: Successful prompt design must account for diverse proficiency levels and learning needs. With well-designed prompts, teachers can guide AI to generate materials suited for various proficiency levels, needs, and backgrounds. To optimize this process, it is advisable to (1) explicitly specify the proficiency level(s) for the expected output; (2) include instructions to provide multiple iterations of the same content, supporting differentiation; and (3) prompt the AI tool to incorporate scaffolding elements in its responses. This fosters a more inclusive and adaptive learning experience.

Directions in the prompts should set the difficulty level to match the learners' specific skills. Beginner-level prompts, for instance, should highlight high-frequency vocabulary and basic grammatical structures and should include instructions for AI to provide suitable scaffolding and break down information into manageable parts. Intermediate-level prompts should ask AI to introduce more complex vocabulary and syntactic structures. These prompts should also incorporate discourse-level features and encourage greater learner independence. Advanced-level instruction requires more complex prompts that challenge learners' linguistic and cognitive abilities. These prompts should direct AI to create complex scenarios that require critical thinking and analysis. They should also provide greater contextual information to help the generated output meet academic and professional language needs.

The implementation of AI prompts in multilevel classrooms requires flexibility and adaptation. Prompts need to accommodate different entry points and completion levels within the same task. They should also result in collaborative learning activities or materials that benefit from diverse proficiency levels.

Cultural Sensitivity and Inclusivity: Because AI tools are trained on human data, they can sometimes generate material that reinforces stereotypes as well as cultural, linguistic, or gender biases, as discussed in Chapter 1. To address this limitation, first, prompts should unambiguously direct AI to generate culturally inclusive content. Second, tasks should emphasize developing pragmatic competence and intercultural knowledge skills. Following the initial prompt to generate materials or activities, teachers can also prompt for a thorough examination of the potential biases and stereotypes that might permeate the generated content. Finally, prompts should instruct AI to generate universally relevant content with broad cultural appeal. Taken together, these strategies help alleviate the risk of cultural insensitivity.

Data Privacy: Clear frameworks for data privacy are indispensable when designing prompts that involve learner interaction, such as AI-facilitated speaking practice or using AI to edit learners' writing samples. In addition, prompts should carefully specify the desired balance between AI-driven assistance and human interaction in order to maintain the central role of teachers and peers in the language learning process.

Interactive Engagement

With well-designed prompts, AI-powered tools demonstrate a noteworthy capacity to generate creative, engaging, and motivating materials that aligns with learners' interests and needs. For instance, teachers can instruct AI to personalize content for learners' specific demographics and connect the generated materials to their real-life experiences, which improves engagement and motivation. Additionally, AI can be directed to generate content that elicits active participation and supports a more dynamic learning experience. Above all, AI can create content with real-world connections and practical applications, bridging the gap between academic knowledge and pragmatic utility.

Pedagogical Alignment

Assessment and Evaluation: Particular care must be taken when utilizing AI tools to design assessments. Prompts should be written with explicit instructions on evaluation criteria, fairness, and ethical standards to avoid any form of bias. Furthermore, prompts must instruct the AI to consider cultural relevance and differentiation in order to generate reliable, useful language assessments.

Core Skills Integration: Designing AI prompts for language teaching requires a systematic approach to both receptive and productive skills.

- *Reading:* Create prompts that specifically support the prereading, reading, and postreading phases. For the prereading phase, ask AI to design tasks for schema activation and prediction. These tasks help learners connect newly received information with their already existing knowledge. For the reading phase, ask AI to generate multilayered comprehension questions. These questions should address both explicit understanding and deeper analytical thinking. For the postreading phase, prompt AI to create tasks that inspire learners to deeply reflect on and critically evaluate the text, moving from comprehension to production.

- *Listening:* Create prompts that follow a similar three-phase structure. Prelistening prompts should direct AI to craft tasks that activate students' background knowledge about the topic and preteach new and key vocabulary. For the listening phase, prompt AI to create tasks that address both bottom-up processing of details and top-down comprehension of general ideas. For postlistening, ask AI to generate tasks that require learners to actively practice their new language.

- *Writing:* Create prompts that address distinct stages of the writing process. At the brainstorming stage, write prompts that direct AI to help learners produce and organize ideas efficiently. At the drafting stage, prompt AI to generate a range of scaffolds for diverse proficiency levels, which encourages independent composition. Revision prompts should direct AI to offer feedback on specific aspects of writing, including organization of ideas, vocabulary choice, and rhetorical effectiveness.

- *Speaking:* Craft prompts that are targeted to the skill area and learning objec-

  design prompts that generate authentic

scenarios for meaningful interaction. These scenarios must reflect communication needs. For a lesson or unit on presentation skills development, prompt AI to generate materials that assist learners through the whole process of planning, organizing, and delivering talks. Finally, for pronunciation instruction, teachers must craft specialized prompts that emphasize specific phonological features and generate targeted practice opportunities.

Technology and Continuous Development

Focus on Outcomes: Successful technology integration means keeping a focus on using AI to achieve comprehensive, high-quality learning outcomes. It is essential to verify that the use of technology supports learning objectives and reinforces rather than detracts from the intended educational goals.

Refinement and Feedback: Successful prompt engineering includes systematic refinement, working toward ongoing improvement in response to learner feedback and measurements of learning outcomes. This entails tracking how well AI-generated content helps students achieve specific language learning goals and changing prompt features accordingly. It is vital to document both effective and ineffective qualities of AI-generated material in response to your prompts. Moreover, developing effective prompts requires multiple feedback sources. In addition to assessments of learning objectives, learner engagement data and direct learner feedback can both generate valuable input for prompt iteration and refinement. This feedback cycle helps teachers refine the specificity of prompts to increase the alignment between AI outputs and targeted learning outcomes.

Adaptive Implementation: During a semester and indeed over the years, teachers must modify their prompts in response to changing classroom dynamics. This involves adjusting prompts based on

- learner progress and achievement,
- varying proficiency levels within the same classroom,
- different cultural contexts and learning styles, and
- emerging language teaching methodologies and approaches.

It is essential to maintain a repository of successful prompts that are regularly refined and curated to address the emerging learning challenges and opportunities that arise in your classroom practice.

A Comprehensive ELT Prompt Template

The following comprehensive ELT Prompt Template is based on the SCRIPT model and is designed to help educators effectively integrate AI into their teaching practice. This template guides you through creating structured prompts that address all critical aspects of language instruction outlined by the SCRIPT model. By following this framework, educators can create materials that are pedagogically sound, culturally responsive, and adjusted to their learners' needs, regardless of which language skills they are targeting.

It is advisable to take this template as an example and to adapt it to your specific context. This template and the example prompt based on it are designed using the SCRIPT model and intended to prompt ChatGPT, or a similar chatbot tool. For a quick start, use the essential version of the template, or refer to the detailed version for more control. You can download both of these templates as well as a prompt library of more than 25 skill- and subject-specific extended templates on the companion website (www.tesol.org/AI-enhanced-ELT-book).

✦✦ Prompt Template: Essential Version (Quick Version)

Strategic Foundation

Goal: I need to create a [deliverable] for [proficiency level] learners focusing on [skill].

— lesson/activity/assessment/resource...

— reading/writing/listening/speaking/grammar...

Context & Objectives

Context: This fits into a lesson on [topic/theme] and aligns with [standard].

— learning standard/curriculum goal...

Responsiveness & Inclusivity

Learning Objective(s): [First measurable objective] [Second measurable objective]

Learner Profile: My students are [age range] with [level] proficiency. They come from [cultural/linguistic backgrounds], and I need to differentiate for [specific learning needs].

— beginner/intermediate/advanced...

Interactive Engagement

Activity Design: The task should be engaging through [grouping]. Provide clear, concise instructions with examples at the right level. Ensure inclusivity by [avoiding bias/using diverse representations]. Include real-world applications to make learning meaningful.

● pair work/group discussion/independent practice...

Pedagogical Alignment

Alignment & Adaptation: Ensure content aligns with [curriculum framework] and difficulty suits [proficiency level]. Support differentiated learning with versions for different skill levels.

Technology & Continuous Development

Technology & Feedback: Suitable for [modality] learning. Include AI-generated feedback/self-assessment methods for learners. Adaptable for different [variables].

● in-person/online/hybrid...

● Levels/cultural contexts/accessibility needs...

 Prompt Template: Detailed Version (Full Version)

Strategic Foundation

Goal: I need to create a [deliverable] for [specific proficiency level] learners focused on [language skill].

● lesson/activity/assessment/resource...

Context & Objectives

Context: This aligns with [curriculum goal] and focuses on [topic].

Learning Objective(s): [First measurable objective] [Second measurable objective] [Optional third objective]

Target Audience: My students are [age] with [proficiency level]. They come from [cultural backgrounds], and I need to differentiate for [specific needs].

Clarity & Structure: Keep language clear and concise for [proficiency level] learners.

Provide step-by-step instructions with concrete examples. Ensure contextual relevance by incorporating real-world situations. Align difficulty with students' proficiency and learning goals.

Responsiveness & Inclusivity

Scaffolding Needs: Adjust content difficulty by using [scaffolds]. ⎯⎯⎯● sentence frames/word banks/visuals/guided practice...

Cultural Sensitivity: Avoid bias and ensure representation of diverse perspectives.

Differentiation: Create versions of the content for different skill levels.

Interactive Engagement

Design the activity for active participation using: [approaches]. ⎯⎯⎯● pair or group work/ gamification/problem-solving/storytelling/ project-based tasks...
Ensure real-world relevance by applying skills to authentic scenarios.

Pedagogical Alignment

Adjust AI-generated content to match [proficiency framework]. ⎯⎯⎯● CEFR/WIDA...
Ensure language complexity aligns with [target level]. Support progression toward broader curriculum goals.

Technology & Continuous Development

The AI-generated content should be usable in [in-person/online/ hybrid settings]. Provide self-assessment or peer-assessment tools to enhance feedback. Adapt prompts based on learner responses and AI-generated feedback. Maintain flexibility by suggesting alternate approaches for varied learning contexts.

✦ Prompt Example Based on Essential Prompt Template (Speaking Activity, CEFR B1)

Create a speaking activity for intermediate (B1) English learners to practice everyday conversations. The lesson should focus on turn-taking and politeness in real-world settings (e.g., ordering food, asking for directions). Ensure clear instructions, scaffolding (sentence starters, word banks), and a short role-play task. Include an AI-driven self-assessment tool for feedback on fluency and pronunciation. Make it adaptable for in-person, online, and hybrid learning.

Prompt Breakdown

SCRIPT Component	How It's Addressed in the Essential Prompt
Strategic Foundation	Defines learner level (B1), skill (speaking), and real-world focus.
Clarity & Structure	Keeps instructions concise while ensuring clear progression.
Responsiveness & Inclusivity	Mentions scaffolding (word banks, sentence starters) and real-world relevance.
Interactive Engagement	Focuses on role-play and real-world scenarios.
Pedagogical Alignment	Implies alignment with CEFR B1 standards without excessive detail.
Technology & Continuous Development	Includes AI-driven self-assessment for pronunciation and fluency.

✦ Prompt Example Based on Detailed Prompt Template (Speaking Activity, CEFR B1)

Generate a communicative speaking activity for intermediate-level (CEFR B1) English learners to develop conversational skills in formal and informal settings. The lesson should align with curriculum standards for spoken interaction and focus on turn-taking strategies, politeness conventions, and real-world communication contexts.

Include culturally inclusive scenarios (e.g., ordering food at a restaurant, requesting information at a tourist center) and ensure differentiation for a mix of proficiency levels. The activity should follow a structured sequence: (1) a warm-up discussion on everyday communication differences, (2) guided practice using sentence starters and model dialogues, (3) a role-play task where students apply learned strategies in real-world interactions, and (4) AI-generated feedback assessing fluency, pronunciation, and accuracy.

Provide clear step-by-step instructions, model answers, and scaffolding tools such as word banks and visual prompts. Include an AI-driven self-assessment tool that allows students to record their responses and receive instant feedback on their speaking performance. Ensure the lesson is adaptable for in-person, online, and hybrid settings.

Prompt Breakdown

SCRIPT Component	How It's Addressed in the Detailed Prompt
Strategic Foundation	Defines proficiency level (B1), lesson goal (spoken interaction), and curriculum alignment.
Clarity & Structure	Breaks the task into clear stages (warm-up, guided practice, role-play, AI feedback) and includes step-by-step instructions.
Responsiveness & Inclusivity	Ensures cultural inclusivity (real-world scenarios), scaffolding (sentence starters, word banks), and differentiation (mixed-proficiency support).
Interactive Engagement	Uses real-world speaking contexts and includes an interactive role-play task for active learning.
Pedagogical Alignment	Tied to CEFR B1 standards and incorporates specific language learning outcomes.
Technology & Continuous Development	Integrates AI-generated feedback, self-assessment tools, and adaptability across different teaching environments.

Teaching Learners to Prompt: Building AI Literacy

Although this book mainly is centered on educator use of AI, it is hard to escape the fact that our learners now interact directly with AI tools and chatbots throughout their language learning journeys. Teaching learners how to write effective prompts enables them to become autonomous learners who can use AI to strengthen their skills via independent practice.

Student prompting is different from educator prompting in various ways. Learners benefit from simpler, more straightforward approaches with a focus on learning goals rather than complete curriculum planning. Successful and efficient student-written prompts should use a dialogue format, specify the student's level of proficiency, and contain explicit description of the type of practice they want.

Essential Student Prompting Skills

- **Define proficiency level:** Learners should learn to identify their level (beginner, intermediate, advanced) and mention the areas they are struggling with.

- **Ask for proper scaffolding:** Teach learners to request sentence starters, vocabulary lists, or guidance when required.

- **Establish practice parameters:** Learners should be clear about the desired length, format, and focus (e.g., grammar, vocabulary, pronunciation) of the generated learning task.

- **Request feedback:** Learners need to understand how to ask for various kinds of correction and clarification.

✦ Sample Learner Prompts for Common Learning Goals

Speaking role-play: "I'm studying the English language at an advanced level. Provide me with exercises to order food at a restaurant. Start with the conversation as the server, keep your language at B2 level, and correct any grammar mistakes in my dialogue."

Writing practice: "I'm studying the English language at an elementary level. For practicing past tense, give me a story prompt about a summer trip. Keep the language simple. After I write, correct my past tense errors and explain why suggested choices are better."

Help with pronunciation: "I'm studying English language pronunciation and struggling with pronouncing *th* sounds. List 10 common words with *th* as an exercise, then tell me if I should concentrate on voiced or voiceless sounds."

Training Strategies for Learner Prompt Engineering

Begin with guided practice using example prompt templates. Gradually inspire learners to change the examples, evaluate the results, and eventually generate their own original prompts. Walk learners through the iterative process. Show them how to improve prompts when AI responses are not in line with the student's intended purpose. Most significantly, highlight that successful prompting is a skill that advances with practice, just like any other language learning skill.

Final Thoughts on Prompt Engineering for ELT

Effective AI prompt design for language learning hinges on careful attention to both task design principles and quality assurance measures. Maintaining quality standards in prompt engineering calls for regular review and modifications, and educators should systematically analyze and evaluate AI outputs for correctness and suitability. This evaluation should involve attention to cultural sensitivity and inclusivity. Each prompt ought to correspond with specific learning objectives and shape part of a coherent development in task complexity. Finally, prompts must incorporate clear feedback or assessment techniques that encourage continuous progress in both teaching and learning.

As we have seen in this chapter, the successful use of AI prompts in English language teaching depends on several key implementation principles, including

- establishing clear pedagogical objectives before prompt creation,
- specifying parameters for AI outputs,
- building in flexibility for diverse learner needs and interests,
- integrating consistent assessment opportunities, and
- upholding a proper balance between AI support and learner autonomy.

Through close observation of these principles, educators can create productive AI-assisted language learning experiences that support learner achievement and preserve high pedagogical standards.

CHAPTER 3

Enhancing Teaching Skills With AI: Setting the Stage for Instruction

Today's educators can harness generative artificial intelligence (AI) systems to design curricula that adapt in real time, manage classroom operations with unique efficacy, and develop a comprehensive picture of their learners' unique profiles and needs. Rather than replacing traditional teaching practices, AI tools can empower educators to create more responsive, personalized, and data-informed learning experiences.

This chapter examines the practical applications of AI across four critical areas of instructional preparation: curriculum design and adjustment, classroom management and administrative efficiency, learner profiling and assessment, and needs analysis with goal setting. Through concrete examples, hands-on activities, and real-world applications, this chapter explores how these tools can foster rather than complicate your teaching practice, freeing you to focus on connecting with and empowering your students to achieve their language learning goals.

Creating Curricula

Integrating AI tools in the process of curriculum design offers English language teachers an unprecedented opportunity to generate more efficient, personalized, and adaptive curricula. Traditional curriculum design in English language teaching (ELT), heavily reliant on teacher expertise and best practices, has its merits. However, the traditional approach struggles to address the diverse needs of language learners in an increasingly globalized world. AI-assisted curriculum design enables educators to build evidence-based, personalized learning pathways and create adaptive content through real time analytics and ongoing data assessment.

AI systems can dynamically adjust curricular content in response to personalized learning pathways and emerging language patterns within global contexts. Furthermore, AI-driven predictive modeling empowers educators to predict learning outcomes with notable precision. This gives teachers the opportunity to design data-based, proactive interventions that address potential learning challenges before they are manifested in assessments. The next section presents an overview of tools for designing and implementing a responsive curriculum.

AI-Powered Tools for Curriculum Design

Teacher-facing, AI-powered tools for curriculum design can assist educators in developing comprehensive learning plans based on an analysis of current educational content, learners' needs, and course objectives. These tools empower educators to quickly and easily structure their instruction in alignment with learning goals (MIT Sloan Teaching and Learning Technologies, 2024). In addition, tools like automated essay scoring can streamline the grading process, and intelligent virtual environments can create an immersive learning experience with opportunities for collaboration (Jiang, 2022; see Chapter 10 for more discussion on immersive learning).

Specific tools currently transforming ELT curriculum design include the following:

- **MagicSchool** offers automated lesson planning and content generation after educators input their learning objectives and standards.
- **Diffit** offers lesson planning automation and educational content creation capabilities.
- **Duolingo** offers adaptive, individualized learning experiences with immediate feedback and progress tracking.
- **Babbel** offers personalized language learning with progress monitoring and adaptive content delivery.
- **Quizizz** offers real-time formative assessment monitoring and instructional adjustment capabilities.
- **Flow Speak** offers responsive assessment tools that enable performance-based instructional modifications.

For more detailed descriptions and links to each tool's website, refer to Appendix B.

Despite their powerful capabilities, the widespread adoption of AI tools for curriculum design must overcome significant resource constraints, including limited implementation costs. In addition, many educators lack adequate training to effectively utilize these technologies, leading them to continue relying on traditional approaches to curriculum design. Ethical concerns surrounding data privacy, algorithmic bias, and the potential reduction of essential human interactions in learning environments present ongoing challenges. Moreover, AI-generated materials may lack the necessary cultural context for effective language learning. All of these limitations reinforce the need to balance AI integration with maintaining meaningful teacher-student relationships.

Real-Time Curriculum Adjustment

ELT educators can leverage AI to continuously polish and improve course content in real time based on learner feedback and performance data. AI-driven adaptive systems automatically regulate lesson plans, modify difficulty levels, and present or eliminate topics to address learners' needs. A recent study on a data mining–based recommendation algorithm for course resources (Zhao et al., 2024) demonstrates the potential of big data-driven approaches in curriculum optimization. The researchers found significant developments in the algorithm's ability to recognize learner needs and offer precise resource suggestions. Though not specifically focused on ELT, this study highlights the growing significance of data-driven approaches in transforming curriculum design and learning experiences across educational domains.

TRY IT OUT: Real-Time Curriculum Adjustment

Track your language learners' progress over a 2-week period as they study with an AI learning platform and use the data to inform your teaching choices.

a. Implement a platform like Duolingo for Schools or Khan Academy. For Duolingo for Schools, create a teacher account, set up a virtual classroom, and invite students via a classroom code. Assign specific skills or units that align with your current curriculum (e.g., "Past Tense" or "Family Vocabulary"). For Khan Academy, create a class, add students by sharing the class code, and assign relevant language exercises or courses. Ensure students complete assigned activities both in class and as homework to generate sufficient data.

b. Monitor the platform's analytics dashboard every day in order to identify which language skills or topics learners are having trouble with (e.g., past tense usage, vocabulary retention, listening comprehension). Note patterns in completion rates and error frequencies across different lessons. Pay attention to where learners spend the most time or request the most hints.

c. Based on the obtained data, adjust your upcoming lesson plans by allocating additional class time to problematic areas, introducing targeted practice activities, and adjusting the pace of instruction.

This approach will help you create a responsive curriculum tailored to your learners' real-time performance data rather than predetermined structures and timelines.

Managing Your Classroom

AI is increasingly being utilized to streamline classroom management and administrative tasks, which often consume a significant portion of teachers' time and energy. AI offers solutions that can substantially reduce the workload of educators and improve overall efficiency. Systems employing computer vision and natural language processing (NLP) show the capability to automate routine tasks, such as tracking attendance and monitoring student participation, in both physical and online learning environments. Such advancements not only simplify administrative tasks but also provide valuable insights into learner engagement and well-being, facilitating early intervention in behavioral issues. The following section shares an overview of tools and approaches for AI-enhanced classroom management.

AI as a Teaching Assistant

Can AI play the role of a teaching assistant? This concept has rapidly evolved from a futuristic idea to a practical reality in many ELT classrooms. By leveraging AI-powered tools, teachers can now offload various administrative and instructional responsibilities to focus more on higher order tasks and high-value interactions with learners. As a result, AI is increasingly becoming an invaluable ally for the modern language teacher.

The power of AI as a teaching assistant extends far beyond simple task automation. These tools can analyze vast amounts of data to identify learning patterns and struggles unique to each learner. They can also facilitate interactive language practice sessions and craft customized learning materials based on learner needs. As a result, educators can find themselves with more time to have meaningful discussions, provide personalized support, and teach critical thinking skills—in other words, to focus on the

human creativity, empathy, and expertise.

The following specific tasks demonstrate how AI can function as an effective language teaching assistant:

- **Automated Grading and Feedback:** Teachers can use AI tools to evaluate quizzes, written assignments, and language exercises, and to provide tailored feedback on grammar, vocabulary, and structure. Platforms like Grammarly for Education, Cambridge English Write & Improve, and Turnitin Revision Assistant provide comprehensive automated writing assessment with instant corrections and suggestions for improvement.

- **Lesson Planning and Content Creation:** Teachers can use AI to craft customized lesson plans, create practice exercises, and develop assessment materials adjusted to particular learning objectives and proficiency levels. Tools like MagicSchool, Diffit, and ChatGPT can produce age- and level-appropriate content aligned with curriculum standards.

- **Language Practice and Conversation:** AI-powered chatbots and virtual tutors can provide learners with opportunities for speaking and writing practice outside the classroom. Platforms like Duolingo, Speechify, and Andy English Chatbot offer interactive conversations and pronunciation feedback in a low-pressure context.

- **Student Progress Tracking:** AI systems can monitor learner performance across multiple skills and gather detailed analytics on strengths and areas needing improvement. Learning management systems like Canvas, Blackboard, and Google Classroom incorporate AI features to track engagement and learning outcomes.

- **Personalized Learning Paths:** AI tools can analyze learner data to suggest activities, resources, and practice exercises based on learners' needs and preferred styles. Adaptive platforms like Rosetta Stone, Babbel, and FluentU tailor difficulty levels and content based on real-time performance data.

- **Administrative Task Management:** Teachers can use AI to streamline various administrative responsibilities such as scheduling, email responses, and report generation. Tools like Calendly for scheduling, Notion for managing projects, and Boomerang's AI Assistant for email management can reduce time spent on routine tasks.

Attendance Tracking and Student Monitoring

AI-driven attendance and monitoring systems mark a significant development in classroom management: They allow educators to track student presence and engagement with increased efficiency and accuracy. Tools like EduPage, ClassDojo, and SchoolPass utilize computer vision and facial recognition capabilities to track student presence and engagement. This technology offers valuable behavioral insights and reduces the routine administrative responsibilities for educators.

How do these systems work? Via the camera on the student's device (if online) or a camera in the classroom (if in-person), these tools can use facial recognition technology to identify students as they enter the classroom or join online sessions (meaning that teachers no long need to spend time on manual roll calls). Then, the tools continuously assess student engagement through various metrics, including eye tracking, body language analysis, and participation frequency. The resulting behavioral data helps teachers understand which students are actively engaged and which may require additional motivation or support strategies. It can also identify potential academic or social concerns before they escalate into crises.

Although these technologies offer significant benefits, teachers or administrators who implement them should give careful attention to privacy regulations, such as FERPA (Family Educational Rights and Privacy Act; United States) and GDPR (General Data Protection Regulation; European Union). Educational institutions must establish transparent and explicit policies for the collection, storage, and usage of student data, ensuring that student privacy rights are protected as schools leverage the advantages of AI-powered monitoring systems.

Knowing Your Learners

Understanding your learners forms the cornerstone of effective English language teaching, yet traditional methods of assessment often offer teachers a narrow scope of information on their learners. AI-powered tools are changing how we gather, analyze, and apply learner data, helping educators move beyond surface-level assessments to understand not only what learners know, but also how they learn, what motivates them, and where their unique competences and challenges lie. This approach is directly in line with Principle 1 of TESOL's *The 6 Principles for Exemplary Teaching of English Learners*, which highlights the significance of knowing your learners to support and ... effectively (TESOL International Association, 2024).

Data-Driven Learner Profiles

AI systems can craft inclusive learner profiles by examining various data points obtained from learners, including performance on assessments, engagement with learning materials, and even affective factors. By leveraging advanced algorithms and data analytics, AI can now dynamically map proficiency levels, adapt content delivery, and adjust learning trajectories, enabling teachers to provide more targeted instruction while reducing preparation time and providing the grounds for learners to progress at their optimal pace. Following are some of the ways it does this.

Multidimensional Proficiency Mapping

A cornerstone of data-driven learner profiles, multidimensional mapping surpasses traditional, single-skill assessment by providing a holistic view of a learner's proficiency. Tools like those listed here employ AI algorithms to analyze and synthesize multiple sources of data, including standardized tests, in-class performance, peer interactions, and self-assessments. The resulting multifaceted profile maps the learner's English proficiency across listening, speaking, reading, and writing skills, as well as their levels of pragmatic competence and sociolinguistic awareness. These profiles can also chart a learner's progression over time, showing areas of rapid improvement, plateaus, and potential regressions. The result is a dynamic picture of learner proficiency that enables educators to tailor their pedagogical practices with enhanced precision by targeting specific areas of need and building on individual strengths.

Following are some multidimensional proficiency mapping AI-powered tools to try:

- **EF Standard English Test** deploys adaptive testing algorithms to assess various language skills. Educators can use this tool to establish basic proficiency levels and trace progress over time.

- Pearson's **Versant** makes use of speech recognition and NLP to evaluate speaking and writing skills in real time, which offers educators the opportunity to track progress on a more frequent basis.

- **ClassDojo's portfolio feature** uses AI-driven analytics to generate a holistic view of learner performance across various activities.

- **Textio** provides AI-powered writing analysis that helps teachers evaluate student compositions for clarity, tone, and effectiveness. The platform offers real-time suggestions for improving word choice, sentence structure, and overall communication impact.

- **Speechace** can be used for pronunciation assessment to provide detailed feedback on learner speech patterns and accuracy. Teachers can assign specific pronunciation exercises and receive automated scoring reports that identify areas where students need additional practice.
- **Blackboard Predict** or **D2L's Brightspace** are learning analytics platforms that can help you mix data from these various sources.

These tools can aggregate and visualize learner data to provide useful insights, identify trends, and help teachers make informed decisions about their teaching. For more details on each of these tools, as well as links to their websites, refer to Appendix B.

> ### TRY IT OUT: Using Versant for Proficiency Mapping
>
> Familiarize yourself and your students with Pearson's Versant assessments.
>
> a. Have students participate weekly in brief, AI-driven tests in Versant, during which their oral and written responses are examined using advanced speech recognition and NLP algorithms.
>
> b. Review the individual proficiency profiles created by the tool right after the test, clearly identifying specific strengths (e.g., pronunciation accuracy, syntactic complexity), as well as areas that need improvement.
>
> c. Equipped with this data, tailor your instruction by designing targeted activities and providing personalized feedback.
>
> This experience demonstrates how AI-driven proficiency mapping empowers learners to conceptualize their progress, often resulting in increased motivation and deeper engagement with the learning process.

Needs Analysis and Goal Setting

Needs analysis and goal setting are the foundation of ELT curriculum design. They are crucial steps for creating tailored instruction, maximized relevance, and elevated educational outcomes. AI-driven tools can revolutionize how educators conduct needs assessments. With more efficient and accurate data collection and analysis, including real-time insights into common mistakes and error patterns, teachers can craft highly personalized, data-driven learning trajectories adapted to individual learners' needs and proficiency levels. This section explores the technology behind these tools, then
analytics phase of curriculum

design—from ELT-specific tools to those designed for general use but adaptable to language education.

Predictive Analytics for Goal Setting

AI technology is increasingly being employed in education to analyze datasets on learner performance. This provides the grounds for designing learning pathways and tailoring content based on learners' profiles. AI tools employing machine learning and NLP can not only identify gaps in learner knowledge but also provide tailored feedback to help set realistic and personalized learning objectives (Woo & Choi, 2021). Through predictive analysis, they create a comprehensive picture of each learner's strengths and weaknesses.

For example, a teacher might use one of the tools listed in this section to track quiz scores, engagement time with reading tasks, vocabulary growth, and participation patterns over the course of several weeks. Using machine learning algorithms, the tool would then identify learning trends and predict future performance trajectories. Based on the emerged patterns, the teacher can establish realistic, evidence-based learning goals and activities to support those goals. If the AI predicts that a student is likely to struggle with complex grammar structures in the upcoming unit, the teacher can preemptively set scaffolded grammar targets, adjust the pacing, or assign preparatory microlessons. Constant review and adaptation of goals based on ongoing performance data are essential features of AI-driven needs assessment, allowing teachers to easily identify and address formerly unobserved performance gaps and learner needs.

Additionally, language learning apps are progressively implementing adaptive algorithms for personalized learning experiences, which predict next content for learners based on past performance (Pikhart, 2020). In the near future, AI systems are expected to gradually incorporate higher order learning skills and interdisciplinary collaboration into their predictive models to create even more elaborate and reliable needs analysis and goal-setting tools (Chen, Zou, et al., 2021).

Critical to this approach is to repeatedly evaluate and refine the AI-assisted needs analysis. To carry this out effectively, it is crucial to collect feedback from learners and educators on the efficiency and practicality of the AI-supported insights. This means it is necessary to compare AI-created assessments with traditional assessment methods; it is also important to stay current on new developments in AI-enhanced language assessment and incorporate the advances as they become available. By following these steps, educators can ensure their AI-generated needs assessment remains accurate and relevant.

AI Tools for Needs Analysis and Goal Setting

AI tools that can be utilized for needs analysis and goal setting include the following:

- **Elsa Speak** offers pronunciation assessment, speech pattern analysis, and individualized identification of speaking skill gaps.
- Cambridge English's **Write & Improve** provides on-the-spot feedback on learners' writing, helping teachers pinpoint recurring grammar, syntax, and vocabulary issues.
- **Cognii** offers diagnostic questioning, knowledge gap detection, and learning readiness assessment capabilities for identifying individual student needs.
- **Duolingo for Schools** offers skill level assessment, progress monitoring, and learning difficulty identification capabilities for determining student placement and support needs.
- **Classtime** offers real-time comprehension checking, knowledge gap detection, and formative needs assessment capabilities for identifying areas requiring additional instruction.
- **Squirrel AI** offers personalized learning path creation, adaptive goal adjustment, and progress milestone setting capabilities for establishing individualized student objectives.
- **D2L's Brightspace** offers learning outcome mapping, competency-based goal tracking, and progress visualization capabilities for setting and monitoring educational targets.
- **Grammarly** offers writing skill progression tracking, personalized improvement goals, and performance benchmarking capabilities for setting language development objectives.

Some of these platforms are available for individuals, but most require institutional adoption. For more details on these applications, refer to Appendix B.

The integration of needs analysis and goal setting via AI tools creates a comprehensive framework that moves from identifying learning gaps to establishing personalized, measurable objectives. By employing real-time data analytics, these tools can track learners' progress and provide constant cyclical adjustments of learning pathways. This approach enhances the effectiveness of instruction and improves engagement by aligning content with learner needs. Moreover, establishing measurable objectives creates a goal-oriented learning environment and encourages accountability and motivation.

TRY IT OUT: Needs Analysis and Response With Write & Improve

To assess your learners' writing proficiency, assign a diagnostic writing task through Write & Improve.

a. Ask your learners to submit their writing through the class dashboard; you will receive immediate AI-generated feedback.

b. Review the common errors (e.g., subject–verb agreement, run-on sentences) that the tool has identified and make note of your learners' weaknesses.

c. Make note of any particular structure that many students struggle with.

d. Adjust your lesson plans accordingly by incorporating targeted grammar instruction and scaffolded writing activities.

This data-driven approach will help you ensure that your instruction is responsive to your learners' needs, creating a more personalized and effective learning experience.

TRY IT OUT: Independent Writing Growth With Grammarly

Assign a diagnostic essay to your students. Have them use Grammarly to highlight error patterns in grammar, clarity, and coherence. Then, have each learner

a. set two improvement objectives based upon the feedback they received,

b. use Grammarly to track their own progress throughout the semester by revising drafts with AI-driven guidance, and

c. reflect on their growth at the end of the course by using Grammarly's reports to showcase their progress.

Be sure to monitor all the changes and adapt your instruction to address your learners' common mistakes and weaknesses. This exercise fosters independent learning and helps learners strengthen their writing skills with personalized feedback.

AI-powered needs analysis and goal-setting tools redefine conventional approaches to understanding and responding to learner requirements—moving from static assessments toward dynamic, responsive learning pathways that are refined in response to each learner's progress. By empowering both educators and learners to identify needs set goals, track progress, and adapt objectives based on real-time data, these technologies can foster student accountability for their own learning and create a learning environment where success becomes observable, and thus, achievable.

Conclusion

The capabilities of AI in ELT extend far beyond everyday task automation. As presented throughout this chapter, AI's most meaningful contributions are in improving human judgment and pedagogical expertise, rather than replacing it. From dynamic curriculum adjustment systems to advanced learner profiling tools, these technologies provide educators with useful insights into both the learning process and learner needs.

The practical applications explored here prove how AI can generate space for what is important in language education: meaningful human interaction, creative problem-solving, and critical thinking development. Perhaps most notably, AI's largest contribution to ELT may be its capability to create individualized learning pathways, accessible at scale, through real-time adaptation and evidence-based goal setting.

Moving forward, the key dilemma for educators should not be whether to embrace AI, but how to integrate these tools to support and extend human creativity, empathy, and expertise.

This chapter established a foundational understanding of AI as a collaborative partner in instruction. In the upcoming chapters, we investigate more detailed uses of AI for specific language functions.

CHAPTER 4

Enhancing Teaching Skills With AI: In the Classroom

Though curriculum design and needs analysis are the foundation of successful teaching practice, the moment teachers step into their classrooms, they must make instant decisions about pacing, difficulty, and learner engagement. This is the next test of the value of generative artificial intelligence (AI) as a tool for English language teaching (ELT): Once you have created your syllabus and established a plan for the semester or session, how can AI continue to support your everyday lesson planning and classroom teaching?

This chapter addresses the practical realities of using AI in active classroom contexts. From intelligent systems that adapt content difficulty to gamified platforms that transform vocabulary study into a collaborative adventure, these tools can help you shift from relying on static lesson plans to leading dynamic, responsive, and engaging classes—all while preserving the human connections that make language learning meaningful.

The applications explored in this chapter prove AI's capacity to improve rather than automate the art of teaching. AI tools can help you differentiate instruction seamlessly, generate compelling interactive experiences, and cut down on administrative work that can sometimes be overwhelming. This chapter offers educators powerful tools that free them to focus on what they do best: inspiring, guiding, and connecting with their learners to best foster language learning and cultural understanding.

Differentiation

The adaptive abilities of AI systems introduce an important step forward in our ability to differentiate language instruction for different levels and learning styles. Using AI-driven intelligent systems that track learners' progress over time, teachers can offer students personalized feedback and suggestions for further development, differentiating the curriculum to match learners' unique needs (Manire et al., 2023). Moreover, AI techniques can provide opportunities to enhance writing and vocabulary learning by analyzing learning behaviors and tailoring the content accordingly (Liang et al., 2021). This technology supports systematic and continuous assessment, determines the learners' language development patterns, and identifies potential challenges.

How does this work? One primary function of AI tools that support differentiation is the intelligent sequencing of learning activities. At the core of this process are adaptive language learning platforms (e.g., Duolingo) that leverage machine learning algorithms to analyze learner performance data and regulate the difficulty of subsequent activities. Learning management systems enhanced with AI capabilities, such as Blackboard AI Design Assistant or Canvas MasteryPaths, provide educators with perceptive interfaces to craft branching learning sequences in response to student performance data. By incorporating these tools, differentiated instruction can be implemented at scale. This can foster more opportunities for teachers to focus on enhancing personalized support and fostering higher order thinking skills while the AI systems handle the complexities of activity sequencing and basic skill reinforcement.

TRY IT OUT: Personalized Learning Pathways With Canvas MasteryPaths

For Canvas users: Set up a sequential learning module within your existing course using the MasteryPaths feature.

a. Design an initial diagnostic activity (e.g., a quiz or an assignment) in Canvas.

b. Using the MasteryPaths feature, set up a module that leads learners to various follow-up activities according to their scores (e.g., advanced learners receive enrichment tasks, and those needing support receive scaffolding practice).

c. Monitor the Canvas analytics dashboard over a 2-week period to track which students are being directed to which pathways and identify patterns in learning needs across your class.

d. Use this data to allocate your in-class time more effectively by providing targeted intervention to students following remedial pathways and facilitating deeper discussions with those on advanced tracks.

This AI-powered sequencing will help you optimize classroom time for personalized attention while ensuring all learners receive appropriate challenge levels for their language learning objectives.

Addressing Different Proficiency Levels

In addition to creating adaptive learning sequences, teachers can use strategic prompt engineering to differentiate instruction by directing AI tools to generate multiple versions of the same content. For instance, when designing reading comprehension activities for a multilevel classroom, teachers can prompt AI to produce three versions of a text in terms of difficulty level, using simplified vocabulary and shorter sentences for beginners, moderately complex structures for intermediate learners, and authentic academic language for advanced students. Likewise, AI writing assistants like Grammarly can be directed to offer various levels of scaffolding.

TRY IT OUT: Multilevel Content Creation With ChatGPT

Design differentiated reading materials for a mixed-proficiency class using a single prompt in ChatGPT.

a. Input a prompt like the following: "Create a 150-word text about climate change at three proficiency levels: beginner (A2), intermediate (B1), and advanced (C1). Include comprehension questions for each level."

b. Review the created content and select the proper version for each group of learners, or use all three versions for various phases of the same lesson.

c. Monitor how learners interact with their level-appropriate materials and adapt future prompts according to what works best for your learners.

This approach allows you to generate personalized content efficiently while ensuring all learners can access the same core concepts at their appropriate challenge level.

Differentiation for Beginning Learners

AI can be an especially powerful tool for students who are just beginning to learn English. AI-driven language learning apps, such as Duolingo, Babbel, Rosetta Stone, and FluentU, can provide structured practice in basic vocabulary, grammar, and pronunciation, scaffolding learners' acquisition through the skills they need, step by step. This tailored practice helps students see their progress and accordingly enhances their confidence. Moreover, AI tools can adjust to each learner's needs, offering an optimal balance of difficulty and support. They are interactive, using stories, games, and simulated conversation practice to make learning fun and meaningful.

Here are some of the practical things AI tools can do in your beginner-level ELT classroom:

- Help learners build vocabulary using pictures, sounds, and interactive games
- Provide support with sentence patterns and grammar via step-by-step instruction
- Use speech recognition to "listen" to learners and offer helpful feedback on pronunciation
- Increase phonemic awareness by analyzing learners' speech and identifying areas for improvement
- Offer engaging, personalized stories that match each learner's vocabulary level
- Use digital characters (like talking avatars) to practice conversations and turn-taking in a safe, guided way
- Reward learners with digital badges and points to sustain their motivation and active participation

Differentiation for Intermediate Learners

Intermediate learners represent a unique position in language acquisition, where foundational skills meet practical application. At this stage, learners are ready to expand their vocabulary knowledge, improve their grammatical accuracy, and develop more advanced pragmatic skills. Tools like Grammarly, Speechace, Andy English Bot, and FluentU become valuable for intermediate learners because they can provide the consistent practice and tailored feedback to bridge the gap between basic communication and advanced-level proficiency.

AI tools offer several key advantages for the intermediate-level ELT classroom. Here are some of the practical things they can do to support your intermediate learners:

- Present new vocabulary in meaningful contexts, rather than word lists
- Offer spaced repetition to support long-term knowledge retention
- Act as a patient tutor for error correction, with clear explanations and relevant examples to help learners understand the underlying rules
- Support speaking practice by actively involving learners in increasingly complex simulated dialogues across diverse topics
- Provide unlimited opportunity for speaking practice outside the classroom, regardless of the availability of tutors or conversation partners

- Offer personalized writing assistance, including feedback on voice and style as well as targeted feedback on coherence, organization, and complexity of ideas

- Differentiate reading instruction by automatically adjusting text difficulty and generating or curating materials related to learners' interests

- Increase learner engagement by fostering a gradual, scaffolded progression toward more challenging authentic materials

Differentiation for Advanced Learners

Advanced learners need AI tools that can match their advanced language abilities while challenging them to move forward. Their goal has shifted from building foundational skills to mastering the subtleties of professional communication. Tools like Textio, ProWritingAid, ELSA Speak, and specialized corpus analysis platforms focus on subtle modifications in style, register, and cultural appropriateness rather than on basic error correction. In addition, accent reduction and prosody training are significant for advanced learners who want to fine-tune their pronunciation for professional or academic contexts.

Here are some examples of AI tools that can support your advanced learners:

- **Textio** and **ProWritingAid** are advanced writing analysis tools that surpass grammar checking to evaluate argument structure, rhetorical effectiveness, and stylistic consistency. They can recognize when a learner's writing fails to strike the appropriate tone needed for academic papers or professional correspondence and offer suggestions for improvement.

- **Immerse** offers a simulated professional environment driven by virtual reality (VR) that helps advanced learners to practice workplace skills, such as presenting to virtual board members, negotiating contracts, or participating in international conferences. The AI agents in these contexts can respond naturally to learner input and provide targeted feedback on their communication.

- **ELSA Speak** uses AI-powered speech recognition technology to identify the subtle variations in intonation, stress patterns, and rhythm that distinguish fluent speakers from advanced learners, following up with targeted training exercises.

For more details on these applications, refer to Appendix B.

Here are additional things that AI tools can do to support your advanced learners:

- Analyze writing for argument structure, rhetorical effectiveness, and tone appropriateness
- Create simulated professional environments for workplace communication practice
- Identify subtle pronunciation patterns in intonation, stress, and rhythm for targeted improvement
- Facilitate complex argumentation and debate practice with cultural awareness components
- Provide corpus-based analysis revealing natural language patterns and collocation usage
- Offer feedback on advanced discourse features like cohesion, coherence, and pragmatic appropriateness

Learning Style and Preference Analysis

AI tools for education excel in differentiating materials and activities for a range of learning styles and preferences, via pattern recognition algorithms and analysis of datasets of learner interactions. They can track and analyze learners' engagement with various media types, their responses to different instructional approaches, and their performance across diverse task formats. Some tools go further, incorporating insights from cognitive science and educational psychology to ultimately create dynamic learner profiles that evolve as learners progress through a set of materials or a learning sequence.

Here are some AI-powered tools for differentiating your teaching according to individual learner preferences or performance data:

- **CENTURY** offers personalized learning paths by analyzing student performance and engagement patterns.
- **Babbel** incorporates AI to recognize and adjust to learner preferences in vocabulary and grammar learning.
- **Nearpod** helps educators create multimodal lessons and generates an analysis of learner engagement data with different modes.
- **ChatGPT** and other large language model chatbots can generate adaptive reading materials or personalized writing prompts.

For more details on these applications, refer to Appendix B.

TRY IT OUT: Adaptive Learning Preferences With Duolingo for Schools

Identify and respond to your learners' diverse needs and preferences. This exercise works best for an intermediate-level class.

a. Have learners complete Duolingo's placement test to establish their starting level. The system will detect strengths and weaknesses across language skills, such as vocabulary, grammar, and listening.

b. Have learners continue to complete adaptive practice activities over several weeks. Review the teacher dashboard insights that show each learner's progress, time on task, and areas of difficulty.

c. Use these data-driven insights to adjust your classroom approach by integrating targeted vocabulary review, collaborative speaking activities, or multimedia resources that align with your learners' identified preferences.

This strategy will help you achieve high engagement, promote learner independence, and enhance language skill development through personalized, adaptive instruction.

TRY IT OUT: Personalized Content With ChatGPT

Use ChatGPT in your reading and writing class to generate personalized content.

a. Create simple written learner profiles for each student, including their reading levels and topic preferences.

b. Then, embed these in a prompt asking ChatGPT to generate customized reading texts and reflective writing prompts for a specific unit (such as "global issues") tailored to each learner's profile.

c. Have learners read their personalized texts in class, then complete their customized writing tasks.

d. Refine your learner profiles for future lessons based on your evaluation of learners' written responses and engagement levels.

This personalized approach will help each learner remain engaged and appropriately challenged while developing both reading comprehension and critical writing skills.

Lesson Planning and Creating Materials

AI-enhanced lesson planning and material creation in ELT presents a revolutionary approach to education, integrating AI-enhanced design of the lesson plans and materials for instruction. These tools streamline the lesson planning by automating the administrative tasks. AI-powered tools also promote the alignment of lesson plans with educational standards and curricula, while assisting with the integration of existing resources and platforms (Generative AI @Harvard, 2024). Furthermore, this methodology allows educators to create dynamic content, catering to diverse student needs and learning styles.

Automated Lesson Plan Generation

AI systems can generate customized lesson plan outlines based on the data obtained from an analysis of learning objectives, learner profiles, and educational standards (Di Mario, 2024; Teaching & Learning Resource Center, n.d.). If provided with well-engineered prompts, generative AI chatbots (e.g., ChatGPT, Microsoft Copilot, Google Gemini) can also curate collections of relevant, level-appropriate materials from across the internet. Together, these capacities can offer teachers significant time savings. Some AI-driven lesson plan generators ask users to input limiting factors, but for others, you'll need to make sure your prompt includes specific details to generate a useful result.

Here are a few AI tools that help with lesson planning:

- **LessonPlans.ai** was designed by teachers, for teachers, and generates detailed lesson plans based on your input of a lesson title, grade level, and detailed description (i.e., prompt).

- **Slidesgo Lesson Plan Generator** offers free, AI-driven text-to-slides lesson plan generation based on educational level, classroom mode, and a detailed prompt.

- **MagicSchool** supports educators with lesson planning, differentiation, writing assessments, and more.

- **Classcraft** is an AI-supported classroom management and lesson-planning platform that can assist teachers with forming learning experiences and monitoring learner engagement. The current version of Classcraft offers features such as behavior tracking, engagement analytics, and teacher-designed "quests" that perform as guided lesson pathways. Its AI-driven suggestions help teachers place learners who may need further assistance and regulate their instructional choices accordingly.

For more detailed descriptions and links to each tool's website, refer to Appendix B.

TRY IT OUT: Lesson Planning With MagicSchool

This activity can be completed using the free version of MagicSchool. Prepare a comprehensive lesson on persuasive speaking and environmental vocabulary using MagicSchool to streamline your planning process.

a. Input your learners' proficiency levels, your learning objectives, and any specific curriculum standards into MagicSchool to generate a structured lesson outline that includes engaging warm-up activities, new vocabulary items, and speaking prompts—all adjusted to your learners' language profiles.

b. Implement the AI-generated lesson plan. For example, you might have learners participate in debates about environmental topics (such as recycling practices), guided by the clear and detailed plan provided by the platform.

c. Use the time saved in lesson preparation to focus your energy on facilitating interactive discussions and providing individualized feedback to learners during the speaking activities.

TRY IT OUT: Unit Planning With ChatGPT

Plan a comprehensive reading and writing unit on digital citizenship for your advanced learners using ChatGPT to generate and structure appropriate and engaging content.

a. Specify parameters such as language proficiency, subject themes, and lesson objectives when prompting ChatGPT to find authentic online articles and videos about digital citizenship, then recommend interactive writing prompts and discussion questions about those materials.

b. Review the collection of level-appropriate materials that ChatGPT generates covering your desired topic, then choose and revise the materials and questions to adapt it to the learners' needs.

c. Implement the revised content in your classroom.

This approach will help you to efficiently develop comprehensive unit materials while guaranteeing the content remains challenging and relevant for your advanced learners.

Multimodal Learning Materials

AI-powered tools excel at creating multimodal learning materials, including illustrations and interactive diagrams. AI image generators like DALL·E, Microsoft Image Creator, and Midjourney can create visual media based on written prompts. Other AI tools can create synthesized speech for listening practice and to model comprehensible pronunciation. Taking advantage of these tools, educators can quickly design creative, engaging, and content-relevant visuals that can help learners make sense of complex concepts (Zhai et al., 2024).

More AI Tools for Lesson Planning and Material Creation

In addition to the tools mentioned earlier for lesson planning and materials generation, the following list provides a selection of other recommended tools. For detailed descriptions for each tool, please refer to Appendix B.

- **QuillBot** offers content rewriting, lesson material paraphrasing, and educational text enhancement.
- **Canva** offers lesson slide creation, educational poster design, and instructional visual content generation.
- **Wakelet** offers lesson resource curation, teaching material organization, and educational content collection.
- **Kami** offers worksheet annotation, lesson material markup, and collaborative document preparation.
- **Gradescope** offers assignment creation, rubric development, and assessment material design.
- **Learnt.ai** offers personalized lesson planning, adaptive curriculum creation, and individualized material generation.
- **Teachology.ai** offers automated lesson planning, curriculum alignment, and educational content creation.
- **Curipod** offers interactive lesson creation, engaging presentation design, and student activity development.
- **Quizlet** offers study materials, flashcard-based lesson content, and responsive practice activities.

- **Kahoot!** offers quiz-based lesson creation, gamified learning activity design, and interactive content development.
- **Edpuzzle** offers video lesson creation, interactive content embedding, and multimedia material development.
- **Wordtune** offers lesson text refinement, instructional content improvement, and educational writing enhancement.

TRY IT OUT: Academic Vocabulary With Quizlet

Prepare a multimodal lesson on academic vocabulary for advanced-level learners using Quizlet.

a. Before class, create a custom Quizlet set featuring key words, definitions, and example sentences relevant to your unit topic (such as environmental issues).

b. Introduce the vocabulary: Use Quizlet Flashcards to teach the new words so learners can hear the pronunciation and see example sentences, then play the Matching Game as a whole class for a quick knowledge check.

c. Assign learners to the Learn Mode, which tracks their progress and adapts the difficulty level based on their performance. Then, facilitate a partner activity: Using Quizlet Live, have students work in teams to match words and their definitions as quickly as possible in a competitive, collaborative format.

d. As a homework assignment, have learners use Quizlet's Test feature to review at their own pace. This will help them to reinforce their learning through self-directed study.

Leveraging Quizlet's AI-driven study tools, students will be actively engaged as they learn new words, receive feedback, and reinforce their learning through multimodal activities that make the lesson both effective and enjoyable.

AI for Lesson Planning: Implementation Checklist

☐ Select an AI tool that aligns with your philosophy of teaching and curriculum standards.

☐ Use the ELT Prompt Template (Chapter 2) to generate a lesson plan and accompanying materials.

☐ Employ the AI-generated lesson outline as a foundation, refining and personalizing it to suit your specific needs.

Providing feedback to AI is vital. This helps AI refine the understanding of your requirements, ensuring the generated content is increasingly tailored to your pedagogy and objectives.

☐ Use AI-curated content to supplement core resources and offer extended learning opportunities.

☐ Select adaptive exercise generators that cover multiple language skills and can effortlessly integrate with your existing learning management system. For assignments, self-study, and in-class practice, employ adaptive exercises and continuously monitor learner progress through the system's analytics.

This iterative approach helps adjust your teaching approach accordingly.

☐ Allow your learners to create their own AI-assisted materials as an extended learning activity. This approach not only expands teaching resources but also engages learners in creative, technology-enhanced learning experiences.

☐ Maintain a balance between AI-generated and human-created materials by using AI as a tool to enhance, not replace, your creativity and expertise.

Frequently review, evaluate, and curate AI-created materials to confirm their value, significance, and relevance.

Interactive Tasks and Gamification

The fusion of gamification with ELT has revolutionized how learners worldwide master English. Rather than relying on traditional vocabulary drills and grammar exercises, today's English language teachers weave task-based, challenge-driven activities into engaging and interactive lessons. Consider how a simple vocabulary exercise can morph into an epic quest, where learners progress through increasingly complex challenges, each perfectly matched to their current abilities. Students might find themselves navigating virtual conversations with fluent speakers, decoding authentic texts, or collaborating with other learners on project-based missions. Game-based language learning goes far beyond basic memorization to create meaningful experiences where language skills develop naturally through authentic interaction. Integrating gamification via edtech tools brings new strengths to the table for teachers. We can see four main areas where AI-driven tools excel in gamification for language learning: adapting game difficulty, building personalized narratives, and supporting competition and collaboration.

Advantages of AI in Gamified Language Learning

Adaptive Difficulty

By utilizing diverse assessment techniques, AI tools can continuously analyze learner behaviors, processing speeds, and accuracy across diverse linguistic skills. Beyond basic performance measurement, AI-driven language learning apps include adaptive content adjustment, where content materials are continuously tailored to align with the learner's proficiency. Notably, these systems recognize differences in proficiency across different linguistic skills, such as recognizing when a learner excels in reading comprehension but struggles with oral communication. The following AI-driven apps exemplify how gamification and adaptive difficulty converge to generate highly engaging, dynamic, and personalized language learning experiences.

- **Duolingo** uses AI to adapt question difficulty, track learner performance, and personalize task content. Gamification is embedded in the platform through streaks, experience points, skill trees, hearts, and badges.

- **EWA** is another app that gamifies language learning. Learners unlock novel obstacles as they progress. EWA uses AI to responsively adjust content complexity, incorporating mini-games, flashcards, and dialogues tailored to learners' proficiency levels and interests.

- **Mondly** uses chatbot-based role-play, augmented reality (AR)/VR environments, and personalized lesson paths. Its gamified features include daily goals, leaderboards, rewards, and conversation simulations. The AI adjusts responses and feedback, and the gamification layer keeps learners motivated.

- **Memrise** combines spaced repetition with gamification through interactive video clips, AI-driven memory cues, and adaptive quizzes and tests. It motivates learners through badges, levels, and speed review obstacles.

For more detailed descriptions and links to each tool's website, refer to Appendix B.

Personalized Narratives and Quests

Another strength of gamification in English language teaching is that games often incorporate adaptive storytelling, which refers to narrative structures, like quests or challenges, that immerse learners in an imagined realistic narrative that is responsive to learner input. These activities can be highly motivating and engaging. Following are some examples of AI-driven language learning platforms that include adaptive storytelling:

- **Mondly,** as mentioned earlier, provides learners a highly interactive experience through AI-powered chatbots and immersive VR scenarios that turn practice into a series of engaging missions. This app adjusts conversation and task complexity to be responsive to learners' interests and skill levels.

- **Speakly** creates contextual learning paths driven from real-life situations. Though not structured as formal quests, its scenario-based method offers learners sequential, dynamic challenges.

- **Immerse** uses virtual environments to generate live, role-based language experiences. Learners take part in guided conversations that evolve dynamically according to their responses, combining storytelling and real-time language use in an immersive, game-like setting.

For more detailed descriptions and links to each tool's website, refer to Appendix B.

A striking feature of many of these apps is their progress-sensitive narrative design, where storylines evolve in direct relation to the learner's mastery of specific language skills. They also track and respond to learner inputs, incorporating cultural context, profession-related scenarios, and personal interests to structure customized learning paths.

Competition

Competitive games foster motivation and cooperative learning. Language learning platforms using AI to drive competition can nurture more immersive and dynamic educational experiences. For example, with intelligent opponent modeling, AI plays the role of a competitor, regulating its skill level to offer learners challenge scenarios at the right level. Another important feature is automated scoring and feedback, where AI delivers prompt results and feedback on both individual and group performance in collaborative tasks.

Following are some examples of AI-driven language learning platforms that include competition:

- **Kahoot!** uses game show–style quizzes with synchronous leaderboards, and recent versions provide AI-powered analytics for supporting differentiated questioning and feedback. Its multiplayer format adds team-based competition elements.

- **Quizlet's** AI-driven Live mode includes adaptive content and generates dynamic team play. Features like Match and leaderboard-driven vocabulary races incorporate gamified competition with spaced repetition algorithms.

- **Memrise** blends spaced repetition with video-based tasks and leaderboards. Its AI adjusts question types and vocabulary review frequency based on learner performance, and its scoring system inspires ongoing progress and competition.

- **Baamboozle** is a team-based language game platform often used in classrooms. Baamboozle+ includes smart scoring, team randomization, and customizable difficulty levels.

For more detailed descriptions and links to each tool's website, refer to Appendix B.

Collaboration

Collaborative learning has long been recognized as an effective method in language education. In collaborative online games, AI eases team formation and role assignment by analyzing participants' powerful and weak areas, thereby generating balanced teams and assigning roles that match individual capabilities. Moreover, AI can support on-the-spot task alteration during group activities, modifying parameters to ensure equal participation and nurturing targeted skill development.

The following tools use AI and game-based elements to support teamwork, problem-solving, and peer interaction:

- **Flip** is an online space that allows teachers and students to share videos with each other. It is not a game in itself; however, its structure allows for challenge-based learning. Built-in AI supports transcription and voice analysis, and teachers often gamify it using structured prompts, points, and response chains.

- **Minecraft Education** offers a rich platform for collaborative, immersive language quests. With AI bots and modded contexts, learners go through obstacles and build shared worlds while using English communicatively. It's one of the most gamified collaborative experiences available in education.

TRY IT OUT: Gamified Language Learning With Quizlet Live and Flip

Combine competitive and collaborative AI-powered gamification by integrating Quizlet Live for vocabulary competition and Flip for video interaction in your classroom.

a. Create a custom Quizlet set with key vocabulary from your unit, then run a Quizlet Live for dynamic team play using vocabulary races and matching games. Quizlet's AI will adjust the items responsively and help you identify which terms learners struggle with most.

b. For recap, assigning a Flip challenge where students record short video responses role-playing how they would use the vocabulary in real-life situations. Tell them to use Flip's AI-powered transcription and voice analysis to track pronunciation and fluency improvements.

c. Gamify the Flip video responses by generating a structured point system for peer feedback, iterative responses, and creative usage examples.

d. Use the combined data from both platforms to recognize learning gaps and adapt your upcoming lessons appropriately.

This approach targets multiple language skills while teaching new vocabulary, encouraging collaboration, and gamifying learning through competing for points. The result is an activity that keeps learners engaged and leads to deeper learning.

Virtual and Augmented Reality

VR and AR platforms offer digital environments with rich sensory engagement and opportunities for authentic, meaningful interaction. These advantages can lead to improved learner outcomes, particularly in their pragmatic knowledge and cultural awareness. These technological frameworks facilitate the navigation of real-life scenarios and provide learners with tailored feedback across multiple linguistic competencies. AR systems, specifically, are redefining language learning by incorporating digital elements into tangible physical contexts.

Virtual Reality

What are some ways that VR platforms can support multilingual learners of English?

- VR **simulates authentic conversations** with intelligent virtual agents, enabling learners to engage in lifelike dialogue across diverse scenarios.

- VR **generates immersive environments** aligned with instructional goals and tailored to each learner's proficiency level, supporting contextualized language practice.

- VR **integrates visual, auditory, and motion-based input**, accommodating a wide range of learning styles through multimodal engagement.

- VR **supports structured language development** in low-stress virtual settings that promote experimentation and fluency building.

- VR **increases learner engagement and motivation** by transforming traditional lessons into dynamic, scenario-driven experiences.

TRY IT OUT: Virtual Reality Conversation Practice With Mondly VR

Integrate VR in your intermediate to advanced classroom to simulate authentic conversations and generate rich contextualized environments for language practice.

a. Set up Mondly VR (or a similar VR language learning app). Encourage students to explore scenarios that require them to engage in lifelike communication with intelligent virtual agents inside the app, such as ordering food in a restaurant, conducting job interviews, or navigating airport conversations.

b. Assign learners specific conversation purposes derived from their proficiency levels, then have students self-report on their interactions through reflection journals or brief verbal check-ins. Expect improvements in fluency, confidence, and eagerness to experiment in this low-stress virtual context.

c. Recap the VR sessions by asking the learners to reflect on the process, including identifying any new vocabulary or phrases they learned through this experiment. Then, integrate these insights into follow-up classroom activities.

This approach reshapes traditional conversation practice into an adaptive, scenario-driven process that enhances learner engagement and motivation and supports structured language development.

Augmented Reality

What are some ways that AR platforms can support multilingual learners of English?

- AR **recognizes real environments** (e.g., classrooms, streets, shops) and provides instant, context-aware vocabulary support.

- AR **identifies objects in the surroundings** and offers lexical prompts based on what students see and interact with.

- AR **anchors digital flashcards to physical locations**, helping students remember vocabulary through spatial associations.

- AR **delivers language support in real-life contexts**, such as transportation hubs or urban areas, to enhance practical understanding.

- AR **uses situation-based analytics** to introduce cultural and linguistic insights tied to specific geographic zones.

- AR **fosters authentic learning experiences** by merging the physical and digital worlds, helping students make meaningful connections to support language acquisition.

TRY IT OUT: Augmented Reality Vocabulary Building With Google Lens

Use AR with your beginner or lower intermediate learners to offer immediate, context-aware vocabulary support.

a. Explore the technology: Have learners use Google Lens (or similar AR translation apps) to scan items around the classroom, school, or local community and receive immediate lexical prompts and translations. This will help them to name items in their surroundings.

b. Assign vocabulary collection projects: Have learners photograph objects using AR apps, then categorize their photographs into digital flashcards that are anchored to locations. This provides them with the opportunity to remember vocabulary through links with real-life context.

c. Extend the activity: Have learners use the collected AR vocabulary in authentic contexts, such as describing their route to school or explaining items in a local store. Ask students to reflect on how merging physical and digital worlds improved their practical language understanding.

This approach helps students learn and reinforce vocabulary in meaningful, situational ways grounded in real-world context.

Emotional Recognition Technology

Recent developments in VR language learning platforms feature noteworthy progress in incorporating emotional recognition technology. Systems equipped with this technology can analyze facial expressions, vocal tones, and engagement patterns to notice delicate changes in learner emotions, then adapt instruction to a learner's level of confidence—helping alleviate anxiety during often high-stress activities, such as conversation practice. Stress-detection protocols allow some VR programs to offer tailored support during phases of anxiety. The platforms are also engineered to accommodate cultural variations in emotional expression, such as differences in cultural values around smiling or eye contact, so they can potentially work across a wide range of educational settings.

The following AI tools use emotional intelligence to generate a more supportive and effective context of language learning:

- **Ellie** is a language learning app built around a virtual character that reads learners' emotions as displayed in their face and voice, then adapts its communication tone and style to generate a low-stress speaking practice setting.

- **ELSA Speak** is a pronunciation and speaking practice app designed specifically to recognize a range of accents and provide personalized feedback. Experimental features use voice-based emotional cues to alter the pacing and complexity of tasks to reduce learner frustration.

TRY IT OUT: Emotion-Aware Speaking Practice With ELSA Speak

Assign your learners to engage in speaking practice with an emotionally intelligent AI-powered tool.

a. Have students use ELSA Speak for pronunciation practice during a classroom session.

b. Observe their engagement levels and willingness to repeat difficult exercises. Notice how the tool's emotionally adaptive approach impacts learners' motivation to practice difficult sounds.

c. Ask learners to reflect on their emotional comfort levels during the activity and compare their speaking confidence before and after using ELSA Speak. Lead a discussion on how learners could bring improved speaking confidence to real-world contexts, too.

Challenges and Limitations

VR and AR technologies are not, of course, without their challenges. Here are a few of the various critical hurdles to integrating these technologies in many ELT classrooms:

- **High up-front equipment costs** limit access for many institutions.
- There is **potential cognitive strain** from immersive virtual environments. Negative physiological effects may result from extended virtual exposure periods.
- The collection of students' emotional recognition data introduces **considerable privacy issues**.
- There is not yet a consensus in our field on best practices for VR and AR **curriculum integration** in ELT.
- **Cross-cultural differences** might also lead to notable variations in the effectiveness and appropriateness of these technologies across global contexts.

To address these challenges requires methodical investigation through empirical methods. Eventually, the progress of VR as a tool for English language instruction depends on sustained cross-disciplinary research that address all these interconnected limitations.

Assessment and Feedback

Advanced analytical tools powered by AI can be valuable assets for assessing learner performance. These tools can provide deep, data-driven insights into learner progress and identify their areas of challenge. In this way, AI-powered assessments provide teachers with useful data they can harness to adapt their lessons and make informed curriculum decisions. Integration of these innovative approaches in ELT can provide the grounds for optimized learning experiences and maximize learner potential (Di Mario, 2024).

Continuous Assessment

One notable development is in continuous assessment. AI tools enable ongoing, formative assessment, providing a more inclusive perspective on learner progress than traditional testing methods. In addition, AI's ability to simulate real-world language scenarios is leading to more authentic assessment practices, such as a shift toward skill-based assessment. Educators are testing how well learners can use AI tools to accomplish language tasks, rather than purely testing memorized knowledge.

TRY IT OUT: Continuous Assessment With Write & Improve and ELSA Speak

Use AI-driven continuous assessment to track learner improvement in multiple skill areas and offer constant feedback throughout a unit.

a. Set up weekly writing assessments using Cambridge English's Write & Improve. Have your students compose and submit short texts on the same theme or topic throughout the unit.

b. Using the Class View dashboard, observe how the AI recognizes patterns and changes in your learners' grammatical accuracy, vocabulary development, and writing coherence across the weekly assignments.

c. During the same unit, assign daily pronunciation practice using ELSA Speak: Ask learners to record themselves reading aloud the same text every week. Use the app's teacher dashboard, with AI-driven phonetic analysis and progress tracking, to review your students' improvements in pronunciation accuracy and fluency.

d. Throughout the unit, continuously apply the data from both platforms to generate personalized learning plans for each learner. You can also show students their progress graphs and engage them in setting data-driven targets for the next assessment.

Progress Tracking and Reporting

AI-powered adaptive learning systems have transformed progress tracking and reporting in education. These cutting-edge platforms provide comprehensive insights into learner progress, enabling teachers to efficiently locate learners' greatest areas of challenge (Khankhoje, 2018). AI algorithms empower these systems to analyze large quantities of learner data and produce detailed reports, leading to more informed decision-making for both educators and learners (Rekha et al., 2024), which ultimately leads to enhanced educational outcomes through personalized, data-driven teaching strategies.

Multiple educational platforms demonstrate how AI analytics can reshape language assessment and progress tracking:

- **Khan Academy** uses machine learning to monitor learner engagement, find knowledge gaps, and suggest helpful exercises.

- **ELSA Speak** offers personalized pronunciation coaching through speech recognition technology and presents measurements of improvement through visual analytics that help with systematic tracking of a learner's phonetic development.

- **Duolingo for Schools** offers educators dashboards displaying metrics of student progress over time in the areas of vocabulary retention, grammatical development, and engagement, provided through user-friendly visualizations.

- **Grammarly for Education** and Cambridge's **Write & Improve** employ natural language processing (NLP) to analyze student writing, offer targeted feedback, and collect longitudinal data on learner progress.

- **CENTURY** has gained extensive adoption in British schools. This platform, which must be adopted by the whole school or institution, generates tailored learning sequences according to performance analysis.

These educational technologies excel at creating evidence of learner progress. This helps with targeted instructional interventions and raises metacognitive awareness.

Employing of AI-generated progress reports provide strong, actionable insights for both teachers and learners. These reports can enhance teaching strategies and help learners establish and track personal goals and progress. Frequent dialogues on these reports with learners can encourage metacognition and learner autonomy, fostering a more self-directed approach to language learning.

Challenges and Limitations

It is essential for educational institutions to offer comprehensive training for teachers and learners on how to effectively employ AI-generated feedback. This training should emphasize the balance between AI insights and human judgments and evaluations, encouraging teachers and learners to be actively involved in setting their own data-driven goals. More broadly, training your students how to use AI ethically and effectively is an important step toward cultivating a culture of digital literacy. This prepares learners to succeed in a technology-driven future while maintaining the fundamental role of human creativity and critical thinking.

Special Note on AI in Assessment

Reliability in assessment is a growing concern in AI-supported language teaching. AI tools often have difficulty consistently evaluating more complex aspects of language, such as writing style or speaking fluency, which require human judgment. In many cases, human teachers are more accurate than AI in assessing student work.

It's also important to note that, as with any online platform used in education, the privacy of students' uploaded work must be protected. Teachers should verify that any tools they choose to implement adhere to robust data protection standards, such as the General Data Protection Regulation (GDPR) in the European Union and the Family Educational Rights and Privacy Act (FERPA) in the United States. Finally, although AI-generated insights and progress reports are valuable, it is vital that educators independently evaluate and analyze this feedback within the broader context of each learner's journey.

Plagiarism Detection

The ability of AI tools to generate extensive written work has resulted in significant challenges for academic integrity in education. Specifically in the field of language teaching, one study found that English language teachers struggle to accurately distinguish between human-written and AI-generated essays, particularly when AI produces technically accurate language with sophisticated expressions (Alexander et al., 2023). It is now increasingly difficult to be sure whether you are assessing your students' true language proficiency via their own writing.

Responding to this issue, there are new AI-driven plagiarism detection tools designed to help educators recognize AI-crafted and plagiarized content in student writing. Two of these tools are Crossplag and the GPT-2 Output Detector, which claim to offer around 89% accuracy in detecting machine-created texts. These are valuable tools for ELT educators, who may use them to check student submissions as well as to teach students to think critically about AI writing generators.

Although plagiarism detection technology is effective, prevention may be a more impactful approach. In this regard, educators should focus on proactive approaches to encourage academic integrity, such as plagiarism awareness workshops, writing templates, and teacher-guided instruction to help learners avoid unintended plagiarism. Relying merely on detection tools may neglect the underlying reasons learners might misuse sources, including a lack of familiarity with citation practices or simply limited language proficiency. By combining AI detection tools with supportive instruction, educators can better promote academic integrity and foster learners' confidence and in proficiency in writing.

Conclusion

The active classroom applications explored in this chapter demonstrate how AI technologies can transform the way English language teachers approach lesson planning, differentiation, materials design, progress tracking, and assessment. From tools that generate personalized, data-driven learning sequences to systems that offer immersive, gamified, authentic communication tasks and challenges, AI tools can add invaluable learning opportunities to your classroom. These tools excel because they adjust dynamically to learner responses, creating a productive balance of challenge and support that keeps learners in their zone of proximal development. Furthermore, many AI tools include embedded progress tracking that offers teachers easy-to-digest, accurate insights on what students have learned and what they need next.

The classroom-specific applications in this chapter show that AI integration fosters rather than complicates the teaching process. Whether through streamlined lesson planning, AR enhancement for vocabulary building, or emotionally supportive pronunciation practice, these technologies free educators to focus on higher order decisions and encourage authentic communication, cultural understanding, and critical thinking.

CHAPTER 5

Focus on Skills: AI Activities for Reading and Writing Instruction

This chapter explores how practical applications of generative artificial intelligence (AI) technology can transform reading and writing instruction. From adaptive text leveling tools that help educators address mixed-proficiency classrooms, to advanced writing evaluation systems that provide immediate, targeted feedback, these tools represent a change from one-size-fits-all strategies for English language teaching (ELT) toward more personalized learning experiences. In addition, rapid progress in natural language processing (NLP), machine learning, and adaptive algorithms has generated a landscape where language learning can be more curated and engaging than ever before. For example, AI-powered text analysis tools can instantly assess and adapt reading materials to fit individual learner proficiency levels, and adaptive questioning systems can dynamically adapt reading comprehension activities in response to learner input.

Through an overview of these and other tools for reading and writing instruction, as well as a number of sample practice activities, this chapter presents both the extraordinary capabilities and significant restrictions that educators must keep in mind when using AI in the ELT classroom. The sample activities illustrate how educators can implement these tools strategically, complementing rather than replacing sound pedagogical practices for teaching reading and writing skills.

AI Theories Relevant to Teaching Reading and Writing

NLP enables AI systems to analyze text structures, identify grammatical patterns, and evaluate sematic coherence. This makes it an essential building block of AI tools for automated essay scoring and reading comprehension assessment. In writing instruction, NLP algorithms can detect errors in syntax, suggest vocabulary improvements, and analyze discourse markers to help students develop coherent arguments. For reading, NLP powers systems that can adjust text complexity in real time and generate comprehension questions tailored to specific passages.

Machine learning algorithms enable AI systems to recognize patterns in student writing over time. They can identify a student's learning preferences and recurring errors, using these to provide increasingly personalized feedback. AI tools use machine learning to track a student's progress from simple sentence construction to complex argumentative writing, automatically adjusting scaffolding levels along the way. In reading instruction, machine learning enables adaptive systems that can predict which texts will challenge students appropriately and suggest reading materials based on individual comprehension patterns.

Neural networks and deep learning technologies, exemplified in large language models like GPT-4, can generate authentic reading passages at a specific level of difficulty and offer detailed feedback on writing quality beyond basic grammar checking. These models can evaluate stylistic appropriateness, suggest organizational improvements, and even engage students in Socratic dialogues about their writing. For reading, they can create personalized summaries, generate discussion questions, and provide instant clarification of complex concepts.

Intelligent tutoring systems are the groundwork of AI applications that offer step-by-step writing guidance, from brainstorming through revision. These systems can model expert writing processes, providing prompts that guide student through planning, drafting, and editing phases while offering just-in-time feedback. In reading instruction, intelligent tutoring systems can provide scaffolded support for comprehension strategies, gradually releasing responsibility to students as their skills develop.

Adaptive learning technologies use continuous assessment of reading comprehension and writing performance to modify content difficulty, text selection, and feedback specificity in real time. This approach ensures that students encounter appropriately challenging texts and receiving writing assignments that build systematically on their developing skills.

Reading Skills

AI is changing how we teach reading by allowing teachers to individualize instruction in ways that weren't possible before. Instead of using the same content and pace for every learner, educators can employ AI-powered tools to adapt reading materials and activities to match learners' needs. This means struggling readers get the encouragement they need while advanced learners stay challenged and engaged.

Tools are already available for everyday classroom use. For example, Newsela allows instructors to automatically adapt the difficulty levels of a provided news article, and ReadTheory provides reading comprehension practice that adapts in difficulty according to learner performance. Tools like these help educators differentiate without spending hours preparing various versions of texts or comprehension questions. Educators are also finding creative ways to use ChatGPT for summarizing complex passages, explaining vocabulary, or helping students rephrase difficult content.

The activities in this chapter show you how to integrate these tools into your practice. You'll discover straightforward approaches that make reading instruction more responsive to student needs without adding complexity to your workflow.

Writing Skills

AI-powered writing tools are changing writing instruction and saving educators' valuable time by offering immediate, tailored feedback that was once only available through one-on-one conferencing. Learners can now upload a writing sample and get on-the-spot, targeted comments on their grammar, word choice, and sentence structure. Using this technology, students have the chance to revise and improve their work on their own at the sentence level. This frees up educators to focus on what matters most: helping learners develop strong arguments, organize their ideas coherently, and find their unique voice as writers.

Today, language teachers are already using various practical tools in their classrooms. Grammarly and ProWritingAid catch surface-level errors while delivering suggestions for tone and clarity. QuillBot and Wordtune help learners experiment with various ways to express their ideas and expand their vocabulary. ChatGPT can support the brainstorming and drafting process. All of these tools are valuable for multilingual learners who may have strong ideas but need support with language.

The activities in this chapter will show you how students can use AI tools to support different stages of the writing process, from early brainstorming to final revision, while still building the critical thinking and communication skills that make them stronger, more confident writers.

AI in Reading and Writing Instruction: In Practice

This section provides an overview of current AI tools for the teaching and learning of reading and writing. You'll discover and practice using specific AI tools that can analyze and adapt reading texts, automate writing evaluation and feedback, and generate interactive reading comprehension activities.

Text Analysis and Adaptation

Text Leveling Algorithms

AI-powered text leveling tools are becoming increasingly advanced, moving beyond simple readability formulas to provide multidimensional analyses of text difficulty. These systems can analyze vocabulary frequency, sentence structure, text cohesion, and conceptual difficulty to ascertain the text's appropriateness for a given proficiency level. Following are some examples of tools for AI-powered text analysis, particularly focusing on text leveling algorithms. The table presents a list of functions, from simply giving a readability score to generating differentiated versions of a text, and indicates whether the tool provides that function. I've also noted whether each text leveling tool is designed in alignment with proficiency levels from the CEFR (Common European Framework of Reference for Languages).

Table 1. Text Leveling Tools

AI Tool	Provides Lexile level or other readability score	Analyzes vocabulary complexity	Analyzes sentence complexity	Analyzes cohesion/ coherence	Automates text editing and simplification	Generates versions at different reading levels	Aligned with CEFR or other standards
Lexile Framework for Reading	✔	✔	◑				
Coh-Metrix	✔	✔	✔	✔			
Newsela	✔	✔	◑		◑	✔	
Rewordify		✔			✔		
Write & Improve		◑	✔	◑	◑		✔
Text Inspector	✔	✔	✔	✔			✔
Lextutor	✔	✔	◑				
ATOS by Renaissance Learning	✔	✔	◑				
Readable.com	✔	✔	◑				

See Appendix B for detailed descriptions and website links for each of these tools.
See "Note on AI Tools" in the front matter regarding evolving tool functionality.

TRY IT OUT: Differentiated Reading With Newsela

Use Newsela to deliver differentiated reading tasks in your reading and writing class.

a. Make a free teacher account at Newsela's website and add your student roster. Assign students to proficiency groups based on prior assessment data.

b. Using the assignment builder, select an article from Newsela's extensive database on a topic relevant to your curriculum (e.g., climate change), then use the AI-driven leveling algorithm to create differentiated versions of the same article. The app can also generate formative assessments and response prompts for each article.

c. Publish the assignment for your students and assign the appropriate version to each proficiency group. Use the embedded AI-driven teacher reporting tools to track your learner's progress.

d. Facilitate follow-up class discussions and writing activities in which all learners can participate, using their shared knowledge of the topic, despite having read various versions of the text. Notice how the differentiated approach fosters more inclusive participation and builds learner confidence.

This activity demonstrates how providing differentiated reading materials for a multilevel classroom guarantees that all learners can access the same core material at their zone of difficulty and creates an inclusive classroom environment.

Dynamic Text Adaptation

Taking text analysis a step further, dynamic adaptation systems modify texts in real time based on learner interaction. These systems monitor reader comprehension through embedded questions or reading speed and adjust text complexity accordingly. Here are some examples of AI-powered tools designed for dynamic text adaptation that can be particularly beneficial for ELT contexts:

Table 2. Text Adaptation Tools

AI Tool	Monitors comprehension in real time	Adjusts reading level dynamically	Provides readability scores	Offers vocabulary support	Automates comprehension checks	Aligned with CEFR or other standards
Lingvist				✔		✔
Text Blaze						
ReadTheory	✔	✔	✔	◐	✔	
Rewordify			✔	✔		
TextHelp Read&Write				✔	✔	
LingQ				✔		✔
Lexia PowerUp Literacy	✔	✔	✔	✔	✔	
ReadWorks	✔	◐			✔	

See Appendix B for detailed descriptions and website links for each of these tools.
See "Note on AI Tools" in the front matter regarding evolving tool functionality.

TRY IT OUT: Adaptive Reading Practice With ReadTheory

Use ReadTheory to provide your intermediate learners with adaptive reading practice.

a. Start a free teacher account on ReadTheory and have your learners complete a placement test. This helps the platform establish a fundamental understanding of each learner's level.

b. Assign students a quiz on a certain theme or topic. ReadTheory will lead students through a series of short reading texts with comprehension questions and dynamically regulate the difficulty level of subsequent texts according to learner responses.

c. Review ReadTheory's analytics and progress tracking features to identify learners who need additional support.

This adaptive learning platform helps you provide personalized instruction for struggling readers and challenge the stronger readers with more difficult texts and extension activities.

Automated Writing Evaluation Systems

Grammar and Mechanics Checking

Automated writing evaluation systems have become increasingly essential tools in ELT, particularly for grammar and mechanics checking. These tools can identify and explain errors in grammar, spelling, and punctuation in a given writing sample, often providing context-aware suggested corrections. Here are some examples of advanced tools in this category:

Table 3. Text Correction Tools

AI Tool	Detects grammar errors	Detects spelling errors	Detects punctuation errors	Provides explanations	Suggests corrections	Checks style and clarity	Aligned with CEFR or other standards
Grammarly	✔	✔	✔	✔	✔	✔	
ProWritingAid	✔	✔	✔	✔	✔	✔	
Ginger	✔	✔	✔		✔	◐	
Criterion	✔	✔	✔	✔	✔		✔

See Appendix B for detailed descriptions and website links for each of these tools.
See "Note on AI Tools" in the front matter regarding evolving tool functionality.

TRY IT OUT: Self-Editing Skills With Grammarly

Familiarize yourself and your advanced writing students with Grammarly as a tool to support independent editing skills.

a. Assign a writing task, such as a short essay.

b. Have learners paste their completed first drafts into Grammarly to receive on-the-spot feedback on their errors. Encourage them to evaluate the app's corrections and suggestions carefully, rather than accepting all comments without understanding the reason.

c. Ask learners to submit their revised drafts, along with error reports on their writing generated by Grammarly's Authorship feature. Track common mistakes that multiple learners are making, such as in article usage, verb tense consistency, or sentence structure.

d. Create targeted mini-lessons to address these frequent errors. The lessons can be designed to encourage independent editing skills through guided Grammarly use.

This approach cultivates self-editing skills among advanced learners and offers you data-driven insights for targeted grammar instruction that addresses the specific needs of your class.

Style and Coherence Analysis

Advanced automated writing evaluation systems go beyond surface-level correction to analyze higher order writing skills for style and coherence. These tools can analyze a text and provide feedback on sentence variety, paragraph structure, use of transition words, and overall text organization—offering particularly useful feedback for multilingual writers at more advanced levels. Some of these tools include the following:

Table 4. Tools for Style and Coherence Analysis

AI Tool	Analyzes sentence variety	Analyzes paragraph structure	Identifies transition word usage	Analyzes cohesion/coherence	Provides clarity/style suggestions	Aligned with CEFR or other standards
Turnitin Revision Assistant	✔	✔	✔	◐	✔	✔
Coh-Metrix	✔	✔	✔	✔		
Hemingway	◐				✔	

See Appendix B for detailed descriptions and website links for each of these tools.
See "Note on AI Tools" in the front matter regarding evolving tool functionality.

TRY IT OUT: Writing Clarity With Hemingway

Lead your writing class through a lesson on editing for style and coherence with assistance from Hemingway.

a. For a given writing assignment, have learners paste their first drafts into Hemingway.

b. Working independently or with a partner, give students time to review the suggested areas for improvement, which might include complex sentences, passive voice, and redundant phrasing.

c. Next, ask learners to revise their drafts and change the highlighted areas to compose a more concise, structured text.

d. Ask learners to submit both their original and revised drafts so you can see how effectively they used the tool's feedback to improve their writing.

e. As you grade the work, provide higher order comments on things like argument, content, and organization. Learners should have already addressed basic clarity and style issues through the editing tool.

This approach helps your learners develop advanced writing fluency and self-editing skills, meaning you can focus your feedback on more substantive aspects of student writing.

Content and Idea Development

The most advanced automated writing evaluation systems are beginning to address the actual content and argumentation of a text. These systems measure whether an essay sufficiently addresses its prompt, if the ideas are fully developed, and if the argument is persuasive. Here are some AI writing tools that focus on content generation and idea development:

Table 5. Tools for Evaluating Writing Content

AI Tool	Analyzes relevance to prompt	Evaluates idea development	Evaluates persuasiveness and argumentation	Suggests content improvements	Gives feedback on organization	Aligned with CEFR or other standards
Intellimetric	✔	✔	✔		◑	✔
PEG Writing	✔	✔		✔	◑	✔
Criterion	✔	✔		✔	✔	✔

See Appendix B for detailed descriptions and website links for each of these tools.
See "Note on AI Tools" in the front matter regarding evolving tool functionality.

TRY IT OUT: Stronger Arguments With PEG Writing

Use PEG Writing to help learners develop stronger arguments and critical thinking skills in your composition class.

a. Have students submit their essay drafts to PEG Writing, which analyzes their work and provides feedback on coherence, idea development, and argumentation strength.

b. Show learners how to use the AI-generated suggestions to revise their reasoning and expand supporting details.

c. When grading the final essays, focus on how well students have incorporated the feedback to strengthen their arguments.

This approach develops critical thinking among learners. It also allows you to save time on giving basic argumentation feedback and dedicate more classroom time for teaching higher level writing skills.

Interactive Reading Comprehension Tools

Adaptive Questioning Systems

Interactive reading comprehension tools with adaptive questioning systems can provide valuable support for multilingual readers. These tools use AI to dynamically tailor the difficulty of texts and questions in response to learner performance. If learners answer correctly, subsequent questions become more challenging; if they struggle, the platform presents simpler follow-up questions or gives hints. Here are some examples of reading comprehension tools with adaptive questioning:

Table 6. Adaptive Questioning Tools for Reading

AI Tool	Adjusts question difficulty in real time	Adapts text difficulty	Provides comprehension checks	Offers hints and scaffolds	Tracks learner progress	Aligned with CEFR or other standards
ReadTheory	✔	✔	✔	✔	✔	
Newsela		✔	✔		✔	
Lexia PowerUp Literacy	✔	✔	✔	✔	✔	
Raz-Plus	✔	✔	✔	✔	✔	

See Appendix B for detailed descriptions and website links for each of these tools.
See "Note on AI Tools" in the front matter regarding evolving tool functionality.

TRY IT OUT: Adaptive Reading Comprehension With Raz-Plus

Explore adaptive reading activities with Raz-Plus and discover its capacity to offer useful instructor data.

a. Assign leveled texts through Raz-Plus and track how the system adjusts follow-up questions based on student responses.

b. Monitor learner progress through the platform's data reports. Note which learners need support and which are ready for more challenges in their reading comprehension skills.

c. Use this data to adjust your classroom instruction through organizing level-targeted reading groups or focusing your lesson planning according to the patterns you observe in learner performance.

This personalized approach challenges learners to practice reading in their zone of proximal development as they develop core reading skills. It also provides you with clear data for instructional decisions.

AI-Generated Summaries and Visualizations

Interactive reading comprehension tools offer valuable support to help multilingual learners grasp complex texts. They can generate simple summaries and visual representations of key ideas, such as mind maps or infographics, as scaffolding to help learners tackle a longer, more challenging reading text. A few notable examples of these tools are the following:

Table 7. Tools to Scaffold Reading Comprehension

AI Tool	Generates text summaries	Simplifies complex texts	Creates visual representations (mind maps/infographics)	Supports paraphrasing and / rewording	Integrates with reading comprehension tasks	Aligned with CEFR or other standards
QuillBot	✔	✔		✔	◐	
Resoomer	✔	✔			◐	
MindMeister			✔		✔	

See Appendix B for detailed descriptions and website links for each of these tools.
See "Note on AI Tools" in the front matter regarding evolving tool functionality.

TRY IT OUT: Guiding Students Through Academic Summarization With QuillBot

Incorporate this paraphrasing tool as a support system in your reading lessons to help learners work through dense academic texts and refine their critical thinking.

- Begin by assigning a challenging academic article for students to read and summarize in their own words, focusing on capturing the central ideas.

- Next, have students use QuillBot's paraphrasing tool to generate an alternative summary of the same article. Ask them to compare their version with the tool's output, noting differences in word choice, structure, and emphasis.

- Lead a class discussion exploring the strengths and limitations of both summaries. Encourage students to reflect on how varied approaches can affect meaning, clarity, and comprehension.

This activity fosters deeper reading skills while giving students hands-on experience evaluating how digital tools can support (but not replace) human interpretation and writing.

Important Considerations for AI in Reading and Writing Instruction

Although AI tools deliver multiple benefits for reading and writing instruction, educators must be aware of their limitations and use these tools judiciously. Keeping the following constraints in mind, educators can make informed decisions about when and how to use AI technologies in their language classrooms.

Superficial Feedback: AI writing tools excel at detecting grammar mistakes and sentence-level errors but often miss deeper writing concerns, such as idea development, coherence, and tone. Learners may use AI tools to produce technically correct texts without developing necessary writing skills or understanding why certain revisions enhance their work.

Constraints on Creative Expression: AI systems may tend to favor predictable, formulaic responses over creative or culturally specific expressions. This tendency could potentially discourage multilingual learners from incorporating their unique perspectives and voices into their writing, possibly constraining authentic self-expression.

Reading Strategy Gaps: Although AI can create effective comprehension questions, it struggles to model advanced reading strategies, such as making inferences, asking critical questions, or evaluating authorial viewpoint. These higher order thinking skills require explicit instruction in the classroom.

Overreliance Concerns: Heavy dependence on AI tools can cause a deskilling impact, where learners lose confidence in independent revision and educators gradually rely less on their professional judgment. Maintaining a balanced approach between AI assistance and human expertise remains vital.

Cultural and Linguistic Bias: Most AI tools are trained primarily on standard American English and other dominant English varieties, which can lead to misinterpretation of culturally specific language patterns or dialectal variations across Global Englishes. This limitation may marginalize learners whose writing is a reflection of their cultural backgrounds or linguistic heritage.

Critical Literacy Gaps: AI tools cannot yet assist learners with analyzing power dynamics, bias, or authorial intent. Educators have a crucial role to play in developing critical thinking skills and media literacy and training learners to actively question what they read. Educators must also guide learners in critically processing AI feedback and identifying when its comments and suggestions may be inappropriate.

Conclusion

The investigation of AI applications for reading and writing instruction in this chapter demonstrates how these technologies can address current challenges in language education. Through exploring a wide variety of AI-powered tools for educators, this chapter illustrates AI's potential to deliver on-the-spot, adaptive reading comprehension activities and to provide intelligent automated feedback, saving instructors' time and opening new avenues for teaching reading and writing skills.

However, our analysis also highlights important limitations: AI's tendency toward superficial feedback, potential limitations on creative expression, and a critical literacy skills gap that requires human guidance. The practical activities presented throughout this chapter highlight that successful AI integration depends on educators who understand these tools' potential and constraints, use them to supplement rather than replace their own expertise, and maintain a clear focus on developing the critical thinking, cultural awareness, and real-world communication skills that define successful language learning. Finally, AI can serve as a powerful amplifier of good teaching practice, freeing educators to focus on the complex aspects of reading and writing instruction that require human insight, creativity, and cultural sensitivity.

CHAPTER 6

Focus on Skills: AI Activities for Speaking and Listening Instruction

This chapter examines the transformative role of generative artificial intelligence (AI) in teaching listening and speaking skills. These central skills, often considered the most challenging areas of language learning, are being transformed by AI-driven apps and learning tools that offer unprecedented opportunities for personalized practice, immediate feedback, and immersive language experiences. For example, AI chatbots help learners engage in conversational practice that enhances fluency, coherence, vocabulary use, and grammar. Because students can practice with AI without fear of judgment, these tools reduce the stress of making mistakes, building learners' confidence as English speakers. In addition, AI is making significant strides in its capacity to assess and provide feedback on spoken language, an area traditionally challenging to address in large classes. This chapter offers an overview of the landscape of AI technologies for speaking and listening instruction and includes a number of sample practice activities.

AI Theories Relevant to Teaching Speaking and Listening

Speaking Skills

Speaking instruction in English language teaching (ELT) is grounded in the theory of meaningful interaction—a capacity that AI language models are continuously improving. ELT's foundational interaction hypothesis (Long, 1996) maintains that language learning is best facilitated through the purposeful negotiation of meaning. AI-driven conversation partners and chatbots put this theory into action.

Moreover, these tools can tailor their interactions to offer learners comprehensible input (Krashen, 1985) by automatically altering the difficulty and pace of conversations according to a learner's proficiency level. Finally, the low-pressure context of speaking practice with AI conversation partners (i.e., learners can make mistakes without fear of criticism) is well-suited to help lower the affective filter (Krashen, 1985) and create a positive learning environment. This allows learners to build confidence through purposeful interactions and adaptive challenge levels.

Listening Skills

AI-powered listening instruction is grounded in the following two frameworks: comprehensible input (Krashen, 1985), which posits that learners acquire language most effectively when exposed to input slightly above their current proficiency level, and adaptive learning, which involves adjusting instructional content and difficulty based on individual learner performance and needs. AI tools can provide authentic and tailored input that enhances listening skills across various situations and accents. AI tools for generating listening materials can adaptively regulate the complexity of the generated content by adjusting speech rates, adding background noise, and tailoring vocabulary difficulty in response to learner input. The adaptive questioning systems built into many of these tools can deliver scaffolded support and progressively build learners' capacity to manage complex listening tasks. In other words, AI tools can create listening materials that are keyed to each learner's zone of proximal development (Vygotsky, 1987).

In addition, AI tools that offer multimodal listening practice are aligned with dual coding theory. Blending auditory input with visual elements, such as interactive transcripts or the real-time highlighting of spoken words, these apps can help learners connect written and spoken forms of language and thus develop stronger auditory processing skills. Finally, AI-generated content can be adjusted to match learners' needs, interests, and preferences, addressing the theory that increasing student motivation through relevant, attention-grabbing material results in higher achievement of learning goals (Dörnyei, 2001).

AI in Speaking and Listening Instruction: In Practice

This section provides an overview of current AI tools and technologies for the teaching and learning of speaking and listening. You'll discover and practice using specific AI tools that provide low-stress, guided conversation practice; offer opportunities to role-play realistic contexts; generate personalized multimodal listening materials; and create interactive, clickable transcripts. In each category, "Try It Out" activities show you how to integrate these tools into your classroom.

AI Conversation Partners

AI conversation partners are chatbot apps, similar to ChatGPT or Microsoft Copilot, but designed specifically for language learning. They use automatic speech recognition and natural language processing to engage students in authentic dialogue practice with immediate feedback, helping develop both speaking fluency and communicative competence. These tools have transformed speaking practice from a predominantly classroom-based activity to one that can be meaningfully extended beyond traditional instruction hours. As mentioned earlier, AI conversation partners offer a low-stress environment where students can make mistakes and receive constructive corrections, accelerating their learning and building their confidence. In the area of AI conversation partners for language learning, several apps are particularly effective at offering scaffolded speaking practice. Here are some tools you can try in your classroom or assign for independent study:

Table 1. Tools for Conversation Practice

AI Tool	Real-time speech recognition	Adaptive dialogue complexity	Corrective feedback	Role-play scenarios	Learner progress tracking	Aligned with CEFR or other standards
Speak	✔	✔	✔	✔	✔	✔
TalkPal	✔	✔	✔	✔	◑	
Rosetta Stone	✔	◑	✔	◑	✔	✔
SpeakPal	✔	✔	✔	◑	◑	

See Appendix B for detailed descriptions and website links for each of these tools.
See "Note on AI Tools" in the front matter regarding evolving tool functionality.

TRY IT OUT: Business Conversation Practice With Speak

Use Speak, an AI conversation partner, to practice professional vocabulary in your business English class.

a. Set up students with Speak accounts and direct them to the Professional Scenarios section. Assign specific business contexts, such as leading a team meeting, negotiating a contract, or presenting quarterly results. Have students practice for 15 minutes daily using Speak's role-play feature, where the AI takes on the role of client, colleague, or supervisor and adjusts its answers based on the selected scenario.

b. Use Speak's unique Conversation Replay feature to have students review their sessions and identify moments where they hesitated or used filler words. Direct students to focus on Speak's Professional Vocabulary Suggestions that appear during conversations when more formal language would be appropriate.

c. Access Speak's teacher dashboard weekly to review the Speaking Confidence Metrics and Vocabulary Usage Reports that show which business terms students are avoiding or misusing.

d. Create targeted classroom activities around these gaps, such as practicing formal email language if students struggle with written business communication prompts or role-playing difficult conversations if the analytics show avoidance of conflict-resolution scenarios.

This approach reduces speaking anxiety and increases confidence while providing valuable data to inform your classroom instruction.

Role-Plays and Simulations

AI conversation partners excel at facilitating role-play exercises, ranging from everyday situations, like ordering in a restaurant, to more specialized scenarios, like a job interview or a medical consultation. Chatbots can play numerous roles, adjusting their persona and language use according to learner feedback, and can introduce unexpected obstacles into the conversation. Practicing speaking via this type of guided role-play challenges learners to adapt and use their language skills flexibly—and the benefits of a consistently available speaking partner cannot be overstated.

ChatGPT is well-known and can be used effectively as an AI conversation partner.

Here are a few additional AI conversation partners specifically designed for role-play and simulation in language learning:

Table 2. Tools for Role-Play Speaking Practice

AI Tool	Provides scenario-based dialogues	Adapts role to scenario	Introduces unexpected obstacles	Provides corrective feedback	Supports speech recognition	Aligned with CEFR or other standards
Immerse	✔	✔	✔	✔	✔	
Mondly	✔	✔		✔	✔	✔
ELSA Speak				✔	✔	
Mango Languages	✔	✔		✔	✔	✔
Gemini (Google)	✔	✔	◑	◑	✔	

See Appendix B for detailed descriptions and website links for each of these tools.
See "Note on AI Tools" in the front matter regarding evolving tool functionality.

TRY IT OUT: Business Negotiation Practice With ChatGPT

Use ChatGPT to simulate challenging client negotiation scenarios for advanced business English learners.

a. Referring to the Prompt Templates in Chapter 2, program ChatGPT to play the role of a demanding international client in 0business negotiation scenarios. Include specific directions asking ChatGPT to have learners practice managing objections, requesting clarification, and proposing compromises.

b. Monitor learners as they interact either in a language lab setting or by reviewing student-submitted recordings. Look for learners who at first struggle with spontaneous professional discourse; note any improvements in use of business vocabulary and formal register as they work through the various role-play scenarios.

c. Use these low-stakes practice sessions to help learners build confidence with advanced business language they might typically avoid when interacting in person. Follow up with in-class tasks or assessments that ask learners to apply their improved professional communication skills in role-plays with peers.

This approach develops advanced business communication skills while allowing learners to experiment safely with complex professional discourse.

✦✦ Sample Learner Prompt for AI Conversation Practice

I'm studying business English at the intermediate (B2) level, and I am getting prepared for client meetings. Role-play as a client who wants to move up our project deadline by 2 weeks. What I need to practice are discussing project time-lines and handling unexpected shifts professionally. I also want to practice using polite language to negotiate and offer alternatives. Adapt your language difficulty to challenge me according to my proficiency level. This means use professional vocabulary, but clarify terms I might not know. Provide me with time to think and change questions if I seem confused. Offer feedback on my professional dialogue and point out areas for improvement after our 10-minute chat. Help me sound confident and diplomatic when discussing complicated topics.

Personalized Listening Materials

Various AI tools can create or curate listening materials that are custom-made for learners' proficiency levels, needs, interests, and learning goals. By analyzing a vast corpus of audio content, these systems can choose or even generate passages that include target vocabulary, grammar structures, or themes pertinent to the learner's current focus. The use of these AI-driven adaptive listening tools benefits teachers by providing a means of differentiating instruction with minimal preparation time. Teachers can assign listening tasks that accommodate diverse proficiency levels within a single classroom. Additionally, the ability to personalize listening materials can foster student engagement by catering content to their interest and motivation.

Here are a few AI tools that can support instructions through personalized listening materials:

Table 3. Tools for Personalized Listening Instruction

AI Tool	Adapts listening level to proficiency	Curates or generates personalized audio	Includes target vocabulary and grammar	Provides transcripts or captions	Tracks learner progress	Aligned with CEFR or other standards
News in Levels	✔	✔	◐			
Lingvist			✔		✔	✔
English Central	✔	✔	✔	✔	✔	
Newsela	✔	✔	◐	✔	✔	
Speechify		✔		✔		
VoiceTube	✔	✔	◐	✔	✔	

See Appendix B for detailed descriptions and website links for each of these tools.
See "Note on AI Tools" in the front matter regarding evolving tool functionality.

TRY IT OUT: Differentiated Listening With News in Levels

Use News in Levels to generate personalized listening comprehension practice on current events topics, curated for different proficiency levels in your class.

a. Create a free teacher account. Browse the current news stories and select one topic that aligns with your curriculum (e.g., environmental issues, technology, health).

b. Click on the story title to access three versions: Level 1 (elementary), Level 2 (intermediate), and Level 3 (advanced). Preview each version to understand the vocabulary and structural differences. Assign students to the appropriate level based on their proficiency, or allow them to self-select after trying a brief sample from each level.

c. Ask learners to listen to their individualized story versions and complete the comprehension activities.

d. Facilitate a class discussion, asking learners to summarize key points from the story.

e. As a whole class, guide learners to compare how the same story was presented at various difficulty levels and inspire critical thinking about how language complexity may affect the content of a story, or our understanding of its meaning.

This approach uses personalized listening practice to support comprehension, create an inclusive classroom, and develop critical thinking skills.

✦✦ Sample Learner Prompt for Personalized Listening Content With an AI Conversation Partner

I'm studying the English language at an upper-intermediate (B2) level, and I'm interested in environmental topics. I need a listening exercise that contains academic vocabulary and difficult sentence structures to prepare me for university lectures. Create or find a 7-minute listening text about renewable energy solutions that fits my proficiency level. The text should include vocabulary related to sustainability, scientific processes, and data analysis. Make sure the speaker's pace is challenging for me, but not too much. After I listen, provide comprehension questions that test both general ideas and some details. If I struggle with a section, explain it and suggest similar listening contents for additional practice. I learn best when content connects to my academic goals and real-world needs and interests. Please track which vocabulary and grammar structures are challenging for me so you can include them in future listening exercises.

Listening Practice With Adaptive Difficulty

As learners engage with online listening exercises, some tools use AI to dynamically regulate the difficulty of the content. This might include increasing or slowing the speech rate, introducing background noise to simulate real-world listening conditions, or changing the difficulty of the text's vocabulary and sentence structure. These systems continuously evaluate the learner's progress through intermittent questions or comprehension checks while listening to confirm that the content remains challenging but not overwhelming.

For ELT educators, AI tools that provide listening practice with adaptive difficulty offer noteworthy benefits for teaching and learning. These tools allow teachers to set broad learning objectives, then rely on the AI to tailor an exercise for each individual learner's needs. Teachers can also monitor learner progress through thorough AI-generated reports in order to identify when learners are ready for more challenge and which need additional support. This level of data-driven insight empowers educators to engage in more strategic lesson planning and interventions.

In addition to English Central and Lingvist, discussed in the previous section, several notable tools for adaptive listening practice include the following:

Table 4. Tools for Adaptive Listening Practice

AI Tool	Adjusts speech rate	Modifies vocabulary/ sentence complexity	Introduces real-world conditions (noise)	Provides comprehension checks	Real-time feedback/ pronunciation modeling	Tracks learner progress	Aligned with CEFR/ standards
Speechling	✔	✔			✔	✔	
Duolingo Stories		✔		✔		✔	
Edpuzzle				✔		✔	
ELSA Speak	✔				✔	✔	
English Central	✔	✔		✔	✔	✔	
Lingvist		✔				✔	✔

See Appendix B for detailed descriptions and website links for each of these tools.
See "Note on AI Tools" in the front matter regarding evolving tool functionality.

TRY IT OUT: Adaptive Listening Practice With Speechling

Use Speechling for guided listening practice activities.

a. Create a free teacher account and set up a virtual classroom. Add your students by sharing the class code or sending email invitations.

b. Navigate to the Listening Exercises section and select content appropriate for your students' proficiency levels. Assign specific listening tasks, such as Daily Conversations or Academic Lectures, and set completion deadlines. Instruct students to complete the listening exercises, which will automatically adjust difficulty based on their comprehension accuracy and response times.

c. View the teacher dashboard to monitor learners' progress through the comprehension checks.

d. Design targeted classroom activities based on the dashboard data showing which listening skills students struggle with most. For example, if data shows students encounter difficulty with connected speech, dedicate class time to practicing listening for contractions and liaisons. You can also create follow-up speaking activities: have students practice using the listening strategies they've developed, such as asking for clarification or summarizing what they've heard in real conversation scenarios.

This approach provides a supportive environment for developing listening comprehension skills through personalized adaptation and feedback.

✦ Sample Learner Prompt for Adaptive Listening Practice With an AI Conversation Partner

I'm studying the English language at an intermediate (B1) level. I can understand slow and clear speech, but I have trouble understanding a natural conversational pace, especially if there is background noise. I want to enhance my listening ability for real-world situations, like coffee shops or busy offices. Create or find a moderately paced and clear conversation about common topics. Check my understanding every 2–3 minutes with questions, and if I answer them correctly you can gradually increase the speech rate and add mild background sounds. If I'm not doing well, slow down or simplify the vocabulary until I'm ready for the next level. My goal is to handle authentic listening situations with confidence. Track my progress and note when I am doing better in processing faster speech or difficult vocabulary. I want to see evidence of my growth over time.

Interactive Transcripts

Tools that offer AI-powered listening practice often come with built-in, interactive transcripts. These transcripts highlight words as they're spoken, supporting audio processing by guiding learners to connect the written and spoken forms of the language. Learners can also click on an unfamiliar word to read its definition or hear its pronunciation.

From an instructional perspective, AI tools with interactive transcripts offer teachers an effective means to enhance listening instruction. They can be used to create engaging, multimodal lessons that cater to different learning styles by combining audio, text, and visual aids. Interactive transcripts enable differentiated instruction by allowing teachers to assign beginner students tasks that focus on identifying key words highlighted in the transcript, while advanced learners can work on inference activities with the transcript initially hidden. Teachers can also use the clickable transcript features to create tiered assignments: Some students might click on unfamiliar words for instant definitions, while others use the transcript to practice note-taking skills by comparing their notes to the written text. Moreover, the ability to replay and isolate audio segments allows for targeted focus on specific listening challenges, such as unfamiliar vocabulary or complex sentence structures, either individually or as a whole class. These tools have transformed traditional listening practice by making natural speech patterns more tangible and comprehensible through visual representation.

Here are some tools to consider:

Table 5. Interactive Transcript Tools for Listening

AI Tool	Highlights words in sync with audio	Clickable word definitions and pronunciations	Generates automatic transcripts	Allows replay and isolating segments	Supports multimodal lesson design	Tracks learner progress	Aligned with CEFR or other standards
YouGlish	✔	✔		✔	◑		
Speechace						✔	
Subly	✔		✔	✔	✔		
Otter	✔		✔	✔	✔	✔	

See Appendix B for detailed descriptions and website links for each of these tools.
See "Note on AI Tools" in the front matter regarding evolving tool functionality.

TRY IT OUT: Interactive Listening With YouGlish

Familiarize yourself and your learners with using YouGlish for listening practice.

a. Have learners watch a video on a topic related to themes in your class. Explain how to view the transcript and notice how it highlights words as they are spoken.

b. Encourage learners to click on any unfamiliar words in the transcript to hear multiple examples from different speakers and see a definition if needed.

c. After the YouGlish session, have students create a vocabulary journal entry with three to five new words they discovered, including the context from the video and at least two example sentences of their own.

d. Then, organize students into small groups to share their vocabulary discoveries and practice using the new words in role-play conversations related to the video topic.

e. Finally, assign students to find one additional YouGlish video on the same topic for homework and prepare to teach one new expression they learned to the class the following day.

This approach reinforces both listening comprehension and vocabulary learning. It also engages learner interest through authentic and interactive content.

Important Considerations for AI in Speaking and Listening Instruction

When implementing AI tools for speaking and listening practice, educators should be aware their limitations and potential for bias. Be aware of the following constraints when adopting AI tools in your classroom.

Understanding the Limits of AI

AI-powered conversation partners (i.e., chatbots) are currently struggling with some aspects of human communication that are necessary for authentic language learning. These systems may misunderstand (or miss altogether) sarcasm, humor, or cultural references, which can lead to responses that sound off-topic or even inappropriate. Research shows that even well-designed chatbots encounter persistent challenges with nuanced language, including irony and sarcasm (Wilhelm et al., 2024). Recent work in sarcasm detection further highlights that AI often fails to capture the subtle cues that signal humor, making misunderstandings more likely and sometimes even harmful, especially in sensitive contexts like mental health support (Sharma & Batta, 2025). As a result, learners interacting with AI chatbots or voice assistants might receive responses that sound off-topic or simply inappropriate because the system doesn't fully perceive the context of their speech.

Educators should make learners aware of these limitations by explaining that, though AI offers valuable practice opportunities, it cannot replicate the full breadth and complexity of human communication. The empathy, cultural knowledge, and real-time adaptability that educators and human conversation partners bring to language learning will remain irreplaceable elements of language teaching and learning.

Addressing Potential Bias

AI tools learn from large datasets that may contain societal biases, which can then appear in the content a system generates or the feedback it provides. This built-in potential for bias presents a significant concern in language learning contexts, where students from diverse backgrounds have the right to equitable treatment as well as culturally sensitive materials and interactions (Jeon et al., 2024; Lewis, 2025).

As much as possible, educators should screen AI-generated materials for unsuitable or biased content. It's also critical to discuss with learners that AI systems are not neutral, do not replicate human intelligence, and may reflect limitations in their training data. Teaching critical thinking activities around AI will help your learners become more selective users of these technologies.

Implementing a Balanced Approach

The most efficient use of AI in speaking and listening instruction is to combine these tools with human interaction and supervision. AI should supplement, not replace, opportunities for authentic human communication practice. Teachers can use AI tools for practice sessions and, at the same time, make sure learners engage in real-world peer work, group discussions, and educator-led tasks. In addition, teachers should provide explicit instruction about both the potential and limitations of AI-powered educational tools, guiding learners to use these tools selectively and develop clear expectations about what AI can and cannot do as a partner on their language learning journey.

Practical Implementation Tips

- ☐ Test AI tools before introducing them in your class.
- ☐ Provide clear guidelines about time and amount of use.
- ☐ Assign learners to compare AI interactions with human communications.
- ☐ Check the feedback offered by AI for accuracy and appropriateness.
- ☐ Maintain a balance between AI-supported practice and human interaction.
- ☐ Teach students to recognize when AI responses seem unusual or inappropriate.

Conclusion

The tools discussed in this chapter, ranging from phoneme-specific feedback to adaptive conversation features and personalized listening content, all show how AI can help manage various challenges in speaking and listening instruction. These tools and technologies offer learners individualized feedback and the chance for authentic practice—two things that can be hard to achieve in conventional classroom settings. The "Try It Out" activities and sample prompts provided in this chapter introduced practical ways to apply the tools we introduced, to extend learning beyond class time, and to gather actionable insights that can guide future instruction.

Successful implementation of these tools, however, requires a thorough understanding of both their advantages and their disadvantages, or limitations. AI should be viewed as a complement to, not a replacement for, human interaction—especially when it comes to spoken communication. Educators must play a key role in helping learners navigate their experiences with AI: Teach them to look for potential bias and unnatural responses, making sure that cultural awareness and empathy remain central to the learning experience. Through informed and judicious use of AI tools for communication practice, teachers can offer students effective and enhanced opportunities to improve their speaking and listening skills.

CHAPTER 7

Focus on Skills: AI Activities for Pronunciation and Grammar Instruction

Pronunciation and grammar have long been considered the most challenging aspects of second language teaching and learning. Traditional methods of pronunciation teaching often relied on repeating sounds after the teacher and offered limited exposure to fluent speaker models. Learners were frequently dependent on the teacher's own accent and phonological awareness, which could limit accuracy and consistency (Derwing & Munro, 2015). In addition, pronunciation instruction has often been underemphasized in many curricula, leaving teachers feeling unprepared or lacking confidence to address it (Foote et al., 2011). Historically, grammar teaching has relied on the highly structured presentation-practice-production model, with worksheets and drills intended to help learners memorize rules. While such approaches may help students internalize basic patterns, they often fail to account for the complexity and variability of authentic language use (Ellis, 2006). Another challenge is that teachers themselves may struggle with balancing explicit rule teaching and communicative approaches, especially when their own knowledge of grammar terminology or pedagogy is limited (Borg, 2015). Though these approaches have their advantages, they are often constrained by time, resources, and the inherent limitations of human perception and feedback.

The arrival of generative artificial intelligence (AI) has transformed the possibilities for teaching and learning these two fundamental language skills. For instance, learners can now receive immediate, individualized feedback on pronunciation through automated speech recognition tools, practice with authentic input at scale, and engage in adaptive grammar activities that respond to their performance in real time. AI technologies offer the potential for highly personalized, data-driven, and interactive pronunciation and grammar instruction. In this chapter, you will discover AI tools that can provide immediate feedback, adapt in response to learner performance, and offer unprecedented levels of practice with and exposure to the authentic sounds and structures of the English language.

AI Theories Relevant to Teaching Pronunciation and Grammar

Pronunciation

Recent advances in machine learning, speech recognition, and natural language processing (NLP) have paved the way for AI systems that can evaluate speech with incredible accuracy, detect nuanced differences in pronunciation, and use that data to offer tailored feedback to learners. These capabilities go beyond evaluating individual phoneme production to encompass advanced linguistic features, such as connected speech, prosody, and the sociolinguistic aspects of pronunciation. In addition, the new field of AI-driven augmented reality (AR) can support immersive articulation modeling, which uses AR technology to overlay visual representations of correct tongue and lip positions onto real-world environments. For example, learners wearing AR headsets can see 3D models of the vocal tract showing proper tongue placement for difficult sounds, such as /θ/ or /r/, while simultaneously practicing with virtual speech therapists who demonstrate mouth movements in real time. One recommended app, SpeechBlubs AR, has the capability to display animated characters modeling correct articulation while learners practice speaking, in addition to providing students with immediate visual feedback on their own mouth movements through the device's camera.

Generative AI grants the potential for unlimited, contextually relevant, tailor-made pronunciation practice, with improved handling of diverse accents. For example, a speech recognition system initially trained on standard British English speech samples can be fine-tuned with a smaller dataset of Indian English speakers, thereby improving its ability to recognize that accent without needing to retrain the entire model from scratch (Pan & Yang, 2010).

These advances in AI's capabilities are highly significant for English language teaching (ELT). At the individual level, learners now have access to tools that can provide detailed analyses of their speech patterns and offer insights and corrections that were previously available only through one-on-one instruction. At the classroom level, AI is reshaping pedagogical approaches by paving the way for a more personalized instruction, while freeing up teacher time for higher order learning activities. On a broader scale, AI is democratizing access to high-quality pronunciation instruction, potentially reducing inequalities in educational resources across diverse regions and socioeconomic backgrounds. For instance, Maria, a Spanish-speaking student in rural Colombia, struggles with the English /v/ and /b/ distinction. Using an AI pronunciation app, she receives immediate feedback and works through targeted practice exercises—a level of personalized coaching previously unavailable in her remote location. Within weeks, her accuracy improves significantly. Though the potential for this type of intervention is high, strong data-driven research and critical examinations are vital to affirm these tools contribute to meaningful language learning outcomes and adhere to sound pedagogical principles.

A review of second language acquisition (SLA) theory lays a robust foundation for the use of AI tools in modern pronunciation instruction. Personalized perception training draws upon the speech learning model and perceptual assimilation model (Best, 1995) to address L1-specific difficulties; noticing mechanisms via advanced speech recognition technologies are grounded in Schmidt's noticing hypothesis (1990), which underlines the importance of recognizing crucial phonetic features; and adaptive learning systems are aligned with Anderson's skill acquisition theory (1982). Although AI is transforming possibilities for how we teach pronunciation, its use should always be grounded in these established understandings of how students learn languages and in ELT best practices.

Grammar

AI-driven tools are transforming grammar instruction by supporting personalized and interactive learning experiences that increase learner engagement during what is sometimes their least-favorite part of class time. Platforms like ChatGPT are especially effective at this: They can create contextualized grammar activities tailored to a learner's areas of interest or professional needs. For instance, educators can prompt ChatGPT to generate practice tasks centered on a sports theme for athletic learners or business scenarios for adult professionals. This customization helps learners connect with grammar in meaningful ways, rather than viewing it as a boring, abstract concept. Moreover, AI chatbots can provide immediate, personalized feedback and correction of errors during practice sessions. This minimizes the delays between performance and feedback that often happen in conventional instruction.

These capabilities are made possible by advances in natural language processing, specifically transformer-based architectures, such as BERT (Devlin et al., 2019) and

GPT models (Brown et al., 2020). Such systems are programmed on large corpora and then fine-tuned to identify incorrect grammatical structures and deliver fluent corrective feedback. From an SLA perspective, this is aligned with Schmidt's (1990) noticing hypothesis: Learners are more prone to internalize grammatical forms when errors are instantly highlighted in meaningful contexts. Similarly, Long's (1996) interaction hypothesis would support the idea that interaction with an AI tool offering corrective feedback can boost negotiation of form, a process central to grammar acquisition.

Furthermore, AI-enhanced writing assistants like Grammarly, when thoughtfully implemented, can play a valuable role in supporting both educators and learners. These tools are effective at catching common problems, such as subject-verb agreement, article usage, and preposition errors, but they often fall short when addressing more specific concerns, such as tense consistency, tone, or clarity. This highlights the vital role of a skilled instructor. Tools like Grammarly should be positioned as an initial editing step, helping learners refine their writing before peer review or instructor feedback. It is critical to teach learners the habit of critically evaluating AI-generated suggestions; such practice can also help learners improve their independent editing skills.

The successful integration of AI in grammar instruction hinges on striking a balance between automation and human guidance. By assigning learners to complete repetitive grammar drills with AI, educators can achieve two goals: making those practice sessions more engaging, and redirecting classroom time toward deeper conversations around clarity, style, and meaning. It's best to start gradually. Begin by using one AI tool in a tailored in-class lesson or activity, observe how your learners engage with it, monitor the impact on learning outcomes, and expand the use of AI tools in alignment with your instructional goals.

AI in Pronunciation and Grammar Instruction: In Practice

AI Applications for Teaching Pronunciation

The integration of AI in pronunciation instruction is characterized by a fast-evolving landscape, with new technological solutions emerging at an exceptional pace. This section presents an overview of the current landscape, introducing specific AI tools that help learners develop awareness of individual phonemes; develop their ability to produce and understand fluent intonation, stress, and connected speech; offer timely and personalized error correction without the need for one-on-one teacher engagement; and increase motivation through gamified activities. Throughout the chapter, you'll find

"Try It Out" exercises that demonstrate how you can take advantage of these AI tools and help your learners succeed.

Developing Awareness and Accuracy With Phonemes

Individual Phoneme Practice

Modern AI-powered speech recognition systems can analyze and parse spoken language at the phoneme level, enabling them to recognize the precise sounds that a learner struggles to produce. This analysis paves the way for targeted practice and feedback that is more accurate and consistent than what even many human teachers can provide. In addition, these systems track a learner's progress over time, identifying persistent pronunciation challenges and areas of improvement and creating longitudinal data that can be invaluable for both learners and teachers in setting goals and measuring progress. This evidence-based approach to pronunciation instruction signifies a noteworthy progress over traditional intuition-based assessment methods.

Several AI-powered tools have proved effective in the realm of individual phoneme practice:

Table 1. Tools for Phoneme-Level Pronunciation Practice

AI Tool	Analyzes speech at phoneme level	Provides real-time corrective feedback	Tracks learner progress	Models correct pronunciation	Personalizes practice by difficulty	Aligned with CEFR or other standards
YouGlish				✔		
Glossika			✔	✔	✔	
Rosetta Stone	✔	✔	✔	✔	◐	✔
ELSA Speak	✔	✔	✔	✔	✔	
Carnegie Speech	✔	✔	✔	✔	✔	✔

See Appendix B for detailed descriptions and website links for each of these tools.
See "Note on AI Tools" in the front matter regarding evolving tool functionality.

Teachers can use these tools to assign targeted practice sessions that complement classroom work, effectively extending focused pronunciation practice beyond traditional contact hours. By providing immediate, personalized feedback on phoneme production, these systems increase students' opportunities for independent pronunciation practice while maintaining a high standard of accuracy.

TRY IT OUT: Phoneme-Focused Instruction With Glossika

Incorporate Glossika into your pronunciation lessons with intermediate learners for phoneme-level practice.

a. Create a free teacher account and set up student profiles. Assign learners to complete the initial placement assessment by speaking into their device microphones.

b. Direct students to focus on the Mass Sentences feature, where they listen to fluent speaker audio, repeat each sentence aloud, and receive immediate pronunciation scoring.

c. Instruct students to spend 15–20 minutes daily practicing sentences that target their identified problem phonemes. Train learners to use the replay function when they receive low pronunciation scores, encouraging them to listen carefully to the fluent speaker model before attempting the sentence again.

d. Have students track their daily scores in a pronunciation journal and note which specific sounds cause difficulty.

e. Access the teacher dashboard weekly to review individual student progress. Use Glossika's analytics data, representing which phonemes learners have difficulty with most, to create targeted classroom activities. For instance, if learners have difficulty with /θ/ sounds, dedicate class time to mouth position demonstrations and minimal pair practice.

f. Create follow-up speaking tasks that incorporate the sentences students have been practicing on Glossika.

This strategy complements your teaching by providing individualized input that enhances learners' pronunciation accuracy and confidence.

TRY IT OUT: Phoneme-Level Pronunciation With ELSA Speak

Use ELSA Speak to boost your learners' accuracy with individual sounds and generate data for future lesson planning.

a. Download ELSA Speak and create a teacher account, then have learners download the app and join your virtual classroom using the class code.

b. Demonstrate how to access the Skills section, where students can select specific pronunciation challenges (e.g., /r/ vs /l/, *th* sounds). Instruct students to complete the initial assessment by reading aloud the prompted sentences.

c. Have students work through the daily lesson recommendations for 10–15 minutes, focusing on the specific phonemes ELSA identifies as problematic. Show students how to use the Practice mode, where they can repeat individual words and sentences until they achieve the target accuracy score.

d. Review ELSA's teacher dashboard to monitor progress and spot persistent pronunciation issues. Use this data to plan focused in-class practice on common problem areas across all learners and to assign targeted independent practice.

This approach increases pronunciation accuracy through personalized feedback and generates data to inform your classroom instruction.

Spectral Analysis and Visualization

Spectral analysis, a key technology in AI-based pronunciation tools, allows for a new approach to teaching advanced pronunciation learners through the precise evaluation and visualization of speech sounds. How does it work? A learner records their speech and uploads the resulting digital file to an app or platform that generates a spectrogram (a visual display of frequencies over time). Then, the app uses AI to compare the learner's spectrogram to a reference model of fluent English pronunciation. Deep learning models trained on large amount of fluent speech datasets can detect the distinctive spectral features of each phoneme. Controlling for the learner's proficiency level and linguistic background, these tools can isolate the main spectral features that differentiate between similar sounds. This novel and scientific approach to visualizing pronunciation may help reach learners for whom traditional teaching methods were ineffective. By integrating spectral analysis into your practice with the help of AI, you can move forward toward a more evidence-based approach to pronunciation teaching. Here are a few notable tools for this approach:

Table 2. Tools for Visualizing Pronunciation Practice

AI Tool	Generates spectrograms	Compares learner speech to model	Identifies spectral phoneme features	Visualizes frequency/pitch	Provides feedback on accuracy	Tracks learner progress	Aligned with CEFR/standards
Praat	✔	✔	✔	✔	◐		
WaveSurfer	✔		◐	✔			
Sonic Visualizer	✔			✔	✔		

See Appendix B for detailed descriptions and website links for each of these tools.
See "Note on AI Tools" in the front matter regarding evolving tool functionality.

TRY IT OUT: Vowel Distinction Practice With Praat

Use Praat to help advanced learners refine their English vowel sound production through experimenting with spectral analysis.

a. Assign learners to record minimal pairs that contain vowel sounds they find hard to pronounce. Have them use Praat to generate spectrograms that visually show the structure of each vowel, called *formants*.

b. Guide them in analyzing the spectrograms, with special attention to the first and second formants (labeled F1 and F2), which are key to vowel quality. Compare their recordings to professional fluent speaker models and stress the visual differences.

c. Use visual feedback from Praat in your instruction. This can help learners recognize delicate differences in vowel production and adapt their articulation accordingly.

This activity helps learners gain a clearer understanding of vowel contrasts while supporting measurable progress through data-informed, individualized practice.

Teaching Prosody and Connected Speech

Although mastery of individual phonemes is imperative, natural and intelligible speech is connected and includes prosodic features, such as stress, intonation, and rhythm. These suprasegmental features present a distinctive challenge for many learners and have traditionally been difficult to teach—but today, AI has opened new windows of possibility. This section explores how AI-powered tools are revolutionizing the teaching and learning of connected speech and prosody in ELT contexts.

Prosody, Stress, and Intonation Training

The acquisition of prosodic features is a multilayered challenge for many multilingual learners of English, as it includes both the placement of stress and the modulation of pitch patterns across utterances. These suprasegmental elements act as critical vectors for the transmission of meaning, conveying delicate gradations of emphasis, emotion, and pragmatic intent. Mastery of these features increases comprehensibility, and inappropriate stress patterns or intonational contours potentially lead to miscommunication.

In the area of prosody and intonation training, various AI-driven language learning applications have emerged that explicitly address the features of stress, rhythm, and intonation. These applications have transformed the teaching of prosodic features from a largely intuitive process (Levis, 2005) to one that can be methodically analyzed and practiced. Explicit instruction in prosodic features, coupled with immediate auditory feedback, can increase learners' ability to internalize and reproduce target language patterns. This has profound implications for both theoretical and practical approaches to language teaching and learning, particularly in contexts where prosodic features differ markedly between the first and target languages.

Here are a few prominent AI tools for helping students practice stress and intonation:

Table 3. Tools for Practicing Prosody

AI Tool	Analyzes stress patterns	Analyzes rhythm	Analyzes intonation contours	Provides visual feedback	Gives corrective feedback	Tracks learner progress	Aligned with CEFR or other standards
SpeechFlow	✓	✓	✓	✓	✓	✓	
Babbel	◐	◐			✓	✓	
ELSA Speak	✓	✓	✓	✓	✓	✓	
Speechace	✓	✓	✓	✓	✓	✓	
Rosetta Stone	◐	◐	◐	◐	✓	✓	✓
Fluency Tutor for Google					✓	✓	

See Appendix B for detailed descriptions and website links for each of these tools.
See "Note on AI Tools" in the front matter regarding evolving tool functionality.

How can teachers integrate these tools into a comprehensive speaking skills curriculum? Start with controlled practice using ELSA Speak's feedback on individual sounds and word stress, then progress toward more communicative practice with its dialogue-based exercises. Through this staged approach, learners can develop both an analytical understanding and practical mastery of prosodic features.

TRY IT OUT: Teaching Prosody With ELSA Speak

One effective way to implement prosody practice is through short learner presentations, which offer a natural context for practicing stress, rhythm, and intonation in extended speech. When assigning an oral presentation with your intermediate or advanced learners, use ELSA Speak to practice prosody.

a. Have your learners record their practice presentations using ELSA Speak's Speech Analyzer feature to receive instant feedback on pronunciation, intonation, and fluency. Ask them to note areas where the app identifies room for improvement.

b. Have students follow this process several times a week, over 3 weeks, each time focusing on the app's feedback regarding word stress and intonation patterns.

c. Encourage learners to treat these presentations as short academic or professional conversations (e.g., introducing a topic, summarizing an article, or pitching an idea) so the practice feels authentic and meaningful.

d. Have learners compare their initial ELSA Score with their score after several weeks of practice so they can track improvement in their presentation delivery and awareness of suprasegmental features.

TRY IT OUT: Intonation Practice for Business English With ELSA Speak

Implement ELSA Speak in a business English class to help learners refine their presentation delivery skills through focused work on pitch and rhythm.

a. Assign learners to record short persuasive speeches using ELSA Speak, which visually maps their intonation patterns as pitch contours.

b. Guide learners in monitoring their intonation patterns and comparing them with proficient speaker models. Help learners identify where falling tones should convey certainty and rising tones suggest nonfinality or inquiry.

c. Offer regular opportunities for learners to rehearse and revise their delivery of short presentations, using ELSA Speak's visual feedback to track progress and reinforce more natural speech rhythms.

This approach strengthens learners' presentation skills by helping them control intonation and express meaning more clearly and confidently.

Rhythm and Timing

The organization of speech timing plays an essential role in language production, especially in stress-timed languages like English, where rhythm and meaning emerge from the interplay of stressed and unstressed syllables. This prosodic framework poses separate cognitive and motor challenges, primarily for learners whose home languages are syllable-timed or mora-timed (a mora is a rhythmic unit smaller than a syllable, as in Japanese, where each mora carries equal weight in timing). Acquiring the rhythm of a new language necessitates complex neurolinguistic modifications that require both perceptual recalibration and motor adaptation. Though fluent speakers reproduce these rhythmic patterns naturally, learners often face struggles (Flege, 1995). Developing an explicit awareness of these temporal features, along with practice in real communicative settings, could improve learners' ability to mimic fluent speech timing. This can foster a more fluid and natural speech style.

Here are some AI-powered tools tailored to help with rhythm and timing:

Table 4. Tools for Rhythm and Stress Timing

AI Tool	Analyzes rhythm patterns	Detects stress timing	Provides corrective feedback	Models fluent rhythm	Tracks learner progress	Aligned with CEFR or other standards
Speechling	✔	✔	✔	✔	✔	
Glossika	◑	◑		✔	✔	
ELSA Speak	✔	✔	✔	✔	✔	

See Appendix B for detailed descriptions and website links for each of these tools.
See "Note on AI Tools" in the front matter regarding evolving tool functionality.

These tools address the complexities language learners face in rhythm and timing learning by providing systematized practice, feedback, and modeling of stress-timed speech patterns. Their integration in language teaching and learning can meaningfully help learners achieve more fluid, fluent rhythm in their speech.

TRY IT OUT: Building Rhythm and Timing With Speechling

Familiarize yourself and your learners with Speechling to improve the natural flow of learners' spoken English through guided practice.

a. Assign learners short speaking tasks using Speechling, where they listen to fluent models and practice mimicking the timing and stress patterns.

b. Encourage learners to repeat phrases and sentences until their pacing matches the model. Speechling delivers instant feedback, which helps learners modify their speech in real time.

c. Revisit frequent rhythm problems with the whole class. For this aim, use learners' Speechling progress to target areas that need refinement and reinforce timing patterns through practice.

This method helps learners internalize the rhythm of English and speak with more fluency, confidence, and clarity.

Connected Speech

The complicated mechanism of connected speech is an intersection of phonological processes and natural language production, wherein separate sound units undergo systematic alterations in continuous discourse, including the seamless linking of adjacent sounds, the strategic elimination of phonemes in rapid speech patterns, and the liaisons that occur when neighboring sounds affect each other. These features exist in many languages.

Connected speech is not simply an artifact of fast, casual speech; rather, it is a complex phonological operation that improves communicative efficacy. Moreover, the rules-based nature of connected speech implies an underlying cognitive framework that fluent speakers unconsciously employ. Understanding these rules has been essential for researchers in the fields of theoretical linguistics, speech pathology, and language pedagogy, predominantly in developing evidence-based approaches to pronunciation instruction and assessment.

Here are some AI tools that address connected speech and phonological processes:

Table 5. Tools for Connected Speech

AI Tool	Visualizes connected speech	Detects linking, assimilation, and elision	Provides real-time corrective feedback	Models fluent connected speech	Tracks learner progress	Aligned with CEFR or other standards
Praat	✔	✔				
Speechling		✔	✔	✔	✔	
Google Read Along		✔	✔	✔	✔	

See Appendix B for detailed descriptions and website links for each of these tools.
See "Note on AI Tools" in the front matter regarding evolving tool functionality.

TRY IT OUT: Exploring Connected Speech With Praat

Use Praat to raise learners' awareness of natural speech patterns through visual and auditory analysis.

a. Assign learners to record sentences containing features of connected speech, including linking, elision, or assimilation. Upload them to Praat to create spectrograms that show these features visually.

b. Ask learners to compare their spectrograms to proficient speaker models and notice where and how their speech diverges from more fluent rhythm and flow.

c. Repeat the previous exercise throughout the course and use Praat's feedback to help learners fine-tune their pronunciation.

This technique deepens learners' perception of how spoken English works in real communication, supporting clearer, more fluent speech over time.

TRY IT OUT: Sharpening Connected Speech With ELSA Speak

Help advanced learners improve clarity in presentations through focusing more on connected speech and intonation using ELSA Speak.

a. Assign learners to record short presentations using ELSA Speak, then ask the program to evaluate their use of linking, vowel reduction, and intonation.

b. ELSA speak will highlight areas that need more practice. Use these results to design short, targeted lessons. Offer AI-generated practice materials that build in difficulty.

c. Support regular practice and use peer or instructor feedback to track progress.

This exercise helps learners develop greater awareness of a range of features of fluent speech, and improves their comprehensibility as they learn to reproduce those features correctly.

Accent Reduction and Dialect Training

In the specialized domain of accent reduction and dialect training for advanced learners (e.g., those studying English for professional or business purposes), several AI platforms have transformed accent training from a previously subjective practice to one that can be tackled methodically while maintaining respect for learner identity. These tools' real-time analysis capabilities allow for immediate feedback on specific dialectal features, and their longitudinal tracking features enable both teachers and learners to monitor development toward individually determined goals. Making use of the objective feedback these tools provide, in balance with sensitivity to sociocultural factors, is an effective way to address the multidimensional relationship between accent, identity, and intelligibility.

Here are some AI-enabled tools that support accent reduction and dialect training in ELT:

Table 6. Tools for Accent Reduction and Dialect Training

AI Tool	Detects accent features	Provides real-time corrective feedback	Offers dialect-specific training	Tracks learner progress	Models target accent and pronunciation	Aligned with CEFR or other standards
ELSA Speak	✔	✔	◐	✔	✔	
Duolingo				✔		
Blue Canoe Learning	✔	✔	✔	✔	✔	
Speechace	✔	✔		✔	✔	
BoldVoice	✔	✔	✔	✔	✔	

See Appendix B for detailed descriptions and website links for each of these tools.
See "Note on AI Tools" in the front matter regarding evolving tool functionality.

TRY IT OUT: Professional Intelligibility With Blue Canoe Learning

Use Blue Canoe in your business English class to increase professional comprehensibility.

a. Ask learners to create an account and access the recording interface. Direct learners to record a technical explanation of something relevant to their field (such as describing a work process, explaining a product feature, or summarizing a project) using the Blue Canoe learning interface. The recording should be 1–2 minutes long. Once finished, the system automatically processes their speech, no file upload is required.

b. Help learners understand the color-coded visual feedback provided by Blue Canoe, which highlights the phonological features of their speech that affect listener comprehension. Explain that green highlights indicate clearly pronounced segments, yellow shows areas needing improvement, and red marks significant intelligibility issues. Have students click on highlighted segments to hear their pronunciation alongside fluent speaker models and view specific articulation guidance.

c. Design focused practice sessions for individual or group study, addressing problematic features (e.g., vowel contrasts, stress patterns) highlighted by the system. Target communication-critical features rather than overall accent reduction.

This data-driven approach helps learners communicate more effectively in business settings while maintaining their unique linguistic identities.

Real-Time Feedback and Correction

Feedback and error correction is another area where AI has transformed pronunciation teaching. AI-powered speech recognition systems can recognize the phonemes uttered by learners and identify errors by comparing these phonemes to models of target pronunciation, determining divergences, and generating personalized feedback. Advanced tools go even further by providing contextual error analysis, meaning that they can recognize errors in phoneme pronunciation depending on adjacent sounds. As with many of the other tools presented in this book, AI systems for pronunciation training can offer personalized feedback that adjusts to each learner's unique error patterns and learning style. Some tools also provide multimodal feedback, such as animated visualizations of speech, slowed-down auditory models, and, in some advanced systems, even haptic feedback to guide learners.

How can these capabilities work in the classroom? When learners interact with AI tools that offer simulated conversations, these systems can provide real-time feedback on a learner's speech. This might comprise slight error corrections, explicit clarifications about the errors, or post-conversation reviews of areas for development. The AI-powered systems might also track patterns in a learner's errors, which helps them start to recognize persistent problems. Finally, they often recommend or generate focused follow-up activities to address problem areas.

Here is a list of AI tools that excel in providing real-time feedback and correction for pronunciation instruction:

Table 7. Error Correction Tools for Pronunciation Instruction

AI Tool	Recognizes phonemes	Provides real-time corrective feedback	Offers contextual error analysis	Provides multimodal feedback (visual/ audio/haptic)	Tracks learner progress	Aligned with CEFR or other standards
BoldVoice	✔	✔	◑	✔	✔	
Speechace	✔	✔	✔	◑	✔	
Talk To Me Technologies	✔	✔	✔	✔	✔	
Duolingo	◑	◑			✔	
ELSA Speak	✔	✔	✔	✔	✔	
Rosetta Stone	✔	✔	◑	◑	✔	✔
Google's Read Along	✔	✔			✔	

See Appendix B for detailed descriptions and website links for each of these tools.
See "Note on AI Tools" in the front matter regarding evolving tool functionality.

TRY IT OUT: Pronunciation of Academic Vocabulary With BoldVoice

Use BoldVoice to support learners working on complicated academic vocabulary by offering targeted pronunciation feedback and animated articulation models.

a. Before launching BoldVoice, dedicate a lesson to presenting key academic terms with difficult consonant clusters, especially word-final combinations (e.g., psychiatrist, interact, manuscript). The pronunciation of these clusters is commonly influenced by home language interference.

b. Assign learners to practice these terms using BoldVoice. The platform uses AI to evaluate learners' pronunciation and offer immediate feedback, with visualizations and animated illustrations to emphasize specific articulation problems.

c. Have learners use the app regularly over several weeks. Monitor progress in clarity and fluency of the pronunciation of the targeted word list. Use in-class check-ins or discussions to reinforce progress and address persistent challenges.

This activity improves learners' confidence and accuracy in pronouncing difficult academic vocabulary, leading to more intelligible and confident participation in academic discussions.

TRY IT OUT: Targeted Pronunciation Practice With ELSA Speak

Use ELSA Speak to capture error patterns and provide personalized pronunciation feedback in your intermediate-level class.

a. Ask learners to work on the ELSA Speak's Pronunciation Checkup assessment, which tests their ability to produce challenging phoneme pairs (e.g., /l/–/r/, /v/–/w/, /θ/–/s/).

- Students should access the Assessment tab in the app, select Pronunciation Checkup, and complete the 5- to 10-minute evaluation where they read aloud prompted words and sentences.

- The app provides immediate feedback showing which specific sounds they mispronounced, with visual cues for correct mouth and tongue positioning.

b. Log into the ELSA Speak teacher dashboard (accessible at teach.elsaspeak. com) and navigate to the Class Analytics section to track your learners' performance data. Review the Common Errors Report, which aggregates pronunciation difficulties across all students and ranks phonemes by frequency of errors. Download the detailed report showing which specific sounds (e.g., final consonants, diphthongs, or consonant clusters) present the greatest challenges for your class.

c. Based on the analytics data, create targeted practice assignments in ELSA Speak by selecting specific phoneme practice modules that address your class's most common errors. Alternatively, design whole-class pronuncia-tion activities focusing on these problematic sounds, using minimal pairs practice or tongue twisters.

This approach provides immediate pronunciation support while helping you identify and address systematic pronunciation challenges across your class.

Unlike the specialized pronunciation tools discussed in previous sections, gener-al-purpose AI platforms, like ChatGPT, can also support pronunciation practice through voice-based conversations, though they lack the detailed phonetic analysis features of dedicated apps. Educators should position ChatGPT as a supplementary tool for flu-ency practice rather than a replacement for dedicated pronunciation software. To do this, educators can guide learners to use ChatGPT's voice mode (available in the mobile app) for conversational pronunciation practice by creating carefully crafted prompts. Here is an example prompt that students can adapt for their own pronunciation goals:

✦✦ Sample Learner Prompt for Pronunciation Error Correction With ChatGPT

Note: To use this prompt, open ChatGPT on your mobile device, tap the voice icon to activate voice mode, then read this prompt aloud or paste it into the text interface before beginning your voice conversation.

I'm studying the English language at an intermediate (B1) level and I'm trying to improve my pronunciation of *th* sounds (i.e., /θ/ and /ð/). Also, I often make grammar mistakes with past tense verbs. I want to have a 15-minute dialogue about my last trip. Correct my pronunciation errors during our chat. Do not interrupt the flow but repeat the correct words for me. For grammar mistakes, note them and give me time to correct myself before stating the right form. Track if I'm improving on the errors you point out during our conversation and acknowledge when I successfully self-correct. After the chat, give me a recap of my errors, highlight any patterns you notice, and suggest follow-up practice exercises. I learn best when corrections are inspiring and contain explanations of the reason they are incorrect.

Gamification of Phoneme Practice

This next set of AI-powered tools for pronunciation training is focused on gamification. With point-based rewards for accuracy, structured levels, and narrative quests, these tools introduce phonemes progressively in a challenging and engaging learning context. Social features, such as leaderboards, add a competitive edge and foster peer interaction. AI enhances these elements by adjusting difficulty in real time, tailoring game scenarios to individual needs, and using NLP to embed pronunciation tasks within meaningful contexts. These gamified tools make phoneme practice both dynamic and adaptive, promoting sustained engagement and leading to measurable improvement.

Here are three AI-driven tools that offer gamified pronunciation training:

Table 8. Tools for Gamifying Pronunciation Practice

AI Tool	Uses game-based rewards/levels	Introduces phonemes progressively	Adapts difficulty in real time	Embeds pronunciation in meaningful contexts	Includes social and peer engagement features	Tracks learner progress	Aligned with CEFR or other standards
Mondly	✔	✔	◑	✔	✔	✔	
Lingokids	✔	✔	✔	✔	✔	✔	
ELSA Speak	✔	✔	✔	✔	◑	✔	

See Appendix B for detailed descriptions and website links for each of these tools.
See "Note on AI Tools" in the front matter regarding evolving tool functionality.

TRY IT OUT: Gamified Phoneme Practice With Lingokids

Use Lingokids with your early and elementary learners to provide engaging and playful pronunciation practice.

a. Start by assigning pronunciation tasks within the Lingokids app.

b. Direct young beginner students to the ABC section, where they should select Letter Sounds, then start with the Phonics Adventure game, which focuses on individual letter sounds and simple phoneme recognition.

c. For slightly older elementary learners, assign the Rhyme Time game under the Reading section, which practices word families and phoneme blending. Students can also use the Say It Right feature, found in the Speaking category, to repeat words after a fluent speaker model and receive immediate feedback through speech recognition technology.

d. Reinforce the learning by adding class discussions or asking students to complete simple progress logs. These allow learners to reflect on their achievements and remain focused on progress.

This activity blends purposeful pronunciation practice with the motivating elements of gameplay.

Adaptive Learning Paths for Phoneme Mastery

Using AI, pronunciation training apps can generate personalized learning paths that dynamically adjust based on an individual learner's needs. How does this work? Most tools use a preliminary assessment activity to examine a learner's phoneme production skills and determine which areas require targeted support. Based on the obtained data, these systems can develop an individualized curriculum made to address the learner's unique challenges. As the learner proceeds, the tool continuously monitors performance and adapts the instructional content as needed. Advanced AI technologies, such as predictive analytics, reinforcement learning, and clustering algorithms, make this kind of support possible. Collectively, these AI-driven techniques create a responsive, individualized learning environment that supports effective phoneme mastery. Here are some of the AI-powered tools that have successfully applied adaptive learning paths for phoneme mastery:

Table 9. Tools for Personalized Pronunciation Learning

AI Tool	Conducts preliminary assessment	Generates individualized curriculum	Adapts instruction based on performance	Uses predictive analytics	Applies reinforcement learning	Tracks learner progress	Aligned with CEFR or other standards
Carnegie Speech NativeAccent	✔	✔	✔	✔	✔	✔	✔
Rosetta Stone	✔	✔	✔			✔	✔
Babbel		◐	◐			✔	
EnglishCentral	✔	✔	✔			✔	

See Appendix B for detailed descriptions and website links for each of these tools.
See "Note on AI Tools" in the front matter regarding evolving tool functionality.

TRY IT OUT: Personalized Pronunciation Paths With NativeAccent

Introduce your learners to Carnegie Speech's NativeAccent.

a. Start by having learners complete NativeAccent's built-in diagnostic task, which evaluates their spoken responses, analyzes pronunciation errors, and identifies areas that need more practice.

b. Guide learners to follow their personalized practice plans within the platform.

c. Use information from the platform to supplement your instruction. Access the NativeAccent teacher portal and navigate to the Class Reports section to view aggregated pronunciation data for your students. For example, if multiple students show difficulty with word stress patterns, dedicate class time to stress-marking exercises and minimal pairs practice.

This approach supports effective pronunciation development by offering targeted practice activities that support each learner's unique learning journey.

AI Applications for Teaching Grammar

Grammar instruction has long been a cornerstone of language teaching, yet it remains one of the most challenging aspects for both teachers and learners. Traditional grammar instruction often relies on explicit rule explanation followed by controlled practice exercises, an approach that can feel disconnected from authentic language use. Though traditional methods have their place, they are constrained by several factors: limited opportunities for individualized feedback, difficulty in addressing each learner's specific error patterns, and the challenge of helping students transfer grammatical knowledge from exercises to authentic communication. The integration of AI into grammar instruction addresses many of these limitations by offering personalized, data-driven feedback that can adapt to individual learner needs. AI-powered grammar tools can analyze writing patterns, identify recurring errors, provide contextualized explanations, and offer unlimited practice opportunities—all while freeing teachers to focus on higher level aspects of language development, such as rhetorical effectiveness and critical thinking. This section explores how AI technologies are transforming grammar instruction in ELT contexts and provides practical strategies for integrating these tools into your teaching.

Automated Error Detection and Correction

Advancements in AI-driven writing tools have notably shifted the way that writers (including language learners) can resolve their grammatical errors. Rather than relying exclusively on fixed grammar rules, AI writing assistants implement advanced language processing models that draw on extensive datasets of writing by both fluent and non-fluent speakers. These models can catch subtle grammatical errors that conventional spell-checkers often miss. For example, they can analyze the context of a sentence to distinguish true errors from typos and offer contextual explanations, not just surface-level corrections.

Here are three AI writing tools that offer advanced error correction and explanation:

Table 10. Tools for Intelligent Grammar Correction

AI Tool	Detects grammar errors	Detects spelling errors	Detects punctuation errors	Provides contextual explanations	Suggests corrections	Checks style and clarity	Aligned with CEFR or other standards
Grammarly	✔	✔	✔	✔	✔	✔	
ProWritingAid	✔	✔	✔	✔	✔	✔	
WhiteSmoke	✔	✔	✔	◐	✔	◐	

See Appendix B for detailed descriptions and website links for each of these tools.
See "Note on AI Tools" in the front matter regarding evolving tool functionality.

One of the key educational advantages of these tools is the quick, thorough feedback they deliver. This can help learners perceive why a revision might be necessary. Still, it's vital that educators encourage multilingual learners of English to think critically about the suggestions these programs can offer rather than adopting them wholesale. At times, these tools may erroneously flag stylistic choices or culturally influenced discourse as mistakes. Students should use these tools as an initial aid in revising their first draft of a writing assignment for correctness, then make use of peer or teacher feedback to check for clear communication of meaning.

TRY IT OUT: Grammar Error Analysis With Grammarly

Use Grammarly to help students identify and understand their recurring grammar patterns.

a. Have students create free accounts, then install the browser extension or desktop app.

b. Assign students to write a 250-word paragraph on a familiar topic, such as describing their daily routine or favorite hobby. Ask them to compose the paragraph directly in word processing software (e.g., Microsoft Word) with Grammarly activated.

c. Instruct students to review Grammarly's highlighted suggestions without immediately accepting them. Have them create a Grammar Error Log documenting (1) the type of error Grammarly identified, (2) Grammarly's explanation, (3) why they made that error, and (4) the corrected version in their own words.

d. After students complete three writing assignments using this process, have them analyze their error logs to identify their three most frequent grammar challenges. Use this data to create differentiated grammar mini-lessons targeting common error patterns across your class, while assigning individualized practice exercises for less common errors.

This approach helps students develop metacognitive awareness of their grammar challenges while providing you with concrete data to inform targeted instruction.

Personalized Grammar Practice and Adaptive Learning

Beyond error correction, AI now powers online grammar instruction via comprehensive online learning platforms. These tools offer adaptive curricula that teachers can harness for supplemental practice or in-class activities. AI-driven grammar instruction excels in generating individualized learning trajectories that adjust to learners' needs and proficiency levels. By continuously evaluating learners' language use, these tools can spot specific grammatical weaknesses and create tailored exercises. These systems track progress over time and adjust difficulty levels dynamically, ensuring that students remain appropriately challenged without becoming overwhelmed.

Table 11. Tools for Personalized Grammar Instruction

AI Tool	Generates individualized grammar practice	Adapts difficulty dynamically	Provides explanations	Integrates into curriculum	Tracks learner progress	Aligned with CEFR or other standards
NoRedInk	✔	✔	✔	✔	✔	
Lingoda	✔	✔	✔	✔	✔	✔
Grammarly	✔	✔	✔	✔	✔	

See Appendix B for detailed descriptions and website links for each of these tools.
See "Note on AI Tools" in the front matter regarding evolving tool functionality.

Because these tools can intelligently adapt their curricula and activities based on student progress, teachers can use them to differentiate instruction for diverse learner needs, such as by addressing multiple proficiency levels simultaneously. By providing unlimited practice opportunities with on-the-spot feedback, AI systems support the repetitive practice required for grammar instruction and set the instructors free to concentrate on more advanced aspects of language use, such as discourse organization and pragmatic appropriateness in different communicative contexts.

Contextual Grammar Instruction With AI Chatbots

Contemporary AI applications in grammar instruction emphasize contextual learning through authentic scenarios rather than stand-alone drills. ChatGPT, Claude, and similar large language models can craft limitless contextualized examples that engage learners' personal interests and academic or professional needs. With well-designed prompts, these AI chatbots can transform abstract grammatical concepts into practical communication tools by embedding practice within real-world scenarios that learners might encounter in their daily lives. This type of practice can help learners understand how grammatical choices affect meaning and appropriateness across different communicative situations.

These AI tools also excel at generating genre-specific practice activities to help learners master the grammatical features of different types of discourse, whether academic writing, business correspondence, or casual conversation. Chatbots can generate an endless variety of linguistic examples and practice questions on demand, offering learners extensive practice without repetitive materials.

I'm studying English at the intermediate (B1) level, and I'm preparing for a job interview in the marketing field. I struggle with using the present perfect tense correctly, especially when talking about my work experience and accomplishments. I need to practice using present perfect in realistic interview scenarios. Please act as a job interviewer and ask me 5–7 common interview questions that would naturally require present perfect tense in the answers (e.g., questions about my experiences, achievements, and skills I've developed). After I respond to each question, give me feedback on whether I used present perfect correctly. If I made errors, explain why the tense I used was incorrect and show me the correct form. If I avoided using present perfect when it would have been appropriate, point that out and explain when and why present perfect would work better. After we finish the mock interview, provide a summary of my most common present perfect errors and situations where I successfully used the tense. Make your feedback encouraging and explain grammar rules in simple terms.

Multimodal Grammar Feedback and Visualization

Advanced AI writing tools have begun to incorporate multimodal approaches to grammar instruction by blending text-based correction with visual representations, audio examples, and interactive elements. Here are two examples:

- **Hemingway** delivers color-coded visual feedback that emphasizes sentence complexity and readability issues.

- **Grammarly** not only flags errors visually but also delivers contextual explanations with voice options for sentence playback.

See Figure 1 for a screenshot of sample feedback from each tool. The integration of visual and auditory feedback addresses different learning preferences and through multiple modalities. This can be especially efficient for complex structures like conditional sentences or passive voice constructions, where visual diagrams can clarify grammatical relationships that may be hard to understand through text alone. However, educators will likely need to help learners interpret and apply this multimodal feedback in their independent writing and speaking tasks.

Hemingway

The cat was sleeping on the windowsill. It was rainin.

The dog don't want to go outside.

The cat likes to watch the rain.

SENTENCE   ADVERB   PHRASE

Readability: Grade 5

Grammarly

The cat was sleeping on the windowsill.

The dog don't want to go outside.

The cat likes to watch the rain.

don't → did not

Some forms of "do' are considered incorrect in this context.

DISMISS

Figure 1. Screenshots of sample interactions with Hemingway and Grammarly (created with ChatGPT; OpenAI, 2025).

Important Considerations for AI in Pronunciation and Grammar Instruction

Despite their considerable benefits, AI tools for pronunciation and grammar teaching must be critically examined. Before bringing any of these tools into your classroom or assigning them for independent practice, consider the following limitations and constraints.

Accent and Dialect Awareness

One major challenge rests in accent variability, as AI-powered pronunciation tools are typically trained on standardized U.S. American or British accents. This is especially relevant in international contexts where multiple English varieties are accepted. Educators should note that these systems may erroneously flag regional or nonfluent accents as mistakes, although they are valid forms of spoken English. This disadvantage can lead to a limited focus on phoneme accuracy (or rather, mimicking the standard accent), that may overshadow broader communicative competence.

To address this issue, educators can pair AI-generated pronunciation feedback with classroom conversations around accent diversity and the significance of clarity and effective communication over rigid conformity to a single-accent norm.

Balancing Technology and Human Interaction

Although AI tools offer valuable on-the-spot feedback, overreliance on these systems can reduce learners' ability to self-monitor their speech in real conversations. Educators should set strict boundaries for AI tool usage and make sure that classroom time includes plenty of human interaction. Regular practice with peers and whole-class discussions are essential for learners to develop the real-world skill of adjusting their pronunciation and correcting their grammar according to conversational context and whether they are understood by their interlocutor.

Privacy and Data Security

Many AI-driven pronunciation platforms work by recording and analyzing learners' spoken input, which triggers key questions about privacy. Before introducing these tools in their classrooms, educators should take the time to investigate how each platform handles user data. This includes looking into how long recordings are stored, whether data is shared with third parties, and if users can opt out. In some cases, tools offer options for local-only processing or enhanced privacy modes. These tools may better align with school or district data protection policies.

Managing Student Expectations

Learners may develop unrealistic expectations about AI tools, either overrating their capabilities or becoming discouraged with their inconsistent feedback. Educators should explain those tools' capabilities and remind learners that AI provides only one form of feedback among many. Establishing realistic goals for progress in pronunciation and explaining the gradual nature of language acquisition may help learners set more practical expectations for how AI can help them.

Technical Integration Challenges

Successful use of AI tools requires thinking about the available technology infrastructure at your school or institution, the ease of learner access to devices, and the level of digital literacy that dominates in your classroom. Educators should have backup plans for when technology fails and ensure that AI tools supplement rather than dominate lesson planning. Consider starting with one tool per semester and gradually expanding according to learner engagement and outcomes.

Contextual Limitations in Grammar Feedback

AI-powered grammar tools are not always perfect when it comes to interpreting language in context. Sometimes, they may flag stylistic variations or awkward phrasing as incorrect, even when those choices are correct ones for the situation. That's why it's vital for educators to help learners become expert users of these tools and encourage them to think about when to follow automated feedback and when to trust their own judgment. This skill has critical value for more advanced writers, who must consider factors like tone, audience, and purpose when crafting their work.

Conclusion

The use of AI in teaching pronunciation and grammar is opening new doors for individualized and adaptive learning. These technologies present immediate, targeted feedback; offer plenty of interactive, engaging practice opportunities; and can generate tailored exercises that match each learner's interests and needs. Whether analyzing individual sounds, helping learners with rhythm and intonation, or detecting specific grammar issues, AI provides feedback and guidance that used to require dedicated one-on-one instruction.

However, thoughtful integration of these technologies is key. Educators need to think carefully about these tools' constraints in recognizing varied accents, safeguarding learner privacy, and more. Ultimately, AI tools can only augment the learning experience when used as a complement to skilled teaching. It is essential to balance the benefits of technology with the insights and care that only educators can provide, resulting in more inclusive and responsive instruction.

CHAPTER 8

Equity and Ethical Considerations

As edtech tools powered by generative artificial intelligence (AI) become increasingly advanced and more prevalent in language classrooms, they prompt teachers to ask important questions about data privacy, algorithmic bias, and human agency. These are more than technical considerations; they cause us to reflect on our core values as educators and on the role of language education in promoting equity and social justice. The actions we take and choices we make today about how AI tools are selected, implemented, and regulated in our classrooms will not only affect our students' achievement of learning outcomes, but also influence wider trends in educational equity.

This chapter explores critical ethical and equity questions related to responsible AI use in English language teaching (ELT). From addressing algorithmic bias that may put learners from diverse linguistic backgrounds at a disadvantage to guaranteeing that the AI tools we choose are accessible to learners with disabilities and students with limited access to technology at home, these challenges call for deliberate, thoughtful responses from educators, institutions, and educational policymakers. The goal is not to remove risk entirely, which is an unfeasible action with any transformative technology. Rather, ELT educators must adopt practices that expand AI's potential to democratize access to quality language education and cautiously protect against its capacity to worsen current inequalities. Through careful attention to transparency, inclusivity, and human-centered design principles, we can work toward a framework for AI-enhanced language pedagogy that effectively supports all learners.

Issues of Ethics and Fairness

Data Privacy and Security

For AI tools to be effective, they must collect and analyze a large amount of learner data, including voice recordings, text inputs, and usage patterns. This brings up important privacy concerns that need to be tackled through well-structured governance frameworks.

To implement AI tools effectively in our classrooms, educators should prioritize tools and platforms that demonstrate transparent data practices. Look for tools where there is transparency about what data is being gathered and how it will be used. Studies indicate that when educational technology companies collect sensitive information, they need explicit consent mechanisms where learners are fully informed before their data is processed (Huang, 2023). This transparency builds trust in AI applications and respects learner autonomy.

Robust data protection is another critical consideration. Educators should evaluate whether AI tool providers implement multilayered security approaches, including anonymization techniques to safeguard learners' identities, particularly when information is used for research or system improvement. Encryption for protecting student data during both storage and transmission, along with strict access controls that limit exposure to authorized individuals only, are essential security features.

When evaluating AI tools, educators should inquire about the vendor's policies on data retention and deletion. Responsible companies outline how long information is stored and when it will be purged, preventing unnecessary collection and storage of sensitive data. Look for providers that conduct regular audits to track and evaluate data usage and guarantee all access aligns with established ethical guidelines. The issue of data ownership becomes particularly critical when AI tools are provided by external vendors, requiring educators to review agreements carefully to understand who controls learner information and how it may be used.

Finally, educators should verify that AI tool providers comply with relevant legal frameworks, such as the General Data Protection Regulation (GDPR) in the European Union and the Family Educational Rights and Privacy Act (FERPA) in the United States. For online courses serving students in multiple territories, adherence to various international data protection laws is fundamental for responsible cross-border data management. Palle (2023) emphasizes that effective digital governance integrates both ethical evaluations and regulatory compliance for comprehensive data protection. When selecting AI tools, ask vendors directly about their compliance certifications and data governance practices to ensure they meet these standards.

What Can I Do?

Here are actionable steps educators can take to manage the data privacy and security concerns related to AI use in language education:

- **Communicate Clearly With Learners and Parents or Guardians:** Clarify what data, including audio or written, the AI tool collects and how it will be used and protected. Use age-appropriate and accessible language for learners.

- **Seek Informed Consent:** Use transparent consent forms before assigning learners to interact with any AI tools that collect their data. Make sure that learners and, when appropriate, their parents or guardians fully comprehend and agree with the terms of consent. Provide options for those who decline.

- **Use Anonymized Data When Possible:** Do not disclose any names or personally identifying data when sharing learners' information or submitted work. Prioritize AI tools with built-in features for anonymization.

- **Limit Data Access:** Make learner data accessible only to individuals with a legitimate educational purpose, such as fellow teaching colleagues or program administrators. Choose AI tools that allow for role-based authorization to view learner data.

- **Follow Your Institution's Data Retention Policies:** Check how long learner data will be stored and confirm that it is removed when storage is no longer necessary. To the extent possible, prevent the AI tool from retaining sensitive learner data longer than needed.

- **Establish Clear Classroom Norms:** Have open conversations about the responsible use of AI tools with learners. Direct them not to share personal or sensitive data about themselves when they interact with AI systems.

- **Use Approved Tools or Platforms:** Work with AI tools that have been vetted and approved by your school or district. Refrain from implementing tools that do not have clear data privacy policies.

- **Ask Vendors Key Questions:** Clarify data ownership policies, users' rights to request deletion of data, and compliance with applicable data protection laws, such as FERPA and GDPR. This is especially relevant when working with international students or when teaching outside of your home country.

- **Stay Informed on Edtech Privacy Trends:** Get involved in professional development programs on data privacy and AI ethics. Engage with educator networks that advocate for safe and ethical technology use.

Algorithmic Bias and Fairness

Bringing AI systems into ELT classrooms can inadvertently perpetuate biases related to language, culture, gender, and race. Such biases undermine inclusivity and impede equitable learning experiences and outcomes. Research shows that bias in AI systems often derives from both the design of the underlying algorithms themselves and from the datasets they are trained on, with the magnification of preexisting societal biases being a frequent consequence (Hall & Ellis, 2023).

The most prevalent forms of bias in AI tools for language learning manifest in several interconnected ways. Cultural bias occurs when AI models favor specific cultural perspectives or communication styles, potentially disadvantaging learners from diverse linguistic and social backgrounds by returning their valid, comprehensible input as incorrect or inappropriate. This is closely related to accent bias, where speech recognition technologies typically perform more accurately for widely recognized accents while struggling to parse regional or nonstandard variations. Next, linguistic bias compounds these issues when AI systems trained primarily on standardized English varieties marginalize speakers of other dialects. Moreover, gender and racial bias can appear in AI-generated course materials, such as reading texts or role-playing scenarios. In such cases, AI tools reinforce existing stereotypes rather than promote inclusivity.

Addressing these biases requires a comprehensive approach, and teachers should look to both technical solutions and ethical oversight. In the realm of technical solutions, certain AI models and technologies are beginning to leverage diverse and culturally representative training datasets, which is a fundamental step toward reducing algorithmic bias. In addition, the incorporation of frameworks for bias detection, such as building diverse product development teams and implementing transparent design processes, has been shown to reduce algorithmic discrimination (Fazil et al., 2024).

Regular audits of AI-generated content and system performance are critical for recognizing unintended biases and responding with corrective measures. The ethical frameworks proposed by Alawneh et al. (2024) put an emphasis on privacy-preserving protocols, fairness metrics, and inclusivity measures as essential for preserving equitable learning environments. Human oversight, often termed "human-in-the-loop," guarantees that AI outputs align with both educational goals and ethical standards. This strategy is widely understood as vital to preventing algorithmic bias (Hall & Ellis, 2023).

Adapting AI tools to various cultural and linguistic contexts can improve their relevance and result in greater inclusivity. Though AI holds transformative potential for language instruction, its application must be accompanied by targeted interventions to address challenges and biases that might otherwise detract from its efficacy (Sharifuddin & Hashim, 2024).

Educators can play a crucial role in this effort by explicitly teaching learners about potential biases in AI systems and encouraging them to think critically about AI-generated content. This pedagogical approach, combined with technical solutions and ethical governance, can create a comprehensive framework for equitable and inclusive use of AI in language teaching.

What Can I Do?

As educators implementing AI in the classroom, it is vital to remain mindful of how these technologies may reflect or reinforce biases. Here are some steps you can take:

- **Evaluate AI Tools for Cultural Representation:** Before introducing an AI system into your classroom, evaluate the tool for inclusivity. For example, review whether the names, stories, and examples it uses in materials and activities reflect a range of cultures, not just one dominant culture.
- **Test Speech Recognition With Diverse Accents:** Test whether the AI tool can successfully process diverse accent variations relevant to your learner population. Check if the tool struggles with certain voices. Then, consider whether it is the right fit for your class.
- **Monitor AI-Generated Content for Stereotypes:** Frequently review the content materials crafted by AI tools. Be alert for any gender, racial, or cultural stereotypes in character roles, professions, or situations learners are exposed to.
- **Provide Alternative Examples:** Replace any biased materials with your own examples that better represent the diverse population of your class.
- **Create Bias-Awareness Activities:** Assign learners to critically evaluate AI-generated content in pair or group discussions. Teach them to spot potential biases and ask questions about representation in digital tools.
- **Engage Students as Coevaluators:** Encourage students to tell you when AI tools generate content that doesn't represent their cultural or linguistic experiences. Use their feedback to make informed decisions about the tools you use in the future.
- **Diversify Your AI Tool Portfolio:** Refrain from depending on a single AI platform. Use multiple tools designed by various companies or teams to reduce the impact of potential biases from one system.
- **Advocate for Inclusive Training Data:** When talking to tech providers, ask about their training data. Does it contain a variety of voices, accents, and cultures?

- **Implement Regular Content Audits:** Schedule time to review AI-generated content being used in your instruction. Share the findings with your team to make smarter choices moving forward.
- **Keep Updated on AI Research:** Attend professional development sessions on AI in education and look for news updates or journal articles on how AI companies are addressing algorithmic bias.

Balancing AI and Human Interaction

Reaching an optimal balance between AI assistance and the role of the human educator is central to effectual AI integration in ELT. AI can be integrated for routine tasks, such as grading assessments, providing personalized feedback on assignments, and monitoring learner progress, to name a few. Using AI for these tasks allows educators to spend more time on higher order aspects of language learning. These include teaching critical thinking, developing intercultural competence, and engaging learners in interactive communication—all areas where human teachers excel. Working together, teachers can use AI-driven tools that are specifically designed for personalizing language instruction, such as adaptive learning systems and intelligent tutoring platforms, to increase engagement and improve learning outcomes. However, without a thoughtful integration strategy, an overreliance on AI tools in the classroom may inadvertently overshadow the essential human elements of empathy, creativity, and cultural sensitivity that are fundamental to language education (Sharifuddin & Hashim, 2024). Human oversight is indispensable for making ethical decisions regarding AI integration and helping learners understand and navigate ethical considerations in their interactions with AI tools.

How can ELT educators achieve the balanced approach described here, especially if they are not yet familiar with many AI tools? Professional development is vital, and should not only equip teachers with the technical skills required to use AI tools but also improve their understanding of how to balance AI's capabilities with traditional teaching methods. Research indicates that educators who are well-versed in the power and limitations of AI are better positioned to incorporate these technologies to support their instructional methods efficiently (Chen et al., 2020). Equally critical is educating learners about the distinct roles of AI tools and human teachers in their learning process. This understanding enables learners to engage usefully with AI tools while maintaining an appreciation for the unique contributions of their teachers, such as building interpersonal relationships and providing moral and emotional support (Ji et al., 2022).

What Can I Do?

Finding the right blend of technology and human interaction is critical to creating meaningful learning experiences. Here are some practical ways to strike that balance:

- **Use AI Tools Strategically:** Use AI where it can support you the most. This could include providing initial grammar and vocabulary feedback, generating practice exercises, or facilitating pronunciation drills. Prefer human interaction over AI tools for things like giving nuanced feedback on writing content, facilitating cross-cultural dialogues, or developing students' critical thinking skills.

- **Set Clear Expectations for AI Use:** Be transparent with learners about when and why you use AI. Ensure learners understand that it is there to support, not substitute for, the richer thinking and conversations that humans can have.

- **Blend AI With Live Teaching:** Create lessons where AI plays a supporting role. For instance, have students review their initial grammar feedback from Grammarly, then dedicate class time for peer review focused on ideas and organization. Assign pronunciation practice with ELSA Speak, then follow up with small-group conversations where students apply what they learned.

- **Use AI to Jumpstart, Not Finalize:** Let AI assist you with brainstorming ideas or drafting exercises. Be sure to personalize what AI generates, making the final product relevant and representative for your learners' needs and your teaching context.

- **Protect Space for Real Human Moments:** Set aside some time in every class for storytelling, culture-sharing, or just checking in. These moments can build trust and connection and cannot be replicated by AI tools.

- **Build Learners' AI Literacy:** Demonstrate wise use of AI to your learners. Teach them how to engineer good prompts, evaluate what the tool delivers, and know when to turn to a human instead.

- **Keep an Eye on Overuse:** Notice if learners are turning to AI to help them complete tasks they should be working on independently. As their skills grow, remind students to gradually ease back on AI usage to build their independence.

- **Reflect Often and Adjust:** Dedicate time to reflect, with colleagues and with your students, on how AI usage and human interaction are balanced in your classroom. Use your reflections to guide your next steps.

Transparency and Explainability

Current trends in AI research include a focus on explainability and social transparency—concepts that matter for teachers selecting AI tools for their classrooms. When choosing an AI platform, educators should look for tools that offer clear explanations of how they work and why they make specific recommendations.

Explainable AI is a field of research focused on making AI systems understandable to users. In practical terms, this means an AI writing tool should explain why it flagged a particular grammar error or suggested a specific correction, rather than simply marking something as "wrong." When AI tools provide clear explanations, both teachers and students can better understand the feedback and learn from it. Research shows that when users understand how AI makes decisions, they're more likely to trust the tool and use it effectively (Rachha & Seyam, 2023; Saeed & Omlin, 2021).

Beyond individual tool features, researchers have proposed social transparency as a framework for evaluating how AI tools function within educational settings. Ehsan et al. (2021) suggest examining how AI systems affect classroom dynamics, institutional decision-making, and community relationships. For teachers, this means considering questions like the following:

- Does this AI tool align with my school's educational values?
- Does it support my teaching goals?
- Will it build appropriate trust with students and parents?

Practically speaking, teachers can evaluate AI tools by asking vendor representatives the following direct questions or by searching for the answers in an FAQ or About page:

- How does your system generate feedback?
- Can students see why they received a particular score?
- What data informs your recommendations?

Tools that provide clear, accessible answers to these questions demonstrate the transparency necessary for ethical classroom use. For those interested in deeper technical details about AI explainability and transparency frameworks, see Olateju et al. (2024), Reddy (2024), and Thalpage (2023).

What Can I Do?

Transparency becomes critically important when using AI to support learning. Here are some practical ways to maintain transparency when working with these tools:

- **Explain How the Tech Thinks:** Help learners comprehend the sources of AI-generated content and feedback. For instance, explain that an AI writing assistant likely draws from datasets dominated by one standardized dialect of English and might therefore misunderstand some of their cultural or stylistic choices.

- **Turn AI Into a Learning Opportunity:** Design assignments where learners investigate the reasons why a tool gave certain suggestions. Ask them to compare it to feedback from a peer or teacher and reflect on the differences.

- **Make Limits Clear:** Keep a shared document or poster that demonstrates what each AI tool is best used for and what its drawbacks are. This helps learners use different tools thoughtfully.

- **Offer a Way to Disagree:** If a learner feels that an AI-generated grade or correction is wrong, ensure that they have the chance to appeal. Ensure that your human judgment is always part of the assessment process.

- **Show How Prompts Affect Output:** Show how small changes to prompt language can lead to very different generated outputs. Build learners' ability to critically evaluate and experiment with AI tools.

- **Talk About Patterns You Notice:** If the AI continuously flags specific types of errors, bring it up in class. Discuss how the system was trained and how learners can navigate its limitations.

- **Ask Vendors for Clarity:** When choosing a tool, seek transparency: What kind of data was used to train it? How does it make decisions? The more you know about the tool, the better you can guide the learners.

- **Show Your Own Process:** Be transparent about how you use AI. Let learners see you questioning AI-generated content. That critical approach sets a strong example for learners.

Authenticity and Academic Integrity

Learners are increasingly turning to AI-powered tools for writing assignments and other academic tasks, and this has important implications for authenticity and academic integrity. First, educational institutions must redefine what qualifies as original work. I recommend a balanced approach that acknowledges AI's role as a learning aid while discouraging an overreliance on AI that weakens critical thinking and creativity. Second, teachers and administrators need to establish clear guidelines that define responsible AI use, ensuring that learners develop their own voice rather than simply rewording AI-created text. Moreover, educators must adopt fair and effective methods for distinguishing between ethical AI-powered learning and inappropriate use.

What Can I Do?

Here are some potential steps educators can take safeguard academic integrity while making use of AI tools for language learning:

- **Define Academic Integrity:** Talk about why it's important for students to go through the stages of the writing process, or to read a full text and not just an AI summary. Remind students that they do not have to avoid all technological assistance, but define academic integrity as submitting work that accurately represents your own learning and effort.

- **Establish Clear Guidelines for AI Use:** Explain when learners can use AI, such as when brainstorming or drafting, and when independent work is required, such as on final essays or exams. Share these boundaries explicitly with all learners.

- **Require Acknowledgement of AI Use:** Require learners to cite or acknowledge when they have used AI tools in their work, and provide models of what such an acknowledgement would look like.

- **Create AI-Resistant Assignments:** Create activities and assignments where students must draw from personal experiences, classroom discussions, or cultural reflections that AI cannot authentically replicate.

- **Assess Learning Process, Not Just Products:** Evaluate the process rather than only final work. Have learners submit outlines and revision histories to track the development of their work.

- **Model Ethical AI Use:** Explain how you integrate AI in your teaching preparation. This can show learners how to use AI for organization, while maintaining an authentic voice.

- **Develop Learners' Original Voices:** Help learners notice their own unique writing styles. You might do this by having students write on a certain topic in class, then ask them to compare and contrast their work with AI-generated samples.

- **Foster Peer Accountability:** Encourage group discussions about ethical boundaries for AI use in teaching and learning. Have groups of learners collectively come up with definitions of responsible use.

Psychological Impact

The psychological effects of AI integration in education can be profound. Overreliance on AI might impact learners' confidence in their own language abilities. Furthermore, concerns about AI potentially replacing human teachers could affect teacher job satisfaction and professional identity. When teachers feel that their skills are being unnoticed or slowly taken over by AI, they may lose motivation and feel less engaged in their work. To ensure that both learners and educators thrive, it is critical to find the right balance between AI assistance and teachers' expertise.

What Can I Do?

Here are some ways to keep the language learning experience human-centered, as you take advantage of AI's capabilities:

- **Celebrate Student Voice:** Hold space in your lessons and assignments for the things only your learners can do. Encourage creative thinking, sharing cultural stories, and reflecting on personal progress.

- **Talk About AI as Support, Not a Shortcut:** Remind learners that AI is there to help them with their progress, not to do the work for them.

- **Showcase What You Bring:** Help learners understand the value you offer: your expertise, your empathy, your ability to adapt to their needs. They need to know that your instructional decisions are driven from their needs and interests, not from data analytics alone.

- **Build Learner Confidence:** If you notice that learners rely too heavily on AI or fell unsure of their own abilities, help them build up confidence.

- **Focus on Human Goals:** Establish clear targets that highlight real communication, intercultural awareness, and emotional intelligence.

- **Promote Self-Reflection:** Assign learners to review their previous work and reflect on how their skills have progressed. Provided guiding questions or activities to help students identify where they are most challenged and where they are showing more strength.

Accessibility and Equity

The Digital Divide and Socioeconomic Factors

Access to technology, or the lack of it, remains a significant barrier across the diverse contexts where English is taught around the world. Many language programs lack sufficient funds to acquire technology for their classrooms, and they may also rely on unstable internet connectivity and limited bandwidth. For example, when attempting to use data-heavy tools like ELSA Speak or SpeakAI in classrooms with poor internet connectivity, learners can experience frustrating delays or even system crashes. These kinds of technological issues can disrupt the learning process.

Socioeconomic factors can affect access to technology, whether for students at home or in the classroom setting. Equitable access to AI tools often depends on technological resources that are not evenly available across different communities. This digital divide can exacerbate existing educational inequalities and should be explicitly considered when teachers or schools decide to adopt AI tools in the curriculum.

In addition to internet access, the cost of subscribing to some AI tools can pose a substantial challenge for teachers and schools. Beyond the initial investment in hardware (i.e., classroom laptops or tablets), there are often ongoing expenses for software licenses, system maintenance, technical support, and regular updates. A 2025 study reported that many higher education institutions are withholding access to generative AI tools primarily because of cost constraints (Robert & McCormack, 2025). Public schools in developing regions often cannot afford subscription-based AI language learning tools, creating a digital divide in educational opportunities (Giannini, 2024). In spite of its promises to democratize education, therefore, AI technologies can sometimes widen the digital divide. When schools with more financial resources and better internet connectivity integrate AI language tools, their learners may have an advantage, while learners in under-resourced educational institutions may fall behind.

The digital divide can also be present within a single classroom. Even if there is adequate in-class access to technology, teachers cannot take for granted that all students have the same access to mobile devices and can pay for subscriptions to the same AI tools. Teachers can take action to push back on this divide through multiple practical approaches, such as completing a "tech equity audit" to better understand their learners' access to AI tools or creating small groups such that each group has access to at least one device.

By recognizing the potential for AI to aggravate inequity and proactively implementing corrective actions, ELT educators can change these tools from obstacles into pathways that connect rather than divide learners.

What Can I Do?

To make sure all learners benefit equitably from AI-powered learning opportunities, it is critical to consider inequalities in access and resources. Here are some practical steps to support digital equity in your classroom:

- **Start With an Access Check:** Before assigning AI-related tasks, check if all learners have equal access to reliable devices and internet. Offer alternative assignment formats to those who do not.
- **Share Tech Smartly:** Assign group and pair work such that at least one student has access to an internet-enabled device. Require students to take turns with the device so that each member has the opportunity to work with the AI tool.
- **Design Materials That Work Both Ways:** Generate lessons that are just as effective with or without AI tools. This leads to equal opportunity for learning.
- **Speak Up for Your Students:** Advocate with school leaders to push for resources, such as shared devices or institutional subscriptions to AI tools.
- **Find the Free Stuff:** Many AI tools are free of cost or have free versions. Explore those options to uncover tools that work for your classroom without breaking the budget.
- **Reach Out Locally:** Check whether your local libraries, community centers, or even small businesses might be able to offer internet or computer access or sponsor some of the costs.

Inclusivity for Learners With Disabilities

Note: This section uses both person-first language (e.g., "learners with visual impairments") and identity-first language (e.g., "learners who are neurodivergent") in alignment with preferences expressed by different disability communities.

To integrate AI systems in ELT inclusively, teachers can refer to universal design principles from the conceptual stage onward. These principles should specifically address the needs of

- learners with visual impairments (e.g., through screen readers and magnification),
- learners who are deaf or hard of hearing (e.g., with captions on audio and visual alternatives),

- learners with learning disabilities or cognitive processing differences (e.g., via adjustable pacing and multimodal presentations), and

- learners with physical or mobility disabilities (e.g., by providing alternative input methods).

Moreover, consideration must be extended to learners who are neurodivergent, whose unique cognitive processing styles may necessitate adaptations in how information is structured, presented, and assessed.

Accessibility cannot be treated as a simply a technical compliance matter. It requires continuous improvement, with insights from with disability experts and members of these communities. When choosing AI tools for an inclusive classroom, look for platforms that undergo regular accessibility audits, conduct user testing with diverse groups of learners, and refine their models based on learner feedback. These are critical parts of building truly inclusive AI-powered learning tools. Educational institutions must also ensure that teachers receive adequate training on digital accessibility tools, such as screen readers or video-captioning software, that can help them support all learners.

When thoughtfully implemented, AI can improve accessibility through features like real-time transcription, personalized learning pathways, and multimodal content presentation. This can potentially make AI-powered language education more accessible than traditional teaching. The ethical imperative is clear: Technological advancement in education must progress in tandem with advancements in accessibility and inclusion.

What Can I Do?

Following are steps educators can take to ensure that their use of AI tools in language learning is inclusive of learners with disabilities:

- **Evaluate AI Tool Accessibility Before Adoption:** Test and determine whether your chosen AI platform is compatible with screen readers and keyboard navigation. Check whether it provides captions for audio content and allows text magnification.

- **Get Training on Assistive Technology:** Learn how your chosen AI tools interact with common assistive technologies. Become familiar with how they work so that you can help students access the support they need.

- **Collaborate With Disability Support Services:** If you are teaching in a school or university with an accessibility office, contact them for help. They may already be working on assessing AI tools for education. You can also find out about accommodation strategies to support your learners with disabilities.

- **Create Multiple Content Formats:** Make use of AI chatbots to generate course materials in various formats. For instance, you could prompt ChatGPT to convert a written grammar lesson into a simplified text version, an audio script, or a dialogue format with clear labeling for screen readers. You might also use an AI tool to generate charts or diagrams—or to create alternative text descriptions for images used in your lessons.

- **Customize Learning Pathways With AI:** Many AI tools for language learning shared in this book offer the capacity to adapt pacing, difficulty level, and methods of presenting based on learner needs. Think about how these personalized learning pathways can support your neurodivergent learners.

- **Provide Alternative Assessment Options:** Use AI tools to create a variety of assessment formats. You might write a prompt that asks AI to generate instructions for an oral presentation, a visual mind map, and a written test on the same topic. These formats accommodate learners with diverse abilities and strengths.

- **Gather Continuous User Feedback:** Check with learners about their experiences with AI tools in your class. Ask about accessibility barriers and consider possible improvements.

- **Advocate for Universal Design Principles:** Call on vendors and institutions to place accessibility features at the forefront.

- **Develop Backup Plans:** Design alternative lessons and assignments for the times technology fails or proves inaccessible. Ensure that no learner's progress is interrupted by technical barriers.

Strategic Implementation for Enhanced Accessibility

For program administrators and educational leaders, attention to accessibility challenges in education requires a multifaceted approach. Institutions should generate clear and comprehensive policies that precisely address AI integration. These policies must ensure that technology improves learning opportunities rather than creating new barriers. Investing in infrastructure that supports equitable access to digital tools is another essential step, as is providing educators with the required training to implement AI in ways that promote inclusivity.

In addition, ongoing assessments should be conducted to evaluate how adopting AI tools has impacted diverse learner populations. The resulting data can provide the grounds for evidence-based improvements. Moreover, educational leaders can collaborate with AI developers to help prioritize accessibility features in newly released and updated technologies. When thoughtfully designed with these concerns in mind, AI has the potential to expand language learning opportunities equitably for all learners.

What Can I Do?

Leaders can take the following strategic steps to support accessibility of AI tools at an institutional level:

- **Develop Institutional AI Accessibility Policies:** Create or push for clear guidelines that mandate accessibility considerations in all AI tool selections.
- **Conduct Regular Impact Assessments:** Examine how AI use affects diverse learner populations through surveys, focus groups, and analyses of performance data. Use the results to inform your choices and to make changes as needed.
- **Participate in Accessibility-Focused Professional Development:** Seek out training on universal design principles and accessibility in learning technology. Share what you learn with your colleagues and consider any takeaways for your institution's use of AI and other edtech tools.
- **Create Cross-Departmental Collaboration:** For educators working in larger institutions and universities, remember that you can partner with the departments of information technology, disability support, and curriculum design to establish coordinated methods for accessible AI use across your institution.
- **Pilot Test With Diverse User Groups:** Pilot your chosen AI tools before launching them with your full class or program by partnering with learners with disabilities to test accessibility features and provide feedback on their experiences.

The Global Perspective

ELT is a global industry, and there is likely considerable variation across national and regional teaching contexts in how quickly teachers have adopted AI tools for language learning. This disparity is influenced by several factors, including economic resources, technological infrastructure, cultural attitudes, government policies, and the specific needs of language learners in different contexts.

In economically advanced countries, AI-enhanced language learning is becoming increasingly commonplace. One reason for this shift is often government policy. For example, in April 2025, U.S. President Donald J. Trump signed an executive order entitled "Advancing Artificial Intelligence Education for American Youth" to promote AI literacy and proficiency among U.S. citizens (Exec. Order No. 14277; 2025). The executive order called for introducing AI into education, offering comprehensive AI training for educators, and developing an AI-ready workforce. In countries where government policy supports access to educational technology and where technological infrastructure is highly developed, students often utilize advanced language learning apps, and schools are progressively implementing AI-driven curriculum planning (Alqahtani & Wafula, 2024). Conversely, in many developing regions, basic digital tools are still being introduced, and the implementation of advanced AI technologies remains limited due to financial constraints and inadequate technological infrastructure (Wei, 2023).

Cultural considerations also play a pivotal role in the use of AI tools in classroom settings. The adoption of these technologies can be significantly influenced by communication styles, teacher roles, and cultural norms related to learning. In some cultures, traditional teaching methods and in-person interactions are highly valued, leading to less acceptance of AI-enhanced learning. In response, adapting AI tools to be culturally responsive is an ongoing challenge and opportunity. When AI applications are tailored to align with local cultural contexts, researchers see higher student engagement and better learning outcomes (Kessler, 2018).

Despite these differences, AI holds an immense potential to bridge educational gaps worldwide, particularly in regions with teacher shortages. In such regions, AI can supplement traditional teaching by delivering adaptive language instruction and individualized learning experiences adapted to each learners' needs (Anis, 2023; Fryer & Carpenter, 2006). AI-driven tools can provide inexpensive learning options, expanding access to quality education across a broader population.

In summary, though AI presents significant opportunities for enhancing language learning globally, it also necessitates careful consideration of economic, cultural, and linguistic factors. The future of AI in ELT lies in developing culturally responsive and linguistically inclusive tools that complement teacher expertise and cater to diverse learner needs.

Ethical Use Guidelines

Teachers and language programs must establish well-structured ethical guidelines that frame their choices of AI tools for ELT. Before adopting any new AI tool, educators should wisely review them to verify they can support teaching goals and protect learner interests. Putting clear rules in place is vital. Educators should ask questions about key ethical concepts, such as keeping learner data secure, addressing built-in biases in AI systems, and ensuring these tools work well for all learners (Homayouni et al., 2024).

Particularly in K–12 education, schools should put measures in place to protect privacy and ensure that AI systems treat all students fairly (Alawneh et al., 2024).

When educators, decision makers, and AI developers work together, they can better verify AI systems match both school goals and community values. With reliable ethical guidelines in effect, schools can build a system that puts fairness, inclusion, and student well-being at the forefront. However, we also need to keep track of how AI affects learning over time. New ethical matters, such as hidden biases or unfairness, often surface slowly and can require ongoing modifications. Our guidelines need to develop and change as AI technology improves, while keeping a focus on openness, responsibility, and human values (Sharifuddin & Hashim, 2024).

What Can I Do?

As AI becomes an indispensable part of language instruction, ELT educators must establish clear policies to guarantee that its use is fair and beneficial for everyone. Following are some steps to take when creating ethical guidelines for AI use at your school or institution.

- **Collaborate on Policy Building:** Be the one who starts the conversation. Partner with your school leaders to develop clear rules around data privacy, storage, consent, and fairness. Begin by reviewing existing school technology policies and identify gaps specific to AI use. Consider starting with a small pilot group to test draft guidelines before implementing them across the school; this would allow you to refine policies based on real classroom experiences.

- **Bring Everyone to the Table:** Ethical guidelines are most effective when they include input from a range of sources. Assemble a diverse policy review committee that includes ELT educators, technology specialists, administrators, and crucially, students and their families. Ensure the committee reflects the linguistic and cultural diversity of your student population. Hold structured feedback sessions where each stakeholder group can voice concerns and priorities.

- **Do Your Homework Before Launching:** Carefully examine any AI tool before introducing it. Reflect on the following questions: Does it protect learner data? Does it represent diverse perspectives? Is it beneficial for your instructional goals? Develop a standardized AI tool evaluation checklist that addresses data privacy policies, accessibility features, cultural representation, alignment with learning objectives, and cost considerations (see the template provided later in this section). Require that all proposed AI tools undergo this evaluation process before approval.

- **Keep Tabs on What Is Working:** Set up systems to track each AI tool's impact on your learners over time. Include student surveys and other forms of feedback. Track learner performance data both within the apps and on larger in-person assessments to help you make informed decisions about whether an AI tool is supporting learning.

- **Be Open About How AI Is Used:** Learners and their families deserve to know about AI use and data privacy. Create clear, jargon-free communications in families' home languages explaining which AI tools are being used, what student data is collected, how it's protected, and what educational benefits are expected. Provide opt-out options where feasible and establish regular communication channels for ongoing updates.

- **Watch for Bias and Let Students Speak Up:** AI content or feedback can contain bias in subtle ways. Create safe, anonymous ways for learners to raise concerns about privacy and bias. Consider establishing a Digital Equity Team with student representatives who can bring forward concerns in a structured way. Develop a clear protocol for investigating and responding to reports of biased AI output, including timelines for review and remediation steps.

- **Keep Learning:** The conversation on ethical use of AI is evolving. Set aside time for professional development and attend conferences to learn about new research and emerging best practices. Schedule quarterly review sessions where your AI policy committee examines new research, discusses emerging ethical concerns, and updates guidelines accordingly. Subscribe to relevant educational technology journals and join professional networks focused on ethical AI in education.

Template for Evaluating an AI Tool for Ethical Use

Use this template when evaluating any AI tool for classroom adoption. Complete all sections and share with your review committee before making a decision.

Tool Name: _____

Evaluator: _____

Date: _____

I. Data Privacy and Security

Yes ☐ | No ☐   Does the vendor clearly explain what student data is collected?

Yes ☐ | No ☐   Is student data encrypted during storage and transmission?

Yes ☐ | No ☐   Does the tool comply with privacy regulations in your country (e.g., FERPA, GDPR)?

Yes ☐ | No ☐   Can student data be deleted upon request?

Yes ☐ | No ☐   Is data shared with third parties? If yes, for what purposes?

Yes ☐ | No ☐   Are there clear data retention and deletion policies?

Notes/Concerns:

II. Accessibility and Inclusion

Yes ☐ | No ☐   Is the tool compatible with screen readers?

Yes ☐ | No ☐   Does it provide captions for audio content?

Yes ☐ | No ☐   Can text be magnified?

Yes ☐ | No ☐   Are there keyboard navigation options?

Yes ☐ | No ☐   Does it support multiple learning modalities (e.g., visual, auditory, kinesthetic)?

Yes ☐ | No ☐   Has the tool been tested with learners with disabilities?

Notes/Concerns:

III. Cultural Responsiveness and Bias

Yes ☐ | No ☐   Does the content reflect diverse cultural perspectives?

Yes ☐ | No ☐   Has the tool been tested for linguistic and cultural bias?

(continued)

Yes ☐ | No ☐   Are there options to customize content for different cultural contexts?
Yes ☐ | No ☐   Does feedback avoid privileging standard American or British English exclusively?
Yes ☐ | No ☐   Are diverse accents and dialects recognized by speech recognition features?

Notes/Concerns:

IV. Pedagogical Alignment

Yes ☐ | No ☐   Does the tool align with your specific learning objectives?
Yes ☐ | No ☐   Can you track student progress meaningfully?
Yes ☐ | No ☐   Does it provide explanations for its corrections and feedback?
Yes ☐ | No ☐   Can content difficulty be adjusted to student proficiency levels?
Yes ☐ | No ☐   Does it encourage critical thinking rather than rote responses?

Notes/Concerns:

V. Transparency and Explainability

Yes ☐ | No ☐   Does the vendor explain how the AI makes decisions or recommendations?
Yes ☐ | No ☐   Can students understand why they received specific feedback?
Yes ☐ | No ☐   Are algorithms and training data sources disclosed?
Yes ☐ | No ☐   Is there documentation on known limitations of the tool?

Notes/Concerns:

VI. Cost and Sustainability

Yes ☐ | No ☐   Are the upfront and ongoing costs clearly posted?
Yes ☐ | No ☐   Is the cost sustainable for our institution?
Yes ☐ | No ☐   Are there hidden fees or required upgrades?
Yes ☐ | No ☐   Is technical support included?
Yes ☐ | No ☐   Is student data deleted if and when the subscription ends?
Yes ☐ | No ☐   Is the tool likely to be supported long-term?

Notes/Concerns:

(continued)

VII. Student and Family Input

Yes ☐ | No ☐   Have students tested the tool and provided feedback?

Yes ☐ | No ☐   Have families been informed about the tool and its data practices?

Yes ☐ | No ☐   Are there opt-out options available?

Notes/Concerns:

Overall Recommendation

☐ Approve for immediate use _____

☐ Approve with conditions:_____

☐ Pilot with small group _____

☐ Reject—concerns outweigh benefits _____

Signatures

Evaluator: _____

Date: _____

Committee Chair: _____

Date: _____

Note: *This template can be adapted for your specific institutional context and should be reviewed annually to incorporate new ethical considerations as AI technology evolves. Download a customizable version on this book's companion site (www.tesol.org/ ai-enhanced-elt-book).*

Conclusion

AI tools are reshaping how we teach and learn languages. Smart systems can now generate unique learning journeys for each individual learner, act as round-the-clock language tutors, and tackle advanced language tasks in ways that were impossible before. But bringing AI into English language classrooms isn't without its barriers. We need to cautiously protect learner information and challenge hidden biases in these systems. We must also find an appropriate balance between computer-assisted learning and in-person teaching. Adopting an AI-powered learning app isn't a one-time decision; we must continuously re-evaluate our choices as technology grows and our understanding broadens.

CHAPTER 9

Professional Development for Teacher AI Use

Teacher training is a critical element for the successful integration of generative artificial intelligence (AI) technologies. Many English language teachers express apprehension about incorporating AI tools into their teaching practices. Even for teachers who are confident with digital tools, the rapid evolution of AI technologies necessitates continuous professional development.

Concentrating on both technical proficiency and pedagogical applications, comprehensive professional development must train teachers to interpret AI-powered learning analytics, design adaptive curriculum pathways, and apply targeted interventions derived from AI-generated feedback. Professional development initiatives must also address the ethical considerations of AI use in language education. In this chapter, you'll discover the difference between digital literacy and AI literacy and learn about effective models for AI-focused teacher training.

Adopting AI tools successfully in English language teaching (ELT) requires more than simply exposing teachers and learners to new tools and technologies for language study. When educators are exposed to such a shallow level of AI education, they frequently fail to utilize the full potential of AI tools. Instead, through continuous professional development that addresses both technical knowledge and strategic curricular integration, teachers can harness the power of AI effectively to create innovative, accessible language learning experiences for all learners.

A Needs Assessment for Teacher Training on AI Integration

What factors lead to resistance or negative attitudes about AI integration among ELT educators, and how can professional development address these attitudes? First, successful AI implementation requires adequate teacher support and technology infrastructure, which many schools currently lack (Chen, Chai, et al., 2021). Second, one study found that many teachers resisted using AI tools due to a lack of training and feelings of computer anxiety (Zulkarnain & Yunus, 2023). Additionally, teachers' attitudes toward AI can vary significantly by age group. Alharbi and Khalil (2023) found that younger teachers (ages 25–35) showed positive attitudes and more willingness to integrate AI, while older teachers (ages 46–55) expressed strong resistance and a preference for traditional methods. Beyond age alone, teacher readiness for AI integration may widely differ by experience level. Early-career educators are often open to experimenting with AI but may need to increase caution in assessing its ethical impact. Those in the middle of their careers may have strong instructional experience but feel overwhelmed by technical demands on top of their other duties. More experienced teachers may resist AI altogether, due to the assumption that it may be misaligned with the relationship-driven practices they have developed over time.

When ELT educators do seek out training on AI integration, there can often be a divide between the skills and topics they pursue and the type of training that would truly impact student learning outcomes. Though AI tools that streamline administrative tasks are valuable for freeing up teachers' time, professional development often stops there. Teachers understandably gravitate toward these efficiency tools because they offer immediate relief from workload pressures. However, this focus can overshadow AI's transformative potential for directly enhancing student learning. Many educators lack sufficient training in AI's pedagogical capabilities, such as providing adaptive feedback, enabling personalized learning pathways, or supporting differentiated instruction. Effective AI integration requires balancing efficiency-focused tools with student-centered applications, but this balance can only be achieved when educators receive comprehensive training addressing both the administrative and pedagogical uses of AI.

Successful AI training for ELT educators starts with building on their existing strengths. For instance, educators skilled in classroom management can benefit from seeing how AI can streamline differentiated instruction without interfering with established classroom routines. Those known for strong learner relationships and classroom communities need to see how technology can strengthen human connection.

Educators who specialize in certain methodologies need transparent explanations and vivid examples of how AI can add to their specific approach.

To encourage meaningful AI adoption, teacher trainers must avoid generic solutions. Instead, they must deliver adaptable paths that build on existing expertise, supporting continued investigation and guided reflection adapted to where each educator is coming from.

Why AI Training for Teachers Matters

TESOL's *The 6 Principles for Exemplary Teaching of English Learners* (TESOL International Association, 2024) offers a valuable structure for grasping AI's role in professional development. See Figure 1 for a detailed comparison.

TESOL Principle	How AI Can Support It
Principle 1: Know Your Learners	AI tools can analyze student language data to identify individual strengths and needs and track learner progress.
Principle 2: Create Conditions for Language Learning	Adaptive AI platforms can personalize practice, offering engaging multimodal activities.
Principle 3: Design High-Quality Lessons for Language Development	AI tools can generate lesson plans, model dialogues, and communicative tasks tailored to learner goals.
Principle 4: Adapt Lesson Delivery as Needed	AI feedback during activities helps teachers adjust pacing, input, or task focus in real time.
Principle 5: Monitor and Assess Student Language Development	AI-driven analytics highlight learner progress, track error patterns, and target areas for intervention.
Principle 6: Engage and Collaborate Within a Community of Practice	Teachers can use AI-supported forums, shared analytics, and collaborative tools to exchange best practices and address ethical challenges.

Figure 1. How AI tools for language teaching and learning can support implementation of The 6 Principles for Exemplary Teaching of English Learners *(TESOL International Association, 2024).*

For teachers working in the United States, the April 2025 executive order on AI in education (Exec. Order No. 14277; 2025) amplifies the urgency of professional development. This directive stresses that the integration of AI in educational settings must prioritize educator agency, rather than substituting for human expertise. The order specifically calls for training initiatives that equip educators to evaluate AI tools critically, recognize their constraints, and retain control over pedagogical decision-making. This policy framework reaffirms that the successful adoption of AI hinges on empowered, well-prepared educators who can make informed decisions on the use of technology in their classrooms.

Defining AI Literacy

AI literacy for ELT educators extends beyond the everyday knowledge of how to use technology. While digital literacy includes fluency with common learning platforms (e.g., Canvas, Google Docs) and the ability to use digital communication technologies, AI literacy includes certain technological skills that support language learning, such as understanding how algorithms process language, identify patterns, and generate responses, and evaluating AI-generated content for relevance to instructional goals.

Four central competencies define AI literacy for ELT professionals:

1. **Technical competency** means understanding how AI tools vary in their functions, data requirements, and output constraints. Educators are not required to become programmers, but they need to understand the basic concepts of natural language processing (NLP), algorithmic pattern recognition, and machine learning. They must also develop skills in prompt engineering.

2. **Pedagogical competency** means integrating AI technologies purposefully into language teaching methodologies. It entails knowing when AI boosts learning goals and when it potentially interferes with them.

3. **Critical competency** means examining AI-generated content for correctness, screening for cultural and pedagogical appropriateness, and spotting potential biases.

4. **Ethical competency** means safeguarding the privacy of students' data as they interact with AI tools, maintaining human agency in decisions on curriculum and assessment, and guaranteeing equitable access to AI-driven learning.

The difference between general digital literacy and AI-related competence becomes apparent in action. A digitally literate educator can make use of email, learning management systems, and presentation software. An AI-literate educator can create effective prompts for activities, diagnose grammatical or cultural problems with generated content, and design learning opportunities that use AI's power while minimizing its drawbacks. This specialized competency is crucial in language teaching, where cultural specificities, contextual factors, and authentic patterns of conversation need human supervision that present AI systems cannot fully replicate.

Effective Models for AI-Focused Professional Development

Workshop-Based Training

When selecting a workshop for AI professional development, look for programs that offer structured contexts for hands-on experimentation and collective problem-solving with immediate feedback from facilitators. The most valuable programs combine technical skill development with critical reflection on pedagogical and ethical considerations. Effective workshop designs also make use of peer collaboration, giving educators the opportunity to share their challenges and achievements with AI tools as they build supportive professional networks.

Consider one of these three established workshop models:

- **SELAR (Supportive Education Lectures AI Resource):** This workshop model provides teachers with graduated exposure to AI tools through scaffolded activities that move from basic awareness to advanced pedagogical applications (Alers et al., 2024). The framework emphasizes collaborative exploration and reflection on ethical implications of AI use in language classrooms.

- **MIT's Responsible AI for Computational Action Workshop:** This program focuses on helping educators understand AI's technical foundations while developing critical perspectives on its ethical implementation (MIT Media Lab, 2020). Participants engage in hands-on activities that balance technical skill-building with discussions of bias, transparency, and accountability in educational AI systems.

- **TESOL's AI in the English Language Classroom Workshop:** Designed specifically for language educators, this workshop explores practical applications of AI tools for language teaching while addressing pedagogical considerations unique to ELT contexts (TESOL International Association, 2025a). The program covers lesson planning, assessment, differentiation, and student engagement through AI-enhanced activities.

Each of these workshops blends technical skill-building with opportunities for reflection, helping educators develop AI literacy and move immediately to classroom applications. Striking a balance between theoretical and practical knowledge, they provide educators with a basic understanding of conceptual frameworks underlying AI tools as well as practical strategies for using AI to support language learning.

Embedded Professional Development and Coaching Models

Institution-based professional development delivers the benefits of contextual relevance. It focuses on specific limitations and opportunities that educators at that institution face in their daily work. Embedded coaching models pair educators with AI-experienced mentors who offer constant support during implementation process. Because thoughtful AI use requires continuous practice rather than one-time exposure, the coaching model can be one of the most impactful.

Language centers often pioneer innovative embedded methods for professional development because their dedicated mission and smaller scale can help with rapid experimentation and adaptation. Successful programs usually include collaborative planning sessions where educators work together to transform familiar lessons by integrating AI tools. This procedure is followed by observation and reflection cycles with other educators that pave the way for continuous improvement.

AI Training for Preservice Teachers

Academic programs in TESOL have identified the need to prepare preservice educators for AI-embedded English language classrooms, starting from the first stage of their professional journeys. Graduate coursework on this topic often blends research-driven frameworks with practical application. This creates the chance for preservice teachers to develop AI literacy alongside other required competencies.

Another strength of these academic programs is that they often focus on critical thinking about technology incorporation rather than tool-specific training. They recognize that AI technologies will continue to evolve during educators' careers. The most effective university interventions help preservice teachers plan for in-service professional development. This approach lays a path for permanent learning that extends beyond early certification.

Online, Self-Paced Courses and Certifications

Online professional development programs offer a level of access and flexibility that is hard to achieve through traditional, in-person workshops. Self-paced modules provide the opportunity for educators to build their AI literacy on timelines that match with their own schedules as well as learning preferences, while still delivering opportunities for virtual peer interaction and collaborative exchange. Consider the following online trainings, current as of publication of this volume:

- **AI Deep Dive for Educators:** This is a structured, 15–hour, self-paced course with instructor support offered through the International Society for Technology in Education (ISTE). Through a university partnership, the course is eligible for graduate-level credit. Visit iste.org/courses/ai-deep-dive-for-educators to learn more.

- **MagicSchool** offers multi-level certification pathways that help teachers progressively integrate this comprehensive AI platform into their practice. Visit www.magicschool.ai/certification-courses to learn more.

- **Google's Generative AI for Educators** is an online certification course that introduces practical applications of generative AI in teaching and learning. Visit grow.google/ai-for-educators to learn more.

These programs deliver formal recognition that can lead to career advancement and establish shared standards of practice across varied educational settings. Thoughtfully designed digital learning contexts blend autonomy with connection, integrating discussion spaces, virtual gatherings, and group projects to foster a sense of community.

Key Components of High-Impact AI Training

Prompt Engineering

Writing effective prompts is a foundational skill for today's educators. Chapter 2 established the crucial role of prompt engineering to link AI-generated materials with instructional goals. Educators must know how to write prompts that produce pedagogically sound responses and avoid inappropriate or confusing results.

The SCRIPT model introduced in Chapter 2 offers a solid foundation for effective prompt design, and its six key elements can serve as a basic curriculum for professional development on this topic (see page 25). Beyond understanding the SCRIPT framework, educators need practical training in applying prompt engineering across different contexts and AI tools.

Understanding Which Tools Require Prompting

Not all AI tools require prompt engineering. Many specialized language learning apps (e.g., ELSA Speak, Duolingo, Grammarly) have preprogrammed AI functionality and don't require user-written prompts—students simply interact with built-in features. However, generative AI platforms (e.g., ChatGPT, Claude, Google Gemini, Microsoft Copilot) rely entirely on user prompts to generate content. Educators need training to distinguish between these tool types and understand when prompt engineering skills are necessary. This knowledge is particularly important because teachers must be able to guide students in writing effective prompts for their own independent learning.

Differentiating Prompt Types and Their Applications

Effective professional development should introduce educators to the following common prompt categories and their pedagogical applications:

- **Instructional prompts** direct AI to create learning materials.
  - » *Example:* "Generate a worksheet on past tense irregular verbs for intermediate learners."
- **Role-based prompts** assign AI a specific persona.
  - » *Example:* "Act as a conversation partner practicing job interview scenarios."
- **Iterative prompts** build on previous outputs.
  - » *Example:* "Now simplify that explanation for beginner-level learners."
- **Exploratory prompts** generate multiple options.
  - » *Example:* "Suggest five different ways to teach the present perfect tense."
- **Evaluative prompts** request assessment or feedback.
  - » *Example:* "Review this student essay for grammar errors and provide constructive feedback."

Training should include hands-on practice with writing each prompt type, comparing outputs, and collaborating with peers to refine prompts based on results.

Promoting Representation and Diversity

Educators require explicit training in crafting prompts that result in output representing diverse voices, registers, and cultural contexts. This includes learning to specify things like register, dialect, or other specific features that should be included in the output course materials. Here are two examples of what this might look like:

- "Include examples from both formal business English and informal conversation."
- "Generate dialogue featuring speakers of various regional Englishes (e.g., British,

American, Nigerian, Indian English)."

Without such specific prompt language, AI often defaults to standard American or British English, potentially marginalizing learners from other linguistic backgrounds.

Training Students as Prompt Engineers

Because students increasingly use AI for independent learning, teachers need strategies for teaching prompt engineering to learners. Professional development should model how to scaffold this skill—starting with analyzing effective versus ineffective prompts, then practicing revising existing prompts, and eventually having students create their own prompts for language practice. When students learn to think critically about the inputs and outputs for AI chatbots and other generative AI tools, they can use these tools strategically and with integrity.

Critical Engagement With AI Output

Educators need specific training to critically evaluate AI-created content for its accuracy, cultural relevance, and instructional value. AI output often appears polished at first glance, but in fact, it can include genuine inaccuracies and incorrect language structures that may impede learner understanding. It can also reinforce cultural biases. Developing a critical eye to spot these matters is essential, along with a healthy skepticism toward AI-generated output.

Identifying Inaccuracies, Hallucinations, and Cultural Mismatches

Professional development programs must include training on how to spot common AI errors. These errors, sometimes popularly called *hallucinations*, can range from fabricated sources and invented facts to grammatically correct but semantically nonsensical sentences and outdated information presented as current. Teachers should practice error-detection exercises, where they review AI-generated content specifically looking for these issues. Particular errors to watch for in the ELT context can include the inclusion of unnatural collocations, the use of an inappropriate register for the context, or an explanation of a grammar rule that sounds authoritative but is incorrect. Teachers also need to learn to identify when an AI tool's output reflects cultural assumptions inappropriate for their learners. This might include idioms unfamiliar to the target audience, cultural references that exclude certain groups, or examples that inadvertently reinforce stereotypes. Educators need practice with recognizing these issues, revising prompts to request more appropriate content, and editing outputs for accuracy.

Adapting Based on Learner Feedback

Effective training includes strategies for gathering student feedback on AI-generated materials and using that feedback to refine prompts. Teachers should learn to ask: Did this resonate with students? What confused them? What engaged them? This iterative process—generate, test with learners, revise prompt, regenerate—is central to effective AI integration.

Framing AI Output as a Starting Point

Critical AI literacy training should emphasize that AI-generated content is never a final authority but rather a starting point for analysis, discussion, and revision. Professional development should model how to use AI outputs to spark classroom conversations: "Let's examine what this AI-generated dialogue got right and what sounds unnatural" or "How might we revise this AI-created reading passage to better reflect our community's experiences?"

This enhanced sensitivity becomes particularly vital in language education, where meaningful human interaction plays a critical role. Educators must be equipped with knowledge and strategies to make professional decisions when integrating AI to ensure that students must still use their critical thinking and creativity, which are essential 21st-century skills.

Tool Exploration vs Pedagogical Application

Well-designed training establishes a clear distinction between knowing how AI tools work and successfully implementing them in educational contexts. Though it is vital for educators to know about the functions of the tools, the emphasis should be on using these technologies to achieve pedagogical goals. Professional development opportunities should provide practice in the art of evaluating and selecting AI tools according to their functions and features, then matching them to the learning objectives they can best support, from building vocabulary to fostering communicative competence. By putting pedagogy—and not the sparkle of new technology—at the core, educators can make informed choices and use AI strategically to support specific teaching and learning objectives.

Designing AI-Integrated Lessons and Assessments

Educators benefit from explicit instruction on applying backward design principles within AI-powered educational contexts (Wiggins & McTighe, 2005). Backward design involves three key steps. First, educators define clear learning objectives and desired outcomes. Second, they determine appropriate assessments that measure whether students have achieved those objectives while accounting for AI use and promoting academic integrity. Third, they select AI tools and design learning activities that support students in reaching the established goals.

Professional development for using AI tools in language assessment should strike a balance between taking advantage of the efficiencies delivered by AI and maintaining the authentic demonstration of learning outcomes. When learners rely on AI tools for writing or translation, educators must develop strategies that measure actual learning rather than the content produced by AI.

Building Communities of Practice and Peer Collaboration

Integrating AI in English language classrooms successfully depends on continuing professional conversations and problem-solving among colleagues. Trainings need to provide the opportunity for educators to share experiences, troubleshoot challenges, and co-construct shared policies and frameworks for using AI in their teaching practices. These communities of practice will only become more significant as AI technologies evolve and are more widely adopted.

Collaboration among teachers helps support experimentation and risk-taking and offers emotional support for sometimes stressful technological transitions. Educators who feel isolated as they try to adopt AI tools can all too easily abandon the effort, while those who are part of supportive professional networks tend to persist and innovate.

Challenges in Professional Development

It is hard to escape the fact that educators across the global ELT community have different levels of access to and support for professional development. Educators in resource-rich regions and schools may be offered adequate financial support and access to workshops and certifications, while those in budget-strapped schools may struggle with limited technology and funding. In a recent report, UNESCO (2025) warns that AI and digitalization risk deepening inequality when deployed without safeguards, particularly if internet connectivity, device access, and training are not equitably distributed. This digital divide threatens to worsen existing educational disparities.

Geographic location can also play a vital role in limiting access to professional development. Educators in rural areas often face restricted in-person training choices or are required to travel long distances to attend trainings; they may also experience internet connectivity problems that impede taking part in online programs. To help alleviate these disparities, educational institutions, school districts, and professional organizations need to take deliberate action to deliver flexible, inclusive training opportunities.

Several approaches can address the needs of rural educators:

- Asynchronous online courses allow teachers to download materials and complete training modules offline, then upload assignments when connectivity is available.

- Regional training hubs can bring professional development closer to rural educators. School districts or state education departments might partner to establish satellite training locations, reducing travel burdens while maintaining in-person interaction benefits.

- Hybrid models combining brief initial in-person sessions with extended online follow-up can minimize travel requirements while building community.

- Mobile professional development, where trainers travel to rural schools rather than expecting teachers to travel, ensures that entire school faculties can participate together.

- Micro-credentialing and modular training allow educators to build skills incrementally through short, focused sessions.

- Peer mentoring networks connecting rural educators with colleagues in similar contexts—facilitated through video calls or messaging platforms—provide ongoing support without requiring physical presence or high bandwidth.

Educational policymakers and funding agencies must also recognize that equitable access requires financial support for rural educators' professional development, including stipends for travel, technology upgrades to improve connectivity, and substitutes to cover classes during training.

A final challenge related to teacher training on AI integration is sustaining ongoing support. Though many trainings include robust introductions, few extend the program into the practical stage—and that is when educators will most likely face difficulties. Without ongoing coaching or structured peer collaboration, early momentum and excitement about new classroom technology can fade when practical obstacles come up. In addition, the rapid advances in AI technologies add to the struggle of long-term sustainability. As tools change and web platforms merge or disappear, previous professional learning risks becoming outdated. Teachers should seek out training opportunities that prioritize transferable skills and critical thinking over tool-specific familiarity so that their knowledge remains applicable regardless of evolutions in AI technologies.

Success Story: A Standout Professional Development Program

At San José State University (California, USA), one faculty-driven initiative shows how context-sensitive professional development can empower educators to maintain pedagogical integrity while using AI tools. Instead of adopting a top-down mandate, the university encouraged collaborative work among writing instructors to modify writing and writing-intensive courses across departments (Writing Across the Curriculum, 2025a). These collaborations focused on increasing faculty AI literacy while also developing their skills in critical thinking, academic authorship, and learner engagement. Faculty participants created a series of workshops titled "Teaching AI for Writing Instructors," which included various AI-related topics, such as linking AI to learning goals and ensuring ethical AI integration (Writing Across the Curriculum, 2025b).

What made this initiative stand out was its deliberate emphasis on reflective practice and collaborative curricular development. Instructors worked together to create assignments that called for AI-powered drafting and maintained the editorial agency of learners. This program centered on framing AI technology as a collaborative writing partner rather than a replacement for human authorship. After participating in the workshop series, writing teachers understood how to inspire learners to critically analyze AI-generated content and make purposeful revisions (Writing Across the Curriculum, 2025c). By encouraging faculty to share instructional materials, rubrics, and policies across departments, the program created a sustainable model for cross-disciplinary collaboration on AI use in writing courses. End-of-program evaluations revealed increased faculty confidence in integrating AI meaningfully and ethically, with heightened awareness of how to evaluate AI-mediated writing assignments.

More Recommendations for Designing Effective AI Training

For teacher trainers and educational leaders, the following additional recommendations can serve as a framework for designing effective training in AI literacy for ELT educators:

- **Align With Institutional Standards and Goals:** Ensure that the content of your AI workshop or training program is aligned with institutional standards and goals in your school or language program, such as existing curricula, school improvement plans, or learner assessment standards. This practice guarantees that the training serves wider educational goals and is not a stand-alone technological initiative; it also provides a transparent rationale for ongoing investment in teacher learning.

- **Incorporate Active Learning:** Ask questions that spark critical thinking about when, why, and how AI might support language learning. Reflective and inquiry-based learning can transform educators from passive technology users into active researchers of AI's pedagogical potential.

- **Use Educator Feedback:** Incorporate educator voices in the design of trainings, and recognize educators as experts in their own learning needs and classroom contexts. Successful programs incorporate teacher feedback continuously, adjusting content and pacing based on participant responses. This collaborative approach increases buy-in while ensuring that training addresses real challenges rather than hypothetical scenarios.

- **Develop Teacher Confidence:** Reinforce educators' authority in choosing whether and how to adopt AI tools in their classrooms. To avoid technological determinism, programs should focus on helping teachers make informed pedagogical choices. Reminding teachers that AI is one tool among many reinforces confidence in their human expertise.

- **Encourage Trial and Error:** Encourage experimentation, creativity, and critical reflection to create a safe space for risk-taking. AI integration should be an iterative progress. Through allowing time for trial and error with AI tools, professional development opportunities become supportive environments for learning. Programs that celebrate innovation attempts, even unsuccessful ones, foster the persistence necessary for meaningful technological integration.

Conclusion: Building Sustainable AI Literacy in ELT

The future of AI in ELT depends less on technological advances and more on educators' readiness to get involved with these tools in successful and purposeful ways. Sustainable competence in this area necessitates continuous professional development that adapts and evolves alongside AI technologies but remains grounded in strong pedagogical principles and a commitment to learning.

AI-focused training must be ongoing, not a one-time event. ELT educators must engage in continuous learning that addresses the dynamic nature of AI technologies as well as developments in ELT methodologies. This approach calls for a robust professional development infrastructure, one that includes flexible entry points, transparent progress pathways, and continued support throughout an educators' career.

The purpose of professional development is not only to help educators adopt new tools, but also to equip them with guidelines for the responsible implementation of those tools. This means cultivating critical evaluation, ethical awareness, and collaborative problem-solving. In this way, educators become active contributors in choosing how AI impacts their classrooms.

Ultimately, AI literacy must surpass the mastery of tools to include professional leadership. Educators who understand the broader implications of AI can advocate for sound institutional policies and model ethical technology implementation. These leaders will help define the role of AI in English language education.

CHAPTER 10

Future Directions and Emerging Trends

The examples in this volume demonstrate how generative artificial intelligence (AI) stands to revolutionize the teaching and learning of English. Educators who are willing to develop the skills to integrate AI technologies with established pedagogical approaches are pushing the field of English language teaching (ELT) forward into a new frontier. Like any new technology, AI tools offer extraordinary opportunities for educators, but they also raise important questions about the future of language teaching and learning. The rapid growth of AI capabilities indicates that we are just beginning to observe the potential effects of these technologies in our classrooms.

Current developments in AI will lead to transformative advancements in language pedagogies. The integration of advanced natural language processing (NLP), coupled with virtual reality (VR) and augmented reality (AR) technologies, promises to generate immersive language learning experiences with contextually aware feedback systems. Moreover, the emergence of emotionally intelligent AI and affective computing forecasts a shift toward more personalized, emotionally intelligent tutoring systems that can adjust to learners' emotional states and provide adapted motivational strategies as they provide enhanced speaking and listening practice.

The trend toward explainable AI addresses the critical need for transparency in AI-driven language learning systems, empowering both educators and learners to understand the underlying decision-making architecture of AI tools. This development, coupled with real-time accent adjustment tools and personalized speech synthesis systems, is setting a framework for more user-friendly language learning experiences. These emerging technologies collectively promise to generate more advanced and inclusive learning environments that can better serve diverse learner needs while supporting transparency and accountability in the learning process.

AI tools have already shown extraordinary success in areas once considered exclusively human domains: real-time translation, personalized feedback, and context-aware language generation. These achievements, although striking, have only laid a foundation for more complicated technologies that could fundamentally reshape ELT. As we look toward that prospect, this chapter provides an overview of key trends and developments in AI that are relevant for English language teachers and the learners they serve.

Current State and Trajectory of AI in ELT

The current state of AI in ELT builds upon a foundation of advanced technologies that have already started transforming language education. As mentioned earlier, NLP is one of the most prominent technologies transforming AI's ability to understand and generate recognizably fluent speech (and writing). Systems employing NLP can assess learners' pronunciation, grammar, and comprehension, providing personalized feedback that adapts to their progress (Crompton et al., 2024), identifies error patterns, and highlights areas for further attention. Today's AI tools also rely on machine learning algorithms that can continuously adapt to learner progress. Finally, modern speech recognition and synthesis technologies have altered pronunciation training by offering learners real-time feedback and corrections that formerly required direct teacher mediation.

Developers have harnessed these foundational concepts to build AI-driven educational tools that combine the best features of traditional instruction with the advantages of new technology. Chapters 4–7 presented some of these tools. Adaptive learning platforms can respond dynamically to learner progress by adapting their content complexity and presentation methods based on individual performance data. Digital assessment systems offer immediate, personalized linguistic feedback that helps learners recognize and address areas of weakness while equipping teachers with necessary tools to track progress more efficiently. Virtual teaching assistants have proven to be valuable supplements to traditional instruction by delivering additional practice and personalized support outside of classroom hours. Teachers should expect more and different types of educational tools to appear online as the landscape of AI expands and new technologies develop.

AI-Driven Pronunciation Instruction: Future Directions

Across the language skills, pronunciation instruction is approaching the greatest moment of transformation in response to emerging AI technologies. Immersive learning environments built on AR and VR allow learners to experience realistic communication scenarios through 3D simulations. For pronunciation teaching specifically, VR platforms can place learners in virtual environments, such as a restaurant, business meeting, or airport, where they must use accurate pronunciation to communicate with virtual characters and complete tasks. These immersive contexts provide immediate consequences for mispronunciation (e.g., a virtual waiter brings the wrong order if pronunciation is unclear) and create authentic motivation for intelligibility. VR environments can also display real-time visual feedback on learners' mouth position, tongue placement, and breath control through avatar mirrors or holographic demonstrations, allowing learners to see and correct articulatory errors as they practice speaking in context. Experimental brain–computer interface systems, discussed later in this chapter, offer novel possibilities for direct neural feedback in pronunciation practice. Another advancement is the development of emotion recognition algorithms, which can approximately measure learners' affective states during pronunciation practice and adjust task design to increase the rates of learner engagement and motivation and build learner confidence (Cheeli, 2024).

Empirical research is needed across multiple domains to better understand the impact of AI technologies on pronunciation teaching, including the following:

- estimating the longitudinal impact of AI-powered pronunciation practice, especially on the transfer of learned skills to authentic communication contexts
- developing cross-linguistic AI models that can address pronunciation complexities across diverse accents, dialects, and language families
- designing AI tools for multimodal learning, combining visual, auditory, and kinesthetic feedback mechanisms

The potential long-term implications of these advances on ELT are extensive. The arrival of personalized language learning ecosystems, adapted individual learning pathways and interests, appears inevitable. This shift requires reforms in teacher education that helps instructors prepare for thoughtful integration of AI technologies. In addition, the increasing quality of AI tools for pronunciation study has the potential to democratize access to learning and reduce socioeconomic barriers. Virtual teaching assistants and chatbots can provide reliable, personalized practice sessions at a large scale and for any student with access to the internet, regardless of geographical or socioeconomic constraints (Istrate, 2018). Perhaps most significantly, ongoing efforts to develop AI systems trained on diverse English varieties, including Indian English, Nigerian English, Singaporean English, and other Global Englishes, are challenging traditional notions of "standard" pronunciation and promoting linguistic diversity. As these multicultural training datasets become more prevalent and accessible, AI pronunciation tools could shift from reinforcing dominant British or American norms to recognizing multiple varieties as equally valid, thereby helping dismantle the linguistic hierarchies that have historically marginalized non-Western English speakers.

Immersive Learning and Multimodal AI

The future of language learning environments is expected to be highly immersive, integrating advanced VR technology with state-of-the-art AI systems. These environments will feature photorealistic virtual spaces populated with AI-generated characters capable of natural, contextually appropriate verbal communication. By allowing learners to practice language skills in real-world contexts simulated virtually, these tools will bridge the gap between theoretical knowledge and practical application (Konyrova, 2024). AI systems are expected to dynamically adapt these immersive scenarios to learners' needs and interests. Incorporating haptic feedback systems will further enhance the learning process by adding a tactile dimension to communication practice, enabling learners to physically practice appropriate gestures and body language in simulated intercultural communication contexts. Engaging with auditory, visual, and kinesthetic stimuli creates a richer, more interactive learning environment (Weihua, 2019).

AR technology is likely to transform language learning by converting everyday experiences into educational opportunities by adding a responsive layer of digital content to real-world contexts through learners' mobile devices. For example, real-time AR language adaptation systems will offer contextually relevant vocabulary and grammar assistance, providing learners with immediate visual feedback as they go about daily activities. AR tools can also deliver instant cultural interpretation features to enhance cross-cultural interactions (Li, 2024). Moreover, AI-powered games and applications will gamify routine activities, increasing learner engagement and retention through interactive and entertaining exercises (Khan & Mishra, 2024).

Advanced systems can include voice recognition to simulate realistic conversations and engage learners in an English language conversation without leaving their homes (Konyrova, 2024).

However, the adoption of these technologies is not without challenges. Equitable access remains a significant issue, with differences in digital infrastructure among learners and across educational contexts. Moreover, ensuring that teachers are adequately trained to use these tools successfully is vital for their efficient use. As discussed in Chapter 10, professional development for educators must focus on AI literacy or an awareness of new tools as well as skills for integrating them into current curriculums. Addressing these challenges in technology access and teacher training, along with ethical considerations around inclusivity, will be critical for the extensive adoption of multimodal AI learning environments.

Emotionally Intelligent AI Tutors

AI tools with built-in emotional sensitivity will shift the way educators approach personalized online learning. AI systems equipped with multimodal emotion recognition technologies, such as facial expression analysis, voice modulation sensing, and behavioral tracking, can immediately adapt to learners' emotional conditions. As an example, if the system notices that a learner is frustrated, the system can make the tasks simpler and easier; in the moments of confidence, the system can introduce more challenging exercises. Tools with this new technology can create an encouraging learning context that mirrors human-like emotional intelligence, which increases learner engagement and achievement of learning outcomes (Fernández-Herrero, 2024). These systems are also capable in integrating adaptive learning pathways that strike a balance between difficulty and support, which ultimately lead to empowering students to persist through challenges (Yu & Chauhan, 2024).

In addition to creating responsive and engaging learning experiences, emotionally intelligent AI tutors also support the social dimensions of language learning. These systems can support peer collaboration on gamified tasks and improve positive group dynamics by evaluating social clues among participants and recommending techniques to resolve conflicts or inspire participation. Research by Fernández-Herrero (2024) underlines how AI can enrich intercultural understanding and improve peer interactions by adapting tasks and interactions based on learners' emotional states and linguistic input. Likewise, AI systems that include conversational agents improve the accessibility and inclusivity of educational contexts by supporting the diverse needs of learners (Yu & Chauhan, 2024).

Despite their advantages, the implementation of emotionally intelligent AI tutors comes with significant hurdles, specifically because of ethical considerations and accessibility. Questions related to data privacy, algorithmic biases, and equitable access to advanced technology continue to be pressing. Research has highlighted the necessity for regulatory frameworks and clear algorithmic practices to protect learner privacy and confirm ethical use of these emotion-sensing technologies (Fernández-Herrero, 2024), as they constitute a new frontier in human–AI interaction. Also, the costly nature of the implementation process and required tools for access to these systems can constraint their reach, demanding innovative strategies to make them available in under-resourced contexts.

As these technologies continue to develop, their ability to copy and respond to human emotions could result in promising innovations for both the cognitive and emotional dimensions of language learning. With advances in their underlying technology, emotionally intelligent AI tutors will become even more adaptive, inclusive, and responsive educational tools. For these systems to extend their full potential, continued collaboration among educators, technologists, and policymakers is indispensable to address challenges and improve capabilities.

Personalized Learning Pathways and Future AI Capabilities

AI's potential for data analysis and personalization has the capability to create advanced individualized learning experiences in ELT. Beyond current tools that adjust learning pathways reactively, predictive analytics could use data gathered from a learner's performance to predict their future learning needs and, accordingly, generate personalized instructional plans. This could potentially include cross-linguistic individualization based on expectations of transfer from a learners' home language(s). Future AI tools may also support interdisciplinary learning by seamlessly combining language instruction with other relevant subjects or skills according to a learner's individual objectives.

Brain–Computer Interface Technology in Language Learning

Brain–computer interface technology refers to systems that establish direct communication pathways between the brain and external devices, typically through sensors that detect neural signals. The integration of this technology with AI systems demonstrates astonishing possibilities for language learning, although this field remains in its early phases. These novel systems show notable potential in monitoring one's cognitive load throughout language learning processes, which would enable real-time adaptations to lesson complexity in response to neurological feedback. For example, Sharma & Ahirwal

(2024) suggest an interesting potential for language learning to take place during states of reduced consciousness, such as sleep or deep relaxation, through AI-driven neural interfaces. Although these applications currently exist mostly in experimental contexts, they exemplify an exciting frontier in educational technology, potentially reshaping our understanding of language learning processes and opening new pathways for faster linguistic development. This convergence of neuroscience and AI might essentially restructure our approach to language education in the coming decades.

Conclusion

Language teachers now stand at a crucial moment, as the rapid advance of AI is leading to central questions about the nature of language learning itself. Drawing from the research discussed in this chapter, we can identify the potential for changes in how language is taught that represent more than mere technological advances. From multimodal immersive environments to emotionally intelligent tutoring systems, AI is posed to create a future in which language learning becomes increasingly naturalistic while remaining methodically structured. Responding to these changes will require rethinking the balance between the human teacher's expertise and the use of mediating technologies.

The arrival of context-aware immersive learning environments, supported by advanced AR and VR technologies, has the potential to fundamentally change the experience of language learning. These systems should not replace traditional pedagogical approaches but can potentially enhance them by creating what might be termed *adaptive learning ecosystems*. Within these ecosystems, learners study language not as an abstract entity but as a living, breathing medium for communication. Research by Konyrova (2024) and Li (2024) underlines how these immersive environments can foster deeper cross-cultural competence, which has long been a challenge in traditional language classrooms.

Yet, as described in Chapter 8, the AI revolution brings with it complicated pedagogical and ethical issues that demand careful consideration. The digital divide remains a notable concern. Furthermore, the development of emotionally intelligent AI systems leads to important questions about data privacy and algorithmic bias. To respond to these challenges, educators, technologists, and educational policymakers must work together to design governmental and institutional policy frameworks that promote equitable access and preserve high standards of educational quality. The work of Crompton et al. (2024) offers key insights into how such frameworks might be structured to increase the educational benefits of these new technologies while reducing their potential disadvantages.

Looking at what's next, the future of ELT will likely be determined by how successfully we can strike a balance between integrating AI and preserving the role of the teacher as an expert in language pedagogy. Throughout this book, we have seen that successful implementation of AI-powered learning platforms requires more than choosing the best technology. It also relies on a teacher's deeper understanding of theories of language acquisition, cultural differences, and learner psychology. Moving forward, we should take care to adopt AI systems that supplement rather than replace human interaction; although resisting technological advances would put our learners at a disadvantage, it's important to remember that using language to connect with others is something deeply human. Pursuing such a balanced approach, informed by continued research and by the careful consideration of ethical concerns, will help ELT professionals realize AI's full potential to advance language learning while ensuring that we continue to serve the diverse needs of multilingual learners in an increasingly interconnected world.

References

Anthropic. (2025). Claude 3.5 Sonnet [Large language model]. https://www.anthropic.com/claude

AI for Education. (2024, October 31). *Prompt framework for educators: The five "S" model.* https://www.aiforeducation.io/ai-resources/the-five-s-model

Alam, S., Usama, M., Alam, M. M., Jabeen, I., & Ahmad, F. (2023). Artificial intelligence in global world: A case study of Grammarly as e-tool on ESL learners' writing of Darul Uloom Nadwa. *International Journal of Information and Education Technology, 13*(11), 1741–1747.

Alawneh, Y., Radwan, E., Salman, F., Makhlouf, S., Makhamreh, K., & Alawneh, M. (2024, April 18–19). *Ethical considerations in the use of AI in primary education: Privacy, bias, and inclusivity* [Paper presentation]. International Conference on Knowledge Engineering and Communication Systems, Chikkaballapur, India. https://doi.org/10.1109/ICKECS61492.2024.10616986

Alers, H., Malinowska, A., Mourey, M., & Waaijer, J. (2024). From chalkboards to chatbots: SELAR assists teachers in embracing AI in the curriculum. *arXiv*, Article 2411.00783. https://doi.org/10.48550/arXiv.2411.00783

Alexander, K., Savvidou, C., & Alexander, C. (2023). Who wrote this essay? Detecting AI-generated writing in second language education in higher education. *Teaching English With Technology, 23*(2), 25–43.

Alharbi, W. (2023). AI in the foreign language classroom: A pedagogical overview of automated writing assistance tools. *Education Research International*, Article 4253331. https://doi.org/10.1155/2023/4253331

Alharbi, W., & Khalil, L. (2023). Artificial intelligence (AI) in ESL vocabulary learning: An exploratory study on students and teachers' perspectives. *Migration Letters, 20*(12), 1030–1045.

Ali, Z. (2020). Artificial intelligence (AI): A review of its uses in language teaching and learning. *IOP Conference Series: Materials Science and Engineering, 769,* Article 012043.

Aljohnai, A., Al-Mamlook, R. E., & Alharbe, N. (2022). AI-based attendance management system using image processing techniques during COVID-19 pandemic. *ICIC Express Letters, 16*(12), 1–13.

Alqahtani, W., & Wafula, R. N. (2024). Artificial intelligence integration: Pedagogical strategies and policies at leading universities. *Innovative Higher Education.* https://doi.org/10.1007/s10755-024-09749-x

Anderson, J. R. (1982). Acquisition of cognitive skill. *Psychological Review, 89*(4), 369–406.

Anis, M. (2023). Leveraging artificial intelligence for inclusive English language teaching: Strategies and implications for learner diversity. *International Journal of Multidisciplinary Educational Research, 12*(6), 54–70.

Best, C. T. (1995). A direct realist perspective on cross-language speech perception. In W. Strange & J. J. Jenkins (Eds.), *Cross-language speech perception* (pp. 171–204). York Press.

Brown, H. D. (1989). *Teaching by principles: An interactive approach to language pedagogy.* Pearson.

Brown, T. B., Mann, B., Ryder, N., Subbiah, M., Kaplan, J., Dhariwal, P., Neelakantan, A., Shyam, P., Sastry, G., Askell, A., Agarwal, S., Herbert-Voss, A., Krueger, G., Henighan, T., Child, R., Ramesh, A., Ziegler, D. M., Wu, J., Winter, C., ...Amodei, D. (2020). Language models are few-shot learners. *Advances in Neural Information Processing Systems, 33*, 1877–1901.

Borg, S. (2015). *Teacher cognition and language education: Research and practice.* Bloomsbury.

Chapelle, C., & Sauro, S. (2017). *Introduction to the handbook of technology and second language teaching and learning.* John Wiley & Sons.

Cheeli, B. (2024). Human elements in pedagogical assistants that aid in english language teaching & learning: An offline study. *Proceedings of the 8th International Conference on Advanced Research in Teaching and Education. 1*(1), 41–54.

Chen, L., Chen, P., & Lin, Z. (2020). Artificial intelligence in education: A review. *IEEE Access, 8*, 75264–75278.

Chen, M., Chai, C. S., Jong, M. S., & Jiang, M. Y. (2021). Teachers' professional development in formal online communities: A systematic review. *Journal of Educational Technology & Society, 24*(2), 151–165.

Chen, X., Zou, D., Xie, H., & Cheng, G. (2021). Twenty years of personalized language learning: Topic modeling and knowledge mapping. *Educational Technology & Society, 24*(1), 205–222.

Cook, J. (2023, June 26). *How to write effective prompts for ChatGPT: 7 essential steps for best results.* Forbes. https://www.forbes.com/sites/jodiecook/2023/06/26/how-to-write-effective-prompts-for-chatgpt-7-essential-steps-for-best-results/

Crompton, H., Edmett, A., Ichaporia, N., & Burke, D. (2024). AI and English language teaching: Affordances and challenges. *British Journal of Educational Technology, 55*(6), 2503–2529.

DeKeyser, R. (2007). Skill acquisition theory. In B. VanPatten & J. Williams (Eds.), *Theories in second language acquisition* (pp. 97–113). Lawrence Erlbaum.

Devlin, J., Chang, M. W., Lee, K., & Toutanova, K. (2019). BERT: Pre-training of deep bidirectional transformers for language understanding. *Proceedings of NAACL-HLT 2019*, 4171–4186.

Derwing, T. M., & Munro, M. J. (2015). *Pronunciation fundamentals: Evidence-based perspectives for L2 teaching and research*. John Benjamins.

Di Mario, M. (2024, May 13). *How to use ChatGPT to support your lesson planning*. Pearson. https://www.pearson.com/international-schools/international-schools-blog/2024/05/how-to-use-chatgpt-to-support-your-lesson-planning.html

Dizon, G. (2020). Evaluating intelligent personal assistants for L2 listening and speaking development. *Language Learning & Technology, 24*(1), 16–26.

Dörnyei, Z. (2001). *Motivational strategies in the language classroom*. Cambridge University Press.

Edmett, A., Ichaporia, N., Crompton, H., & Crichton, R. (2023). *Artificial intelligence and English language teaching: Preparing for the future*. British Council. https://doi.org/10.57884/78EA-3C69

Ehsan, U., Vera Liao, Q., Muller, M., Riedl, M. O., & Weisz, J. D. (2021). Expanding explainability: Towards social transparency in AI systems. *Proceedings of the 2021 CHI Conference on Human Factors in Computing Systems,* Article 82, 1–19. https://doi.org/10.1145/3411764.3445188

Ejjami, R. (2024). The future of learning: AI-based curriculum development. *International Journal for Multidisciplinary Research, 6*(6).

Ellis, R. (2006). Current issues in the teaching of grammar: An SLA perspective. *TESOL Quarterly, 40*(1), 83–107. https://doi.org/10.2307/40264512

Exec. Order No. 14179, 3 C.F.R. 8,741 (2025). https://www.federalregister.gov/executive-order/14179

Exec. Order No. 14277, 3 C.F.R. 17,519 (2025). https://www.federalregister.gov/executive-order/14277

Fazil, A., Hakimi, M., & Shahidzay, A. (2024). A comprehensive review of bias in AI algorithms. *Nusantara Hasana Journal, 38*(8), 1–11.

Fernández-Herrero, J. (2024). Evaluating recent advances in affective intelligent tutoring systems: A scoping review of educational impacts and future prospects. *Education Sciences, 14*(8), Article 839.

Flege, J. E. (1995). Second-language speech learning: Theory, findings, and problems. In W. Strange (Ed.), *Speech perception and linguistic experience: Issues in cross-language research* (pp. 229–273). York Press.

Flege, J. E. (2003). Assessing constraints on second-language segmental production and perception. In A. Meyer & N. O. Schiller (Eds.), *Phonetics and phonology in language comprehension and production: Differences and similarities* (pp. 319–355). Berlin: Mouton de Gruyter.

Flodén, J. (2024). Grading exams using large language models: A comparison between human and AI grading of exams in higher education using ChatGPT. *British Educational Research Journal, 51*(1), 201–224.

Foote, J. A., Holtby, A. K., & Derwing, T. M. (2011). Survey of the teaching of pronunciation in adult ESL programs in Canada, 2010. *TESL Canada Journal, 29*(1), 1–22. https://doi.org/10.18806/tesl.v29i1.1086

Fryer, L., & Carpenter, R. (2006). Bots as language learning tools. *Language Learning & Technology, 10*(3), 8–14.

Generative AI @Harvard. (2024). *Teach with generative AI: Resource for faculty.* https://www.harvard.edu/ai/teaching-resources/

Giannini, S. (2024). Use of AI in education: Deciding on the future we want. *UNESCO.* https://www.unesco.org/en/articles/use-ai-education-deciding-future-we-want

Grammarly. (2025, January 13). *Prompt engineering explained: Crafting better AI interactions.* https://www.grammarly.com/blog/ai/what-is-prompt-engineering/

Hall, P., & Ellis, D. (2023). A systematic review of socio-technical gender bias in AI algorithms. *Online Information Review, 47*(7), 1264–1279.

Hearst, M. A. (2000). The debate on automated essay grading. *IEEE Intelligent Systems and Their Applications, 15*(5), 22–37.

Hidayat, M. T. (2024). Effectiveness of AI-based personalised reading platforms in enhancing reading comprehension. *Journal of Learning for Development, 11*(1), 115–125.

Hockly, N. (2023). Artificial intelligence in English language teaching: The good, the bad and the ugly. *RELC Journal, 54*(2), 445–451.

Homayouni, L., Hejazi, Y., & Zarifsanaiey, N. (2024, February 27–29). *A review of ethical considerations in using artificial intelligence in e-learning* [Poster presentation]. 17th International and the 11th National Conference on e-Learning and e-Teaching (ICeLeT), Isfahan, Iran. https://icelet2024.ui.ac.ir/files_site/files/r_24_240225125046.pdf

Huang, L. (2023). Ethics of artificial intelligence in education: Student privacy and data protection. *Science Insights Education Frontiers, 16*(2), 2577–2587.

Huang, X., Zou, D., Cheng, G., Chen, X., & Xie, H. (2023). Trends, research issues and applications of artificial intelligence in language education. *Educational Technology & Society, 26*(1), 112–131.

Istrate, A. M. (2018). Artificial intelligence and machine learning: Future trends in teaching ESL and ESP. *Proceedings of the 14th International Conference eLearning and Software for Education, 2*, 471–476.

Jacobs, G. M., & Farrell, T. C. (2003). Understanding and implementing the CLT (communicative language teaching) paradigm. *RELC Journal, 34*(1), 5–30.

Jeon, J., Lee, S., & Coronel-Molina, S. M. (2024). Rethinking AI: Bias in speech-recognition chatbots for ELT. *ELT Journal, 78*(4), 435–445. https://doi.org/10.1093/elt/ccae035

Ji, H., Han, I., & Ko, Y. (2022). A systematic review of conversational AI in language education: Focusing on the collaboration with human teachers. *Journal of Research on Technology in Education, 55*(1), 48–63.

Jiang, R. (2022). How does artificial intelligence empower EFL teaching and learning nowadays? A review on artificial intelligence in the EFL context. *Frontiers in Psychology, 13,* 1–8. https://doi.org/10.3389/fpsyg.2022.1049401

Kasneci, E., Sessler, K., Küchemann, S., Bannert, M., Dementieva, D., Fischer, F., Gasser, U., Groh, G., Günnemann, S., Hüllermeier, E., Krusche, S., Kutyniok, G., Michaeli, T., Nerdel, C., Pfeffer, J., Poquet, O., Sailer, M., Schmidt, A., Seidel, T., … Kasneci, G. (2023). ChatGPT for good? On opportunities and challenges of large language models for education. *Learning and Individual Differences, 103,* Article 102274. https://doi.org/10.1016/j.lindif.2023.102274

Kessler, G. (2018). Technology and the future of language teaching. *Foreign Language Annals, 51*(1), 205–218.

Khan, A., & Mishra, V. (2024). Empowering English language learners: Harnessing AI for enhanced ESL education. *Journal of Advances and Scholarly Researches in Allied Education, 21*(3), 208–218.

Khankhoje, R. (2018). The power of AI driven reporting in test automation. *International Journal of Science and Research, 7*(11), 1956–1959.

Kim, N. Y. (2018). A study on chatbots for developing Korean college students' English listening and reading skills. *Journal of Digital Convergence, 16*(8), 19–26.

Kirana, S. N., & Gupta, Y. M. (2022, April). Utilising natural language processing to assist ESL learners in understanding parts of speech. *International Journal of Innovative Technology and Exploring Engineering, 11*(5), 12–15.

Konyrova, L. (2024). The Evolution of language learning: Exploring AI's impact on teaching English as a second language. *Eurasian Science Review, 2*(2), 133–138. https://doi.org/10.63034/esr-42

Krashen, S. (1985). *The input hypothesis: Issues and implications.* Longman.

Kuddus, K. (2022). Artificial intelligence in language learning: Practices and prospects. In A. Mire, S. Malik, & A. K. Tyagi, *Advanced analytics and deep learning models* (pp. 1–17). Scrivener.

Lee, J. H., Shin, D., & Noh, W. (2023). Artificial intelligence-based content generator technology for young English-as-a-foreign-language learners' reading enjoyment. *RELC Journal, 54*(2), 508–516.

Levis, J. (2005). Changing contexts and shifting paradigms in pronunciation teaching. *TESOL Quarterly, 39*(3), 369–377. https://doi.org/10.2307/3588485

Lewis, A. (2025). Unpacking cultural bias in AI language learning tools: An analysis of impacts and strategies for inclusion in diverse educational settings. *International Journal of Research and Innovation in Social Science, 9,* 1878–1892. https://doi.org/10.47772/IJRISS.2025.9010151

Li, H. (2024). The current state and future trends of AI-assisted higher vocational English education. *Higher Education and Practice, 1*(5), 29–35.

Li, L., Chen, C. P., Wang, L., Liang, K., & Bao, W. (2023). Exploring artificial intelligence in smart education: Real-time classroom behavior analysis with embedded devices. *Sustainability, 15*(10), Article 7940. https://doi.org/10.3390/su15107940

Liang, J., Hwang, G., Chen, M. A., & Darmawansah, D. (2021). Roles and research foci of artificial intelligence in language education: An integrated bibliographic analysis and systematic review approach. *Interactive Learning Environments, 31*(7), 4270–4296.

Liao, H., Xiao, H., & Hu, B. (2023). Revolutionizing ESL teaching with generative artificial intelligence: Take ChatGPT as an example. *International Journal of New Developments in Education, 5*(20), 39–46.

Long, M. H. (1996). The role of the linguistic environment in second language acquisition. In W. Ritchie & T. K. Bhatia (Eds.), *Handbook of second language acquisition* (pp. 413–468). Academic Press.

Loyola Innaci, D., & Helan Jona, P. (2024). AI in second language learning: Leveraging automated writing assistance tools for improving learners' writing task assessment. *JARJ, 5*(1), 134–138.

Manire, E., Kilag, O. K., Cordova, N., Jr., Tan, S. J., Poligrates, J., & Omaña, E. (2023). Artificial intelligence and English language learning: A systematic review. *Excellencia: International Multi-Disciplinary Journal of Education, 1*(5), 485–497.

McCarthy, K. S., & Yan, E. F. (2023). Reading comprehension and constructive learning: Policy considerations in the age of artificial intelligence. *Policy Insights from the Behavioral and Brain Sciences, 11*(1), 19–26. https://doi.org/10.1177/23727322231218891

MIT Media Lab. (2020). *Responsible AI for computational action: Workshop resources.* Massachusetts Institute of Technology. https://raise.mit.edu/resources/curricula/raica/

MIT Sloan Teaching and Learning Technologies. (2024). *Getting started with AI-enhanced teaching: A practical guide for instructors.* https://mitsloanedtech.mit.edu/ai/teach/getting-started/

MIT Sloan Teaching & Learning Technologies. (2025). *Effective prompts for AI: The essentials.* https://mitsloanedtech.mit.edu/ai/basics/effective-prompts/

Mohamed, A. M. (2024). Exploring the potential of an AI-based chatbot (ChatGPT) in enhancing English as a foreign language (EFL) teaching: Perceptions of EFL faculty members. *Education and Information Technologies, 29*, 3195–3217.

Mohammad Ali, A. (2023). *An intervention study on the use of artificial intelligence in the ESL classroom: English teacher perspectives on the effectiveness of ChatGPT for personalized language learning* [Master's thesis, Malmö University]. DiVA. https://urn.kb.se/resolve?urn=urn:nbn:se:mau:diva-61339

Monika, M., & Suganthan, C. (2024). A study on analyzing the role of ChatGPT in English acquisition among ESL learners during English language classroom. *Bodhi International Journal of Research in Humanities, Arts and Science, 8*(2), 75–84.

Nazari, N., Shabbir, M. S., & Setiawan, R. (2021). Application of artificial intelligence powered digital writing assistant in higher education: Randomized controlled trial. *Heliyon, 7*(5), Article e07014. https://doi.org/10.1016/j.heliyon.2021.e07014

Olateju, O., Okon, S., Samuel-Okon, A., & Asonze, C. (2024). Exploring the concept of explainable AI and developing information governance standards for enhancing trust and transparency in handling customer data. *Journal of Engineering Research and Reports, 26*(7), 244–268.

Oliver, S. (2024). *AI prompt writing for ELT teachers: 7 ingredients of a successful prompt.* World of Better Learning, Cambridge. https://www.cambridge.org/elt/blog/2024/03/09/ai-prompt-writing-for-elt-teachers-7-ingredients-of-a-successful-prompt/

OpenAI. (2025). ChatGPT [Large language model]. https://chatgpt.com

Palle, R. R. (2023). Investigate ethical challenges and considerations in the collection, analysis, and use of data for IT analytics, addressing issues related to privacy, bias, and responsible AI. *International Journal of Science and Research, 12*(1), 1246–1252.

Pan, S. J., & Yang, Q. (2010). A survey on transfer learning. *IEEE Transactions on Knowledge and Data Engineering, 22*(10), 1345–1359. https://doi.org/10.1109/TKDE.2009.191

Park, H. (2022). Effects of virtual reality-based English learning on Korean university students' speaking ability. *Multimedia-Assisted Language Learning, 25*(4), 93–119.

Park, J. (2019). An AI-based English grammar checker vs. human raters in evaluating EFL learners' writing. *Multimedia-Assisted Language Learning, 22*(1), 112–131.

Park, Y., & Doo, M. (2024). Role of AI in blended learning: A systematic literature review. *The International Review of Research in Open and Distributed Learning, 25*(1), 164–196.

Pikhart, M. (2020). Intelligent information processing for language education: The use of artificial intelligence in language learning apps. *Procedia Computer Science, 176*, 1412–1419.

Pokrivcakova, S. (2019). Preparing teachers for the application of AI-powered technologies in foreign language education. *Journal of Language and Cultural Education, 7*(3), 135–153.

Qin, L., & Zhong, W. (2024). Adaptive system of English-speaking learning based on artificial intelligence. *Electrical Systems, 26*(6), 267–275.

Rachha, A., & Seyam, M. (2023, April 1–16). *Explainable AI in education: Current trends, challenges, and opportunities* [Conference presentation]. SoutheastCon, Orlando, FL, United States. https://doi.org/10.1109/SoutheastCon51012.2023.10115140

Ramalingam, S., Yunus, M., & Hashim, H. (2022). Blended learning strategies for sustainable English as a second language education: A systematic review. *Sustainability, 14*(13), Article 8051.

Rebolledo Font de la Vall, R., & Araya, F. G. (2023). Exploring the benefits and challenges of AI-language learning tools. *International Journal of Social Sciences and Humanities Invention, 10*(1), 7569–7576.

Reddy, S. T. (2024). Human-computer interaction techniques for explainable artificial intelligence systems. *Recent Trends in Artificial Intelligence & It's Applications, 3*(1).

Rekha, K., Gopal, K., Satheeskumar, D., Anand, U. A., Doss, D. S., & Elayaperuma, S. (2024, May 14–15). AI-powered personalized learning system design: Student engagement and performance tracking system [Conference presentation]. *4th International Conference on Advance Computing and Innovative Technologies in Engineering (ICACITE)*. Greater Noida, India. https://doi.org/10.1109/ICACITE60783.2024.10617155

Richards, J., & Rodgers, T. S. (2014). *Approaches and methods in language teaching*. Cambridge University Press.

Robert, J., & McCormack, M. (2025). *2025 EDUCAUSE AI landscape study: Into the digital AI divide*. EDUCAUSE. https://library.educause.edu/ resources/2025/2/2025-educause-ai-landscape-study

Rudik, I. V., & Onyshchuk, I. Y. (2024). Artificial intelligence tools for developing educational resources: Enhancing digital learning experience for teachers and learners. Закарпатські філологічні студії [Transcarpathian Philological Studies], *2*(33), 89–94.

Saeed, W., & Omlin, C. (2021). Explainable AI (XAI): A systematic meta-survey of current challenges and future opportunities. *Knowledge-Based Systems, 263*, Article 110273.

Schmidt, R. (1990). The role of consciousness in second language learning. *Applied Linguistics, 11*(2), 129–158.

Schmidt, T., & Strassner, T. (2022). Artificial intelligence in foreign language learning and teaching. *Anglistik, 33*(1), 165–184.

Shabara, R., ElEbyary, K., & Boraie, D. (2024). Teachers or ChatGPT: The issue of accuracy and consistency in L2 assessment. *Teaching English with Technology, 24*(2), 71–92.

Sharifuddin, N. S., & Hashim, H. (2024). Benefits and challenges in implementing artificial intelligence in education (AIED) in ESL classroom: A systematic review (2019–2022). *International Journal of Academic Research in Business and Social Sciences, 14*(1), 146–164.

Sharma, V., & Ahirwal, M. K. (2024). An end-to-end brain computer interface system for mental workload estimation through hybrid deep learning model. *Human-Centric Intelligent Systems*, 4, 599–609.

Sharma, S., & Batta, P. (2025). Decoding sarcasm: Machine learning and its effect on mental health. In S. K. Swarnkar & Y. K. Rathore (Eds.), *Proceedings of the International Conference on Advances and Applications in Artificial Intelligence (ICAAAI 2025), Advances in Intelligent Systems Research* (Vol. 194, pp. 1189–1207). Atlantis. https://doi.org/10.2991/978-94-6463-738-0_91

Sotlikova, R. (2023). Design thinking in education: Empowering students in ELT class. *Proceedings Series on Social Sciences & Humanities, 13*, 196–199.

Srinivasan, V., & Murthy, H. (2021). Improving reading and comprehension in K–12: Evidence from a large-scale AI technology intervention in India. *Computers and Education: Artificial Intelligence, 2,* Article 100019. https://doi.org/10.1016/j.caeai.2021.100019

Sumakul, D. Y., Hameid, F. A., & Sukyadi, D. (2022). Artificial intelligence in EFL classrooms: Friend or foe? *LEARN Journal: Language Education and Acquisition Research Network, 15*(1), 232–256.

Sweller, J. (1988). Cognitive load during problem solving: Effects on learning. *Cognitive Science, 12,* 257–285.

Tai, T. Y., & Chen, H. J. (2023). The impact of intelligent personal assistants on adolescent EFL learners' listening comprehension. *Interactive Learning Environments, 31*(3), 1485–1502.

Teaching & Learning Resource Center. (n.d.). *AI considerations for teaching and learning.* Ohio State University. https://teaching.resources.osu.edu/teaching-topics/ai-considerations-teaching-learning

TESOL International Association. (2024). *The 6 Principles for Exemplary Teaching of English Learners: K–12* (2nd ed.). TESOL Press.

TESOL International Association. (2025a). *AI in the English language classroom workshop.* https://www.tesol.org/professional-development/education-and-events/live-online/artificial-intelligence-workshop/

TESOL International Association. (2025b). *TESOL zip guide: AI in English language teaching.* TESOL Press. https://bookstore.tesol.org/tesol-zip-guide--ai-in-english-language-teaching-products-9781953745484.php

Thalpage, N. S. (2023). Unlocking the black box: Explainable artificial intelligence (XAI) for trust and transparency in AI systems. *Journal of Digital Art and Humanities, 4*(1), 31–36.

Tomasello, M. (2003). *Constructing a language: A usage-based theory of language acquisition.* Harvard University Press.

UNESCO. (2025). *AI and education: Protecting the rights of learners.* UNESCO. https://doi.org/10.54675/ROQH4287

University of San Francisco Gleeson Library. (2024, July 5). *FLC: Pedagogy for the age of AI: Crafting prompts for GenAI.* https://library.usfca.edu/ai/promptengineering

Vančová, H. (2024). AI and AI-powered tools for pronunciation training. *Journal of Language and Cultural Education, 11*(3), 12–24.

Vijayakuma, N. M., & Chellapandiyan, N. G. (2024). Language learning through AI technology - LLA (language learning apps). *International Research Journal on Advanced Engineering and Management (IRJAEM), 2*(4), 957–962.

Vygotsky, L. S. (1987). *The collected works of L. S. Vygotsky* (Vol. 1; R. W. Rieber & A. S. Carton, Eds.). Springer.

Wei, L. (2023). Artificial intelligence in language instruction: Impact on English learning achievement, L2 motivation, and self-regulated learning. *Frontiers in Psychology, 14*, Article 1261955.

Weihua, L. (2019). Multimodal construction of artificial intelligence technology in modern teaching of foreign languages. *Bulletin of Luhansk Taras Shevchenko National University, 7*(330), 147–155.

Wiggins, G., & McTighe, J. (2005). *Understanding by design* (Expanded 2nd ed.). Association for Supervision and Curriculum Development.

Wilhelm, M., Schwaetzer, E., Otten, T., Schumacher, K., & Zobel, T. (2024). Troubleshooting conversations: Exploring chatbot repair strategies. In *Proceedings of Mensch und Computer 2024 (MuC '24)* (pp. 386–391). ACM. https://doi.org/10.1145/3670653.3677496

Woo, J. H., & Choi, H. (2021). Systematic review for AI-based language learning tools. *arXiv*, Article 2111.04455. https://doi.org/10.48550/arXiv.2111.04455

Writing Across the Curriculum. (2025a). *Generative AI for writing instructors*. San José State University. https://www.sjsu.edu/wac/writingwithai/

Writing Across the Curriculum. (2025b). *Join a faculty workshop*. San José State University. https://www.sjsu.edu/wac/writingwithai/workshops/index.php

Writing Across the Curriculum. (2025c). *Learn about our research project*. San José State University. https://www.sjsu.edu/wac/writingwithai/about/index.php

Xia, Y., Shin, S. Y., & Kim, J. C. (2024). Cross-cultural intelligent language learning system (CILS): Leveraging AI to facilitate language learning strategies in cross-cultural communication. *Applied Sciences, 14*(13), Article 5651.

Yang, H., & Kyun, S. (2022). The current research trend of artificial intelligence in language learning: A systematic empirical literature review from an activity theory perspective. *Australasian Journal of Educational Technology, 38*(5), 180–210.

Yu, J. H., & Chauhan, D. (2024). Trends in NLP for personalized learning: LDA and sentiment analysis insights. *Education and Information Technologies, 30*, 4307–4348. https://doi.org/10.1007/s10639-024-12988-2

Zaghlool, Z. D., & Khasawneh, M. A. (2023). Incorporating the impacts and limitations of AI-driven feedback, evaluation, and real-time conversation tools in foreign language learning. *Migration Letters, 27*(7), 1071–1083.

Zhai, C., & Wibowo, S. (2023). A systematic review on artificial intelligence dialogue systems for enhancing English as foreign language students' interactional competence in the university. *Computers and Education: Artificial Intelligence, 4*, Article 100134.

Zhai, X., Zhao, R., Jiang, Y., & Wu, H. (2024). Unpacking the dynamics of AI-based language learning: Flow, grit, and resilience in Chinese EFL contexts. *Behavioral Sciences, 14*(9), 1–18.

Zhao, H., Guo, H., Wang, S., & Wei, S. (2024). Professional curriculum adjustment and system optimization based on big data. *Proceedings of the 2023 International Conference on Information Education and Artificial Intelligence*, 447–452. https://doi.org/10.1145/3660043.3660123

Zou, B., Du, Y., Wang, Z., Chen, J., & Zhang, W. (2023). An investigation into artificial intelligence speech evaluation programs with automatic feedback for developing EFL learners' speaking skills. *Sage Open, 13*(3). https://doi.org/10.1177/21582440231193818

Zou, B., Guan, X., Shao, Y., & Chen, Y. (2023). Supporting speaking practice by social network-based interaction in artificial intelligence (AI)-assisted language learning. *Sustainability, 15*(4), Article 2872.

Zulkarnain, N. S., & Yunus, M. M. (2023). Primary teachers' perspectives on using artificial intelligence technology in English as a second language teaching and learning: A systematic review. *International Journal of Academic Research in Progressive Education and Development, 12*(2), 861–875.

Appendix A

AI Tools for English Language Teaching: A Functional Matrix

Note: Such tools evolve rapidly; the information presented here should be understood as a comparative snapshot, not a guarantee of current or complete functionality.

Tool Name	Needs Analysis	Goal Setting	Lesson Planning & Materials Creation	Text Analysis & Adaptation	Writing Evaluation	Reading Comprehension	Speaking & Pronunciation	Listening
Andy English Chatbot							✔	
ATOS by Renaissance Learning				✔				
Baamboozle			✔			✔		
Babbel							✔	✔
Blackboard AI Design Assistant			✔	✔				
Blue Canoe Learning							✔	✔
BoldVoice							✔	✔
Calendly		✔						
Canva			✔					
Canvas MasteryPaths	✔	✔						
Carnegie Speech NativeAccent							✔	✔
CENTURY	✔	✔						
ChatGPT			✔	✔		✔	✔	
Classcraft	✔		✔					
ClassDojo		✔						
Classtime	✔							
Cognii	✔				✔			
Coh-Metrix				✔				
Criterion					✔			
Crossplag					✔			
Curipod			✔					
D2L Brightspace	✔	✔						
DALL·E			✔					
Diffit			✔	✔		✔		

Tool Name	Needs Analysis	Goal Setting	Lesson Planning & Materials Creation	Text Analysis & Adaptation	Writing Evaluation	Reading Comprehension	Speaking & Pronunciation	Listening
Duolingo / Duolingo for Schools		✔				✔	✔	✔
Edpuzzle			✔			✔		✔
EduPage		✔						
EF Standard English Test	✔					✔		✔
Ellie							✔	
ELSA Speak							✔	✔
EnglishCentral							✔	✔
EWA								
Flip							✔	✔
Flow Speak	✔						✔	
Fluency Tutor for Google							✔	
FluentU						✔		✔
Gemini			✔	✔		✔		
Ginger				✔	✔			
Glossika							✔	✔
Google Read Along						✔	✔	
Gradescope	✔	✔						
Grammarly		✔		✔	✔			
Hemingway				✔	✔			
Immerse							✔	✔
Intellimetric					✔			
Kahoot!			✔					
Kami			✔		✔	✔		
Khan Academy		✔	✔			✔		
LearnCube							✔	✔
Learnt.ai			✔					
LessonPlans.ai			✔					
Lexia PowerUp Literacy	✔					✔		
Lexile Framework for Reading				✔				
Lextutor				✔				
Lingokids							✔	✔
LingQ				✔		✔		✔
Lingvist				✔		✔		✔

Tool Name	Needs Analysis	Goal Setting	Lesson Planning & Materials Creation	Text Analysis & Adaptation	Writing Evaluation	Reading Comprehension	Speaking & Pronunciation	Listening
MagicSchool			✔					
Mango Languages							✔	✔
Memrise						✔		✔
Microsoft Image Creator			✔					
Midjourney			✔					
MindMeister			✔					
Minecraft for Education			✔				✔	
Mondly							✔	✔
Nearpod			✔			✔		✔
News in Levels						✔		✔
Newsela				✔		✔		✔
NoRedInk					✔			
Notion		✔	✔					
Otter							✔	✔
PEG Writing					✔			
Praat							✔	
ProWritingAid				✔	✔			
QuillBot			✔	✔		✔		
Quizizz			✔			✔		
Quizlet			✔			✔		
Raz-Plus						✔	✔	
Readable.com				✔	✔			
ReadTheory	✔					✔		
ReadWorks			✔			✔		
Resoomer				✔		✔		
Rewordify				✔		✔		
Rosetta Stone							✔	✔
SchoolPass		✔						
Slidesgo Lesson Plan Generator			✔					
Speak.com							✔	✔
Speakly						✔	✔	✔
SpeakPal							✔	✔
Speech Analyzer							✔	

Tool Name	Needs Analysis	Goal Setting	Lesson Planning & Materials Creation	Text Analysis & Adaptation	Writing Evaluation	Reading Comprehension	Speaking & Pronunciation	Listening
Speechace							✔	✔
SpeechFlow							✔	
Speechify								✔
Speechling							✔	✔
Squirrel AI	✔	✔						
Subly						✔		✔
Talk To Me Technologies							✔	
TalkPal							✔	✔
Teachology.ai		✔	✔					
Text Blaze			✔	✔				
Text Inspector				✔				
TextHelp Read&Write						✔		✔
Textio				✔	✔			
Turnitin Revision Assistant					✔			
Versant	✔				✔	✔	✔	✔
VoiceTube						✔		✔
Wakelet			✔			✔		
WaveSurfer							✔	
WhiteSmoke				✔	✔			
Wordtune				✔	✔			
Write & Improve	✔			✔	✔			
Writesonic			✔	✔				
YouGlish							✔	✔

Appendix B

AI Tools for English Language Teaching: A Practical Glossary

Andy English Chatbot (andychatbot.com) is a simple AI-powered tool that offers learners the chance to practice English conversation in the real world. It simulates interactive dialogues to help learners build confidence in a low-pressure environment. For ELT educators, Andy can be used as a supplementary practice tool for everyday conversations and to reinforce vocabulary or grammar introduced in class. Because it responds instantly, learners get a sense of real-time interaction, which supports fluency development. Teachers might assign Andy as part of homework tasks or recommend it for extra practice to learners who need more speaking exposure. Its accessibility and informal style make it a practical companion for ongoing language practice.

ATOS (renaissance.com/products/atos) by Renaissance Learning employs machine learning to analyze text difficulty based on features like the length of the word, the frequency of the word, and the length of the sentence.

Baamboozle (baamboozle.com) turns language review into a lively classroom game. Teachers can use it to review vocabulary and grammar or to comprehension while keeping learners engaged. The team-based format boosts collaboration, and Baamboozle+ adds options for smart scoring and random team assignments. Games can be made from scratch or selected from the large library of existing sets, so teachers save time on preparation. Quick to set up, Baamboozle works well for warm-ups, revision, or lesson endings, giving learners an engaging way to practice English and fostering collaboration.

Babbel's (babbel.com) AI-powered adaptive learning system uses clustering algorithms to generate personalized phoneme practice sequences, focusing on learner performance patterns to identify specific pronunciation challenges and modify the curriculum accordingly. The system integrates spaced repetition principles with AI-driven content selection, ensuring challenging phonemes receive attention at optimal intervals for retention. Its prosody training module represents an advanced application of AI in suprasegmental instruction, incorporating context-aware feedback mechanisms that reflect the communicative intent behind utterances. For instance, when practicing the sentence *I didn't say she stole my money*, the system examines both acoustic features and efficient stress placement. Finally, the system's ability to group learners with similar pronunciation profiles helps teachers use more targeted instructional strategies for specific learner populations.

Blackboard AI Design Assistant (blackboard.com) helps teachers build efficient courses by suggesting activities, resources, and assessment ideas based on learners' needs. Tracking learner progress, it can create branching pathways to make delivering differentiated instruction easier at scale. For ELT educators, this means routine practice tasks or remedial activities can be created quickly, while teachers focus on personalized support and higher level skills. By automating sequencing and reinforcing basics, Blackboard provides the opportunity for educators to spend more time engaging learners in meaningful communication and critical thinking activities.

Blue Canoe Learning (bluecanoelearning.com) stands out among AI-powered pronunciation teaching tools through its advanced and novel Color Vowel System and well-developed speech recognition technology. The application combines gamified learning with research-based methodology to address English pronunciation challenges, especially vowel sounds, stress, and rhythm. Through its adaptive AI technology, the platform offers detailed feedback on pronunciation, creates progress analytics, and provides targeted activities.

BoldVoice (boldvoice.com) provides AI-powered accent coaching, focusing particularly on American English pronunciation. It offers video lessons combined with instant AI-powered feedback on learner production. The system employs advanced neural networks trained on extensive datasets of fluent and nonfluent speech to provide timely feedback on pronunciation errors. What sets BoldVoice apart is its error pattern recognition system, which not only recognizes pronunciation errors but also examines the phonetic environment in which these errors happen. Language educators can utilize this tool to help learners understand how adjacent sounds affect pronunciation. This enables learners to gain more detailed and context-specific correction strategies.

Calendly (calendly.com) helps educators manage scheduling without endless back-and-forth emails. By sharing a simple booking link, learners or colleagues can choose available time slots that sync with the educator's calendar. For ELT educators, this is useful for setting up office hours, speaking practice sessions, or parent-teacher meetings. With less administrative hassle, teachers can spend more time on preparing lessons and supporting learners, as well as keeping their calendars clear and organized.

Canva (canva.com) is an advanced online design platform, with a user-friendly interface and AI-driven design recommendations. In the ELT context, Canva is particularly valuable for developing high-quality educational posters, interactive flashcards, infographics, and presentations. Teachers can especially use resources designed in Canva to make vocabulary and grammar teaching more engaging. By leveraging Canva's capabilities, educators can craft materials that not only deliver linguistic information effectively but also stimulate visual learners and enhance retention.

Canvas MasteryPaths (instructure.com/canvas/mastery-paths) helps teachers adapt lessons automatically. After a quiz or task, learners are instructed to complete personalized follow-up work that matches their results—meaning remedial practice for some, enrichment for others. In an ELT class, Canvas MasteryPaths helps teachers ensure that stronger learners stay challenged while those needing support receive targeted help. Its built-in analytics show patterns in progress. This makes it easier for teachers to identify learning gaps and focus classroom time on important tasks.

Carnegie Speech (carnegiespeech.com), developed through extensive research at Carnegie Mellon University, utilizes proprietary speech recognition technology to analyze learner pronunciation at the individual phoneme level. Its specific strength resides in identifying slight variations in phoneme production that may influence intelligibility. For instance, when a learner has difficulty distinguishing between /ɵ/ and /s/, the software provides thorough acoustic analysis and targeted correction strategies. Its **NativeAccent** system uses advanced diagnostic algorithms and predictive analytics to anticipate pronunciation difficulties based on learners' L1 backgrounds, serving as a proactive intervention strategy. Teachers can employ this data to cultivate individualized intervention plans while monitoring learner progress through the platform's analytics dashboard.

CENTURY (www.century.tech) is a school-wide learning platform that leverages AI to provide data-driven insights, create adaptive learning pathways, and track student progress. This AI-powered tool constantly adapts lessons supported by data from ongoing performance analysis. It is designed for British and international curriculum schools.

ChatGPT (chatgpt.com) is OpenAI's generative AI chatbot that can support language educators with lesson planning and materials curation. When provided with well-crafted prompts, the chatbot can synthesize pedagogical concepts, frame educational content, and suggest instructional tasks tailored to curricular specific areas or learner requirements. It also excels in producing assessments, clarifying grammatical concepts, and crafting contextualized scenarios for conversation tasks. For teaching reading, ChatGPT can adapt and adjust texts to a learner's needs and proficiency level, making changes to vocabulary items, adding paraphrases, or providing context via explanations or definitions. For teaching speaking, ChatGPT is a highly adaptable AI conversation partner for role-play scenarios. Its capability to maintain character consistency while adapting language complexity makes it an asset for ELT contexts. Educators can create custom role-play situations, from basic to professional scenarios, with the AI preserving proper register and vocabulary. However, it should be noted that the system needs careful prompt engineering to maintain an educational focus.

Classcraft is an AI-enhanced instructional platform developed to assist educators develop and deliver lessons, monitor student engagement, and support behavior management. The tool delivers engagement analytics, behavior tracking, and customizable lesson pathways ("quests"). Though previous versions highlighted gamified classroom experiences, the current platform functions primarily as a teacher-facing tool for planning instruction and identifying learner needs as opposed to a game-based application.

ClassDojo (classdojo.com) can automate the tracking of attendance, behavior, and engagement in real time. Its AI features ease routine tasks, like monitoring participation, giving feedback, and recording presence, which reduces the administrative load. ClassDojo offers clear insights into learner engagement. It also strengthens communication with parents by sharing progress updates, creating a transparent system that keeps learners motivated and accountable.

Classtime (classtime.com) offers a state-of-the-art formative assessment platform. This tool enhances needs analysis through real-time feedback on learner performance, enabling educators to identify areas of challenge across various language skills. By providing insights into learner progress on its diverse assessment types, Classtime helps teachers make data-driven changes to pedagogical strategies and curriculum content. For both individual and class-wide learning, Classtime enables educators to tailor their instruction rapidly, ensuring a responsive and effective language learning environment.

Cognii (cognii.com) leverages NLP and AI to support comprehensive language assessment and provide contextualized feedback. This tool conducts precise analyses of learners' language production across tasks, then offers deep linguistic insights, adaptive feedback, and precise skill gap identification. By scrutinizing linguistic features, tracking progress over time, and adapting assessments, Cognii offers educators an in-depth understanding of each learner's language proficiency.

Coh-Metrix (cohmetrix.com) provides an inclusive multilevel evaluation of text features, encompassing syntactic complexity, word concreteness, and cohesion. It employs AI to measure more than 100 indices of text complexity. The Text Ease and Readability Assessor (TERA) is a tool that uses the Coh-Metrix program to analyze a text by providing measures of text readability. It focuses on referential cohesion, latent semantic analysis, and syntactic complexity. Educators can apply Coh-Metrix to foster learners' explicit understanding of their word choices and sentence structures that contribute to overall text coherence.

Criterion (ets.org/criterion), developed by ETS, is an automatic writing evaluation tool especially designed for educational purposes. It supplies detailed feedback on essay flow and organization, grammar, usage, and mechanics It also measures whether an essay covers all the essential features of successful argumentation, comprising a clear thesis, supporting evidence, and persuasive counterarguments. In an advanced ELT course focused on academic writing, Criterion could be used to teach learners how to write a well-structured and finely argued essay. The system might encourage a student to improve the quality of their thesis statement, add more supporting details, or consider alternative perspectives, thus leading them towards more advanced and persuasive writing.

Crossplag (crossplag.com) is an AI-powered plagiarism detection tool that helps educators spot copied or machine-generated text in learner work. For ELT classrooms, it offers a quick way to check writing assignments for originality while also opening discussions about the responsible use of AI tools. By highlighting questionable sections, Crossplag inspires learners to develop authentic writing skills and critical thinking. It saves educators time on manual checks and supports academic integrity in a digital learning environment.

Curipod (curipod.com) is a novel AI-powered platform designed to generate interactive lesson plans that integrate engaging activities, assessments, and multimedia. By blending traditional pedagogical methods with these dynamic features, Curipod boosts learner participation and creates a more immersive learning experience. The tool enables educators to design lessons that actively engage students by integrating interactive quizzes, videos, and group work activities, which encourages deeper understanding and long-term retention of content. Curipod promotes critical thinking and collaboration, supports diverse learning styles, and fosters active learner participation, making it an asset for language instruction.

D2L Brightspace (d2l.com/brightspace) is a powerful tool that provides real-time data analysis and goal setting for educators. With data-driven insights into learner performance on language tasks, teachers can make educated decisions about curriculum design including writing short- and long-term learning objectives tailored to their learners' demonstrated needs. D2L Brightspace fosters a more responsive and adaptive teaching and learning environment, enabling personalized support for learners and, ultimately, augmenting learner outcomes.

DALL·E (openai.com/dall-e) is an AI-powered image generator that works via text prompts. ELT educators can use this tool to create custom visuals for lessons, from flashcards and visual story prompts to illustrations that match specific vocabulary items or course themes. For speaking and writing practice, teachers might show learners AI-generated images and ask them to describe, compare, or come up with stories around them. By tailoring visuals to class needs, DALL·E makes lessons more engaging and sparks creative language use.

Diffit (diffit.me) helps teachers create ready-to-use lesson materials. By entering a topic or learning objective, educators can generate reading passages, questions, and activities at different levels of difficulty. For ELT classes, this makes it easy to adapt content to mixed-ability groups, ensuring all learners can access the same theme at the right level. Diffit saves planning time while supporting differentiated instruction, giving teachers more space to focus on interaction and language practice.

Duolingo (duolingo.com) is an advanced language learning platform that adjusts materials and complexity to each learner's proficiency level and delivers individualized practice outside the classroom. It reinforces grammar, vocabulary, and comprehension through interactive exercises. **Duolingo for Schools** offers educators thorough analytics on learner progress and helps educators provide targeted support and modifications. The platform also features speaking exercises that offer on-the-spot feedback on pronunciation and basic grammar, with a gamified approach to error correction. Though useful for basic pronunciation practice, Duolingo is not as specialized as other accent training tools. **Duolingo Stories** offers story-based listening and reading practice, and it tailors the complexity of narratives and comprehension checks based on learner responses. Overall, Duolingo is a valuable supplementary resource for language learners and educators, offering personalized learning experiences and immediate feedback.

Edmodo (edmodo.com) was a K–12 educational technology platform for teachers, students, and parents to communicate and collaborate. It permanently shut down on 22 September 2022.

Edpuzzle (edpuzzle.com) offers a library of thousands of interactive video listening lessons. With an innovative approach to adaptive listening, Edpuzzle allows teachers to embed questions, comments, and explanations at strategic points throughout a video. This interactive feature engages learners actively and provides immediate feedback on their understanding. The platform uses AI to identify patterns in responses and modify the difficulty of follow-up questions or of the vocabulary used in the video, maintaining a balance between challenge and comprehension. Edpuzzle supports the development of critical listening skills by providing a multimodal learning experience that combines visual and auditory elements.

EduPage (edupage.org) helps educators to spend less time on roll calls and schedules by letting EduPage handle those tasks automatically, instead. Its AI-powered attendance and tracking tools provide fast insights on attendance and student engagment. For ELT classes, this means more time for interaction and less for administration.

EF Standard English Test (efset.org) uses adaptive testing to measure reading and listening skills. It tailors subsequent questions based on learners' responses. Results provide a clear snapshot of the learners' level of proficiency, which is a great source for placement data or for tracking growth. In ELT classrooms, this test works well for benchmarking at the start of a course and can also be used to check progress later.

Ellie (elliespeak.com) is an AI-powered conversational practice app that incorporates an emotionally responsive virtual character. Ellie uses facial recognition and voice analysis to detect learners' emotional states, then adjusts its communication style accordingly. This creates a personalized, stress-free conversation setting. Teachers can recommend Ellie to learners who need additional speaking opportunities or struggle with performance anxiety in traditional classroom contexts. This approach helps build learners' confidence before live interactions with peers or instructors.

ELSA Speak (elsaspeak.com) employs state-of-the-art speech recognition algorithms to test learners' oral production and offer immediate feedback on individual sounds, stress, and intonation patterns, using speech recognition technology to detect pronunciation errors and suggest corrections. It even offers visual representations of speech patterns to help students see their errors. The platform also includes role-play scenarios with adaptive listening features that adjust complexity according to learner performance. What sets ELSA Speak apart is its use of deep learning algorithms trained on a large number of datasets of nonstandard English speech styles; as a result, it can generate individualized practice based on recognized pronunciation patterns in a learner's first language background. This is valuable in mixed-nationality classrooms where educators must address diverse phonological interference patterns at the same time. This paramount tool in integrated pronunciation instruction engages machine learning algorithms to generate personalized progression paths that address specific pronunciation challenges while providing sustained, focused practice outside traditional classroom settings.

EnglishCentral (englishcentral.com) offers a huge library of authentic videos for listening and speaking practice with AI-driven adaptive playback capabilities. The platform makes modifications to videos based on learner performance, including raising or lowering speech rates, adding caption support, and targeting vocabulary and grammar according to their level. This focused approach guarantees that learners are exposed to language that is relevant to their present proficiency level, which fosters both motivation and retention. EnglishCentral has developed a flexible learning platform that blends multiple AI technologies to optimize phoneme mastery and utilizes both predictive analytics and real-time performance data to adjust learning pathways. Its algorithm focuses on pronunciation accuracy as well as learning speed, error patterns, and practice consistency when changing content complexity and sequence. Educators can monitor student progress through comprehensive analytics.

EWA (appewa.com) is a gamified language learning platform that employs AI to adapt content complexity based on learner proficiency and interests. Through progressive challenges, mini-games, flashcards, and interactive dialogues, it provides personalized language practice opportunities. Educators can utilize EWA as supplementary homework or independent study material, particularly for learners who benefit from game-based motivation. The adaptive algorithms ensure appropriately leveled practice, making it useful for differentiated instruction and maintaining student engagement outside classroom hours.

Flip (info.flip.com) is a video-sharing platform for asynchronous classroom interaction. Its built-in AI provides automatic transcription and voice analysis to support assessment. Educators can design speaking activities via prompts and response chains, often incorporating gamified elements, like points or challenges. Flip is effective for developing oral skills in a stress-free environment, allowing learners to record and re-record responses while giving teachers accessible documentation for feedback and evaluation.

Flow Speak (flowspeak.io) is an AI-powered speaking assessment tool that provides real-time feedback on learner performance. Its responsive assessment features allow educators to identify specific speaking challenges and adjust instruction accordingly. The platform evaluates pronunciation, fluency, and communicative effectiveness, generating actionable data for performance-based modifications to assessments. Teachers can use Flow Speak for diagnostic assessment, progress monitoring, or targeted practice assignments, enabling differentiated instruction based on individual speaking profiles and supporting data-driven pedagogical decisions in oral skills development.

Fluency Tutor for Google (fluencytutor.com) is a reading-assistance tool that provides immediate feedback on aspects of pronunciation, such as stress and intonation. Students can record passages, receive feedback, and track their progress over time. Fluency Tutor can be adopted to assign reading tasks and track pronunciation improvements in stress and intonation. It can potentially help students focus on natural speech patterns in a supportive environment.

FluentU (fluentu.com) is an AI-powered language learning platform that uses authentic video content to provide contextualized learning experiences. The app analyzes learner performance and adapts the difficulty level of its content to offer personalized practice and feedback. Particularly valuable for intermediate learners, FluentU helps bridge the gap between basic communication and advanced proficiency through consistent, tailored practice with real-world materials. Educators can assign specific videos aligned with curriculum goals, while the platform's interactive subtitles, vocabulary lists, and adaptive exercises support autonomous learning and skill development outside classroom instruction.

Gemini (gemini.google.com) is Google's generative AI chatbot that supports lesson planning and material curation for language educators. When provided with well-crafted prompts, including learning objectives, learner profiles, and proficiency levels, Gemini can generate customized lesson plan outlines and curate level-appropriate materials from across the internet. Educators can use Gemini to streamline preparation time, discover diverse authentic resources, and adapt content to meet specific educational standards. Its ability to analyze multiple parameters simultaneously makes it particularly useful for differentiating instruction and creating targeted materials for varied learner needs.

Ginger (gingersoftware.com) is an outstanding tool that not only corrects grammar and spelling but also suggests sentence rephrasing. This particular feature is advantageous for learners that are struggling with English syntax, as it provides alternative ways to express the same idea. Ginger includes a text reader and translator, making it an inclusive tool for language learning.

Glossika (glossika.com) is a language learning platform that has set itself apart with its AI-driven spaced repetition system for pronunciation training. The platform utilizes NLP to evaluate learners' pronunciation patterns and automatically regulates the complexity and frequency of practice items derived from their performance. Glossika's repetition model helps learners internalize rhythm patterns via recurring exposure. Language educators can leverage Glossika's adaptive technology to create personalized phoneme practice regimens that respond to each student's specific challenges and learning pace. The platform can generate authentic contexts for pronunciation practice and keeps systematic records of learner progress.

Google Read Along (readalong.google.com) is a tool designed to help young learners with reading. It uses speech recognition to provide instant feedback on mispronunciations, skipped words, and pauses. Because the main focus is on reading aloud, it's especially helpful for beginners and younger students. The tool isn't as advanced as others specifically for speaking practice, but it still offers a solid way to work on pronunciation and fluency. Teachers can upload simple texts or even short conversations for students to read out loud. The system also points out when speech isn't flowing smoothly, making it a useful resource for practicing both reading and speaking, helping students improve fluency and correct themselves in real time.

Gradescope (gradescope.com) is an advanced AI-driven assessment tool. This platform utilizes machine learning algorithms to accelerate the grading process for both objective and subjective assignments. The system rapidly processes quizzes and written assignments, which not only reduces the time spent on grading tasks but also increases consistency in assessment criteria. Moreover, Gradescope collects comprehensive data on student performance, facilitating the accurate tracking of learner progress. This equips educators with the data necessary to identify areas of challenge and tailor their pedagogical strategies accordingly.

Grammarly (grammarly.com)is a powerful tool for improving writing skills. Students can compose directly within Grammarly's online text editor or install the browser extension. Grammarly utilizes sophisticated AI algorithms to assess texts for errors in spelling, grammar, punctuation, and style; offers detailed explanations of errors; and suggests corrections for learners. Its context-aware feature takes into consideration the overall meaning and tone of a text when recommending modifications. Together, these features offer a robust framework for learners to engage in self-correction, encouraging the development of critical writing skills and nurturing autonomy in language learning. For teachers' own use, Grammarly can also function as a proofreader of lesson materials.

Hemingway (hemingwayapp.com)is a digital writing assistant that excels in analyzing writing for clarity and concision. A simpler tool than other automated writing evaluation systems, it focuses on simplifying complex sentences and avoiding passive voice and adverbs, resulting in clearer, more direct writing. Educators can use Hemingway to show learners how to simplify complex sentences without losing meaning. This tool can be advantageous for learners who tend to translate directly from their L1, which usually results in overly complex English sentences.

Immerse (immerse.online) represents an advanced approach to speaking practice through its VR-based language learning environment. The platform generates immersive role-play scenarios where learners interact with AI characters in visually contextualized contexts. Immerse stands out for combining visual, auditory, and interactive features to create authentic speaking experiences while reducing learner anxiety.

Intellimetric (vantagelearning.com/products/intellimetric), designed by Vantage Learning, employs AI to analyze the strength of ideas, relevance of content, and quality of argumentation in written texts. High-quality ideas often lead to meaningful discussions, augment innovation, and support effective problem-solving. Educators can adopt this tool to foster idea generation that can significantly improve the quality of the essay at the end.

Kahoot! (kahoot.com) is an engaging, gamified platform that lets educators easily create and launch quizzes and other interactive activities. This tool is particularly appealing for younger learners. Its competitive environment boosts participation and creates an enjoyable educational experience. The platform supports a wide range of topics and is well-suited for improving classroom engagement through real-time participation. Kahoot! offers educators a dynamic and interactive way to strengthen language skills, particularly vocabulary and grammar. Kahoot! is tailored for various language levels, allowing instructors to design quizzes and activities to meet the specific needs of multilingual learners.

Kami (kamiapp.com) is an innovative AI-powered annotation and collaboration platform that facilitates cooperative reading and writing tasks. By leveraging AI to improve the process of document annotation, this tool creates a more interactive and collaborative approach to textual analysis and written assignments in ELT. For reading, Kami allows students to interact with digital texts in a dynamic manner, engaging in real-time annotations, comments, and discussions. This tool extends to written assignments, where learners can work cooperatively on documents. These interactive features not only promote active engagement with language materials but also cultivate critical thinking and peer-to-peer learning, essential components of effective language acquisition.

Khan Academy (khanacademy.org) offers a flexible digital classroom where teachers can assign curriculum-based exercises through class codes. Its adaptive system adjusts task difficulty as learners progress. Teachers gain access to detailed analytics that highlight strengths, gaps, and overall progress. Khan Academy can support flipped learning by allowing independent practice before class, or it can be used for targeted follow-up after lessons. With immediate feedback and self-paced pathways, it helps with managing mixed-ability groups while giving learners ownership of their progress and practice.

Learnt.ai (learnt.ai) assists educators with creating lesson plans, course outlines, feedback, and assessments. Learnt.ai allows for inclusive lesson planning, with built-in options for projects, quizzes, and surveys, making it highly adaptable for ELT classrooms. This adaptability enables teachers to construct robust and engaging curricula that address diverse learning styles, potentially fostering student engagement and enhancing language learning outcomes.

LessonPlans.ai (lessonplans.ai) streamlines the lesson preparation process. It employs advanced algorithms to quickly create complete lesson plans based on specific input parameters, such as proficiency level, subject matter, and intended learning outcomes. The platform produces interactive, objective-aligned lesson plans, providing a foundation upon which teachers can shape and modify their instructional approach. This flexibility allows for the integration of personalized teaching strategies while maintaining a structured framework. By providing an efficient technique for generating pedagogically comprehensive lesson plans, LessonPlans.ai empowers educators to allocate more time to other critical aspects of instruction, potentially enhancing overall teaching effectiveness and boosting learner engagement.

Lexia PowerUp Literacy (lexialearning.com/powerup) is a beneficial tool for struggling readers as well as multilingual learners. It tailors instruction in real time based on student performance on personalized practice activities, with an emphasis on word study, grammar, and comprehension. Lexia PowerUp Literacy is primarily designed for fluent English speakers. However, this tool offers valuable features for multilingual learners of English. Its adaptive system not only regulates text complexity but also delivers scaffolded support for comprehension questions. Lexia supports struggling readers while challenging more advanced learners, making it a useful tool for mixed-ability classrooms. The system might offer simplified explanations or visual aids to students who are having hard time, gradually decreasing this support as they improve.

Lexile Framework for Reading (lexile.com) analyzes text difficulty derived from syntactic and semantic features. The analysis provides a Lexile measure to direct text selection informed by reading proficiency.

Lextutor (lextutor.ca) evaluates vocabulary in texts and identifies word frequency and categorizes words in various difficulty levels (e.g., academic word lists). This tool enables teachers to evaluate the suitability of vocabulary for learners at diverse proficiency levels.

Lingoda (lingoda.com) is an online language school that offers live classes with certified, native-speaking teachers, with courses aligned with CEFR (Common European Framework of Reference). Recently, Lingoda launched Lingobites, an AI-driven interactive tool for post-class language review. Though the content for Lingobites is created using AI technology, it is carefully reviewed by language experts, including Lingoda teachers, to ensure accuracy and quality.

Lingokids (lingokids.com) has developed a cutting-edge gamification system particularly designed for phoneme acquisition. The platform utilizes machine learning to create adaptive game scenarios that target specific pronunciation difficulties while sustaining a playful learning environment. Lingokids integrates social learning elements, engaging students in collaborative pronunciation challenges and providing individualized AI-powered feedback. The system's potential to balance entertainment with learning makes it particularly valuable for motivating learner persistence.

LingQ (lingq.com) is an online language learning platform where students interact with authentic language samples, such as podcasts, books, TV shows and more. It incorporates dynamic text adaptation and allows for inserting any text and getting rapid translations. Moreover, this tool tracks vocabulary learning and adjusts content difficulty accordingly.

Lingvist (lingvist.com) is a language learning platform that employs AI to dynamically adjust vocabulary and reading texts based on learner performance, increasing engagement and providing an optimal challenge. Though primarily designed for vocabulary acquisition, Lingvist also incorporates adaptive listening by curating audio content that aligns with a learner's language proficiency. By analyzing individual performance data, it chooses audio materials that not only match the learner's proficiency but also emphasize areas requiring further practice, such as specific vocabulary sets or grammatical patterns. This adaptability encourages targeted learning and fosters students' listening skills relevant to their current language goals. The tool's ability to introduce progressively complex language while still ensuring comprehensibility makes it highly effective for learners aiming to transition from basic to advanced listening skills.

MagicSchool (magicschool.ai) is designed to reduce the time teachers spend on planning and paperwork. By entering objectives or key standards, educators can quickly generate lesson outlines, activities, and assessments. This frees up time that can be used for direct student interaction. English language teachers might use MagicSchool to create differentiated reading tasks, draft writing prompts, or design practice questions that match specific language goals. The tool is flexible enough to adapt materials for different learner levels, helping educators focus less on routine preparation and more on meaningful instruction.

Mango Languages (mangolanguages.com) offers guided role-play experiences, highlighting cultural context and practicality. Though its scenarios are more scripted than truly adaptive AI conversations, the system performs remarkably in providing culturally appropriate language practice, with detailed attention to register and pragmatics.

Memrise (memrise.com) blends spaced repetition with real-world input to make vocabulary learning more memorable. Instead of relying only on flashcards, the app introduces words and phrases through short videos of fluent speakers, helping learners connect language to authentic contexts. Its AI personalizes review cycles so that tricky items reappear until mastered, while easier ones fade into long-term memory. Memrise works well as a supplement for self-study or homework, giving learners extra practice beyond the classroom. It helps learners expand vocabulary, improve listening comprehension, and feel more confident using English in real situations.

Microsoft Image Creator (bing.com/images/create) allows teachers to generate original visuals from text prompts using AI. This makes it especially useful in ELT, where tailored images can bring vocabulary lists, reading passages, or storytelling prompts to life. Instead of relying on stock pictures, teachers can request specific contexts, like a café in Paris or a busy airport check-in, to match the language being taught. Students can also use the tool for creative tasks, such as generating images for group projects or presentations. By integrating visuals directly tied to lesson themes, Image Creator makes practice more engaging and memorable.

Midjourney (midjourney.com) is an AI image generator that creates detailed, artistic visuals from short text prompts. For language teachers, it offers a creative way to design unique lesson materials, from story prompts to cultural scenes that fit specific vocabulary sets. Learners can also use it to generate visuals for projects, presentations, or writing tasks, with teachers encouraging them to describe and discuss what they see. Because Midjourney's images often feel more imaginative than stock photos, they spark curiosity and conversation. This makes it a powerful tool for turning abstract language input into vivid, engaging classroom experiences.

MindMeister (mindmeister.com) is an advanced tool that offers AI-assisted mind mapping capabilities for visual learners. Though learners design their own mind maps, this tool uses AI to suggest related concepts and connections, helping learners expand and organize their ideas. In an English composition class, MindMeister can guide students through the prewriting phase of an essay, and its AI suggestions could help them discover new viewpoints or supporting points learners hadn't considered, enriching their understanding.

Minecraft for Education (education.minecraft.net) transforms language learning into an immersive, game-based experience. In its virtual worlds, students collaborate, solve problems, and build projects while using English to communicate. Teachers can set tasks that require teamwork and discussion, such as designing a city, creating role-play scenarios, or completing quests. The platform also offers ready-made lesson plans aligned with curriculum goals, which can be adapted for ELT. By combining creativity with purposeful language use, Minecraft encourages authentic communication, critical thinking, and collaboration, making it an engaging tool for both classroom projects and remote learning contexts.

Mondly (mondly.com) distinguishes itself as a pioneering platform in gamified pronunciation practice, leveraging AI to make an immersive learning environment. The system employs high-tech speech recognition algorithms within a game-like framework that gradually familiarizes learners with new phonemes through well-designed challenges. Mondly's adaptive difficulty system automatically modifies exercises based on learner performance while also fostering engagement through digital rewards and achievement milestones. This tool can be utilized by language educators to create structured pronunciation practice sessions that feel more like interactive games than traditional drilling exercises. Going beyond a standard language learning app, Mondly offers VR and AR speaking practice experiences that deliver structured role-play scenarios with AI-powered characters. The system is notable for creating realistic situational dialogues where learners can practice specific language functions in a controlled yet authentic environment. Its branching dialogue system supports multiple conversation paths, encouraging learners to experiment with diverse language choices.

Nearpod (nearpod.com) makes lessons engaging by incorporating interactive slides, polls, quizzes, and virtual reality experiences. Instead of passively following along, students respond in real time on their own devices, giving teachers instant insights. For ELT classrooms, this can mean quick vocabulary checks, comprehension quizzes after listening tasks, or interactive discussions around reading passages. Teachers can also embed videos, images, or VR tours to spark conversation and contextual learning. The platform works equally well in-person or online, making it a versatile choice for blended and remote teaching while keeping learners engaged and actively participating.

News in Levels (newsinlevels.com) presents AI-curated news content at diverse proficiency levels. Its strong point is providing current news content, which enhances engagement. The platform is capable of adjusting authentic news stories into three different difficulty levels, while maintaining thematic relevance and adjusting vocabulary complexity as well as speech rate. Educators can employ these leveled materials to design differentiated listening activities within the same thematic unit. This makes learning tasks appropriate for a mixed-ability classrooms.

Newsela (newsela.com) exploits AI algorithms to automatically customize news articles to different reading levels while maintaining core content and meaning, making it exceptional for academic English practice. Though primarily known for offering reading materials drawn from current events, Newsela also includes AI-adapted audio content at multiple levels. In this way, Newsela content can be used to develop both listening skills and subject matter knowledge. Recently, Newsela added an adaptive questioning system in which learners answer comprehension questions that get progressively more and more challenging if they respond correctly. The adaptive nature of the questions helps students recognize areas where they need more practice, whether in making inferences, understanding vocabulary in context, or identifying core ideas. This tool can particularly help students prepare for standardized tests like the TOEFL or IELTS.

NoRedInk (noredink.com) supports writing instruction through personalized practice and adaptive feedback. Students work on grammar, sentence structure, and composition tasks that adjust in difficulty based on their responses. The platform also includes guided writing activities where learners build essays step by step, with hints and examples. For ELT classrooms, NoRedInk helps strengthen accuracy and writing fluency while reducing the time teachers spend correcting the same errors. Progress reports highlight common trouble spots, allowing teachers to tailor follow-up lessons. Its engaging interface and clear guidance make writing practice less intimidating and more effective for developing language skills.

Notion (notion.so) is an all-in-one administrative workspace that combines notes, databases, task lists, and collaboration tools. Teachers can use it to organize lesson plans, track student progress, and share resources with colleagues or learners. Its flexible structure allows educators to build customized pages for different classes, projects, or skills, while its AI tools help summarize text, draft content, or generate ideas. For ELT contexts, Notion can serve as a digital portfolio where students collect writing samples, vocabulary items, and reflections. It can also serve as a project hub for group work. Notion's adaptability makes it a powerful tool for streamlining both teaching and learning.

Otter (otter.ai) is primarily designed as an audio transcription tool. Usefully for ELT contexts, Otter also supplies advanced visualization features, such as waveforms and pitch contours. These visual aids can assist learners to literally "see" aspects of speech, such as stress, rhythm, and intonation patterns. The visual feedback on pitch contours can enhance learners' understanding of the tonal aspects of pronunciation, which are often hard to discern by ear alone. This visual representation of speech is particularly advantageous for advanced learners aiming to refine their intonation and naturalness in speaking.

PEG Writing (pegwriting.com) is a web-based formative writing practice and automated scoring environment (powered by the Project Essay Grade engine) typically implemented in licensed educational services/institutions. Direct teacher sign-up may require institutional/ district arrangements.

Praat (fon.hum.uva.nl/praat) is a foundational tool in spectral analysis for pronunciation instruction with advanced capabilities for speech visualization and analysis. This software employs cutting-edge signal processing algorithms to create spectrograms and formant displays, equipping educators with the tools to display the acoustic properties of phonemes with exceptional precision. Language educators can employ Praat's visualization qualities to help learners understand the nuanced differences between similar sounds. Praat with AI integration now includes machine learning algorithms to recognize and analyze phonological processes in continuous speech. This can be particularly beneficial for educators in visualizing and demonstrating various aspects of connected speech, such as assimilation, elision, and liaison. The AI component simplifies the process of recognizing these phenomena in speech samples and makes it more accessible for pedagogical purposes.

ProWritingAid (prowritingaid.com) is a powerful tool that goes beyond grammar checking to focus on more advanced elements, such as sentence structure, vocabulary usage, and readability. For multilingual learners of English, ProWritingAid offers detailed and comprehensive reports on writing style and consistency. The suggestions for improving sentence variety and word choice are particularly helpful for advanced learners.

QuillBot (quillbot.com) is a digital writing assistant that goes beyond simple paraphrasing to provide AI-powered, sophisticated summarization. QuillBot can shorten wordy articles or academic papers into concise summaries, adjusting the length and complexity based on user preferences. In an academic reading class, QuillBot can help learners tackle challenging research papers. Learners can be instructed to summarize a text on their own, then critically compare the AI-generated summaries with their own words and identify key elements that they might have missed, leading to a discussion on what makes a successful summary. Educators can use QuillBot to automatically adjust the reading level of linguistically complex texts for multilingual learners, scaffolding comprehension for different proficiency levels.

Quizizz (quizizz.com) is an interactive quiz platform that turns language practice into a game. Teachers can create their own quizzes or choose from a large library of ready-made ones, and students can play individually or in teams on their devices. With real-time feedback, reports, and leaderboards, the tool keeps learners motivated while giving teachers clear data on performance. Quizizz is effective for reviewing vocabulary, grammar, or comprehension in a lively way. Its homework mode also allows students to practice outside class, making it a flexible option for both in-person and online learning.

Quizlet (quizlet.com) is a well-known platform for vocabulary building and interactive language practice. It helps learners to engage with various practice and study tools, such as flashcards, matching games, and multiple-choice quizzes, nurturing a more engaging and effective learning process. The platform offers both self-paced study and teacher-led classroom activities. Quizlet is especially effective in ELT contexts for reinforcing vocabulary acquisition and reading comprehension. The tool also offers individualized learning paths, providing support for learners with diverse proficiency levels.

Raz-Plus (raz-plus.com)**,** part of the Learning A–Z suite, is an online literacy platform for young learners that presents an extensive library of leveled books with accompanying adaptive quizzes. What distinguishes Raz-Plus is the diverse question types, including multiple choice, short answer, and even recording options for evaluating speaking skills. Raz-Plus helps learners develop both reading and speaking skills. Students might read a story, answer comprehension questions that adapt to their previous performance and replies, and then record themselves retelling the story. This tool offers an all-inclusive language learning experience.

Readable.com (readable.com; formerly Readability-Score.com) is a text leveling tool that evaluates text using machine learning algorithms and readability metrics. It scores writing based on clarity, sentence length, and word choice, making it widely used by educators, writers, and content creators. In ELT classrooms, teachers can use it to adapt authentic materials for learners at different proficiency levels or to check the accessibility of their own lesson texts. Students can also analyze their own writing with Readable.com, gaining feedback on how easy their work is to read and learning to adjust style for clarity and audience.

ReadTheory (readtheory.org) is an online reading comprehension platform that uses AI to regulate texts dynamically and adjust them to the learner's comprehension skills. For instance, a more advanced learner might face increasingly complex texts, while a beginner might start with simpler narratives, both moving forward at their own pace. Educators can use ReadTheory to provide learners with opportunities for individualized reading comprehension practice across proficiency levels.

ReadWorks (readworks.org) provides a digital library with adaptive elements. Reading text recommendations are informed by student reading level and progress. It also supports vocabulary learning and offers comprehension questions that adjust according to student responses. Moreover, ReadWorks helps teachers assign and track reading activities.

Resoomer (resoomer.com) uses AI to summarize the most relevant details from texts. What distinguishes this tool is its capability to generate hierarchical summaries emphasizing main ideas and supporting details. In a content-based English language course, such as business English, Resoomer can be applied to help students quickly grasp the main points of industry reports or case studies. This can free up more class time for in-depth discussions and language practice related to the content.

Rewordify (rewordify.com) is an online tool that engages AI to simplify complex texts by replacing complex and low frequency vocabulary words with simpler synonyms. Rewordify also revises complex sentences into simpler structures, which yields easier-to-understand text and promotes both reading fluency and comprehension.

Rosetta Stone (rosettastone.com) delivers an inclusive approach to pronunciation practice with its speech recognition technology, TruAccent. The platform assists learners in refining their pronunciation by focusing on stress, intonation, and phoneme accuracy. It adapts to each learner's needs through dynamic practice sessions and adjusts content complexity and timing according to their progress. The system also offers structured conversation exercises with immediate feedback, engaging learners in low-pressure speaking practice outside of class. Rosetta Stone focuses on communicative success over perfect accent reproduction and provides focused corrections that help learners improve at their own pace.

SchoolPass (schoolpass.com) is a school management platform that uses AI to automate attendance and other daily routines. Its facial recognition and tracking tools allow schools to monitor student presence with accuracy, reducing the time teachers spend on administrative tasks like roll calls. This means smoother lesson starts and fewer interruptions, giving more time for instruction. The system also provides useful insights into student engagement and patterns of absence, helping educators identify learners who may need extra support while ensuring a safe, well-organized environment for teaching.

Slidesgo Lesson Plan Generator (slidesgo.com/ai-presentations) helps teachers design structured, visually appealing lesson plans in minutes. By entering the topic and objectives, educators receive a ready-made slide deck that outlines activities, goals, and timing. For ELT educators, this means less time formatting materials and more time focusing on content, whether it's a grammar lesson, vocabulary set, or skills practice. The templates can be customized with examples, images, or prompts to suit classroom needs. Its professional design makes lessons clearer for students while reducing the workload of creating engaging, organized teaching materials from scratch.

Speak.com (speak.com), powered by GPT-4 technology, distinguishes itself as a leading AI role-play platform. The application provides wide-ranging scenario-based conversations, from casual to complex interactions. What sets Speak apart is its capability to dynamically adjust the difficulty level of the role-plays while maintaining communicative authenticity. Educators can make use of its predesigned role-play situations or craft custom scenarios aligned with their curriculum goals.

Speakly (speakly.me) is a language learning app that teaches vocabulary and phrases based on frequency and real-life use. Instead of memorizing isolated word lists, learners are introduced to the most practical language first and then reinforce it through listening, writing, and speaking activities. Speakly uses AI to track learner progress and adapt lessons to each learner's needs. For multilingual learners of English, this approach builds communicative ability quickly, focusing on the words and expressions they are most likely to use. Teachers can recommend Speakly as a supplement for independent study, giving learners structured, real-world practice outside the classroom.

SpeakPal (speakpal.ai) merits attention for its emphasis on authentic conversation patterns. The app regulates its speaking rate and language complexity based on learner responses while maintaining natural discourse features. This helps learners develop both linguistic competence and conversational fluency in a supportive environment.

Speech Analyzer (sil.org/computing/sa), developed by SIL International, merges traditional spectral analysis with AI to create comprehensive visualization options for pronunciation instruction. Speech Analyzer uses machine learning to generate representations of speech sounds across multiple dimensions. Educators can use this tool to visually demonstrate the relationships between articulatory movements and speech sounds, which can ultimately facilitate a deeper understanding of pronunciation mechanics.

Speechace (speechace.com) is an AI-powered platform for accent training that delivers comprehensive feedback on pronunciation, rhythm, and intonation. Speechace utilizes advanced speech recognition technology to analyze speech at both segmental and suprasegmental levels and offer real-time, multimodal feedback. Visual representations of speech patterns and pitch contours help learners visualize and understand pronunciation. Its adaptive algorithm tailors feedback according to the learner's proficiency, allowing educators to personalize pronunciation instruction. Speechace also integrates with various learning management systems and supports mobile and web applications, making it adaptable for various educational settings. Its API integration enables flexible use in custom language learning solutions.

SpeechFlow (speechflow.io) has gained significant interest in the ELT community for its novel approach to rhythm and stress training. The neural networks for this application have been trained on wide-ranging datasets of natural speech, which makes possible the precise analysis of speech rhythm patterns. Teachers can apply its specialized practice exercises centering on thought groups, linking, and stress timing—aspects that are often challenging to teach explicitly. The system's ability to recognize and provide feedback on inappropriate pausing or stress placement offers learners explicit and clear guidance for progress.

Speechify (speechify.com) converts written text into spoken language using AI-powered text-to-speech technology. Texts can be attuned to include specific linguistic features based on learner proficiency. This tool is useful for integrating targeted vocabulary or grammar into listening exercises, as educators can choose texts that cover the desired language focus and have them read aloud at a pace and tone appropriate for learners' levels.

Speechling (speechling.com) is a language learning platform that employs AI to give learners feedback on rhythm and timing in their speech. Learners record their pronunciation, which is then compared to fluent recordings for accuracy. The platform delivers immediate feedback on core features of connected speech, helping raise learner awareness of spoken English patterns. Educators can implement Speechling during online or in-person classes for shadowing practices, listening discrimination tasks, and focused pronunciation exercises. One of its unique features is the capability to increasingly introduce background noise and varied accents, with the aim of simulating authentic listening conditions. Teachers can monitor student progress through the platform's detailed performance analytics and modify classroom instruction accordingly.

Squirrel AI (squirrelai.com) is a comprehensive online learning platform that leverages AI to create custom learning pathways, equipping educators with the necessary data to continuously refine and adjust objectives based on learner performance. By identifying learners' strengths and areas for improvement, Squirrel AI helps foster a dynamic approach to assessment and instruction as well as a targeted learning experience, enhancing learner engagement and optimizing learning outcomes.

Subly's (subly.com) AI-powered transcription technology, though primarily designed for content creators, also has valuable application in ELT contexts. The system supports accurate, time-aligned transcripts with interactive features that allow learners to navigate through audio content and see the corresponding text highlighted. Educators can utilize this tool to create accessible listening materials with synchronized visual support.

Talk To Me Technologies (talktometechnologies.com) has developed a high-quality real-time speech correction system that incorporates both acoustic and articulatory feedback. The platform uses computer vision and speech recognition technologies to provide feedback on both sound production and mouth positioning. Educators can benefit from this dual-modality approach to address pronunciation errors from multiple perspectives, enhancing learners' awareness of both the acoustic and physical aspects of correct pronunciation. This makes it especially useful for teaching the pronunciation of sounds that are challenging to describe verbally.

TalkPal (talkpal.ai; developed by Kalpora) provides AI-driven conversational practice with adaptive features that adjust complexity founded on learner performance. The system facilitates structured dialogue scenarios while regulating its speech rate and vocabulary complexity to match learner proficiency levels.

Teachology.ai (teachology.ai) is an advanced AI-powered platform that offers quizzes, assessments, and personalized feedback. It substantially boosts engagement and reinforces active learning by empowering educators to assess learning progress and tailor instruction in real time. This tool equips ELT educators to plan engaging, dynamic lessons and tailored assessments and quizzes. The platform's potential to offer immediate, personalized feedback allows learners to reflect on their learning and improve their language skills, developing learner autonomy. By reducing time spent on lesson preparation, Teachology enables educators to focus more on personalized instruction and learner interaction.

Text Blaze (www.blaze.today) is an AI-driven browser extension that allows users to save snippets of frequently typed text and insert them as templates, using quick shortcuts. Educators can utilize this tool, for example, to streamline providing feedback on student work or offering customized explanations or examples during language lessons.

Text Inspector (textinspector.com) assesses vocabulary, grammar, and text complexity specifically for multilingual learners of English. It adopts the CEFR (Common European Framework of Reference) scale to help teachers match course reading materials to learners' proficiency levels.

TextHelp Read&Write (texthelp.com/products/read-write) is primarily an assistive technology tool. It offers text-to-speech with synchronized highlighting, vocabulary support with pictures, and simplified idioms and figures of speech that are useful for language learners.

Textio (textio.com) is an AI-driven writing assistant that reviews texts for clarity, tone, and inclusivity. Widely used in professional communication, it can also support teachers and students. Educators can refine lesson instructions, assignment prompts, or feedback to ensure messages are clear and accessible. In ELT contexts, Textio helps simplify complex phrasing, adjust vocabulary for different proficiency levels, and highlight areas where tone could be improved. Students can use it to polish drafts, making their writing more accurate, engaging, and audience-focused.

Turnitin Revision Assistant (turnitin.com/products/revision-assistant) makes use of machine learning algorithms to analyze text structure, argumentation, and use of evidence. This tool provides targeted feedback on essay organization, including the strength of thesis statements and topic sentences and the organization of supporting details. Educators can use Revision Assistant to boost learners' understanding of how to construct well-organized essays.

Versant (www.pearson.com/languages/hr-professionals/versant), developed by Pearson, is an AI-powered testing tool that evaluates speaking, listening, reading, and writing skills in English. Using advanced speech recognition and automated scoring, it provides quick, reliable results without the need for a human examiner. For teachers, Versant can be used for placement data, progress checks, or certification of proficiency levels. In ELT classrooms, it helps track learner development over time and ensures consistent assessment across groups. Because results are immediate, educators can use the data to plan targeted lessons, address specific weaknesses, and give students clear feedback on their progress.

VoiceTube (voicetube.com) offers a vast range of video content with integrated AI to personalize listening practice, with level-adjusted topics to choose based on learner interest. This feature not only improves motivation but also guides learners to better comprehend spoken language in contexts that are both familiar and relevant. The tool supports ELT educators by providing a wide selection of listening materials that can be customized to align with lesson objectives.

Wakelet (wakelet.com), an AI-powered content curation platform, helps educators organize and distribute digital resources. This system employs AI algorithms to aid educators in curating comprehensible and thematically relevant online materials, streamlining the process of lesson planning and resource management. Materials can include reading texts, audiovisual content, and scholarly articles; Wakelet helps teachers and learners collect them into cohesive units, enriching the efficiency of lesson planning or research projects. This feature enables educators to curate inclusive resource collections that students can access individually, fostering autonomous learning along with digital literacy skills.

WaveSurfer (wavesurfer.xyz) uses speech visualization technology to provide spectral analysis of recorded speech and pronunciation. The system's adaptive thresholding mechanism repeatedly fine-tunes visualizations to account for individual speaker variation while maintaining accuracy in phoneme recognition. Educators can leverage WaveSurfer's interactive interface to offer visual pronunciation feedback during speaking classes.

WhiteSmoke (whitesmoke.com) is an AI-powered writing assistant that checks grammar, style, punctuation, and word choice. Unlike basic spellcheckers, it offers suggestions for improving clarity and fluency, making it useful for both teachers and learners. In ELT contexts, WhiteSmoke can support students as they draft essays, reports, or emails by catching common errors and recommending more natural phrasing. Teachers may also use it to quickly review student work or refine their own instructional materials. Its translation and plagiarism-check features add extra value in academic settings.

Wordtune (wordtune.com) is an AI-powered digital writing assistant that can analyze learners' written output, then offer recommendations for enriched clarity, coherence, and style. This is an invaluable tool for developing students' written English proficiency. By providing alternative phrasing, vocabulary suggestions, and structural improvements, Wordtune provides the guidelines and feedback for learners to improve their writing in real time. Wordtune helps advanced learners experiment with more complex linguistic constructions and idiomatic expressions. This highlights the importance of immediate feedback and iterative improvement in language acquisition, in line with the current approaches to writing instruction.

Write & Improve (writeandimprove.com), developed by Cambridge English, harnesses advanced NLP algorithms to analyze learner writing samples; identify recurrent error patterns and gaps in grammar, syntax, and vocabulary; and provide feedback. By generating a linguistic profile for each learner, Write & Improve informs and significantly improves the needs analysis process. This tool empowers educators to locate specific areas for instruction and curriculum refinement.

Writesonic (writesonic.com) enables the development of instructional materials, pedagogical resources, and compositional tasks with minimum user input, simplifying lesson planning and materials creation. Writesonic excels in creating level-appropriate writing prompts and constructing reading materials tailored to diverse language proficiency levels. This makes it a valuable tool for differentiated instruction in ELT contexts.

YouGlish is a searchable online video library offering a wide array of authentic media samples enhanced with interactive transcript visualization. Learners can search for a word, then view and listen to many examples of that word in natural contexts, spoken by fluent speakers of various Global Englishes. YouGlish uses AI to deliver contextual pronunciation practice for individual phonemes. The system evaluates millions of authentic video content pieces to offer learners real-world examples of specific sound usage. ELT educators can incorporate YouGlish into their teaching practice by focusing on targeted phonemes and demonstrating their articulation in various authentic contexts, providing learners with multiple reference points for correct pronunciation.

Index

About the Author

Dr. Samaneh Eslamdoost is an internationally experienced educator and innovator in language teaching. Holding a PhD in English language teaching, she blends expertise in curriculum design and teacher training with a deep interest in the transformative power of AI and a passion for shaping the future of learning. Currently advancing her knowledge with an MA in instructional design and technology, she bridges cultures, classrooms, and technologies to inspire educators worldwide.